RESILIENCE
— in the Face of —
ADVERSITY

A Suffolkian's Life Story

Margaret Ellen Mayo Tolbert

BALBOA.
PRESS

A DIVISION OF HAY HOUSE

Balboa Press books may be ordered through booksellers or by contacting:

Balboa Press
A Division of Hay House
1663 Liberty Drive
Bloomington, IN 47403
www.balboapress.com
1 (877) 407-4847

Because of the dynamic nature of the Internet, any web addresses or links contained in this book may have changed since publication and may no longer be valid. The views expressed in this work are solely those of the author and do not necessarily reflect the views of the publisher, and the publisher hereby disclaims any responsibility for them.

The author of this book does not dispense medical advice or prescribe the use of any technique as a form of treatment for physical, emotional, or medical problems without the advice of a physician, either directly or indirectly. The intent of the author is only to offer information of a general nature to help you in your quest for emotional and spiritual well-being. In the event you use any of the information in this book for yourself, which is your constitutional right, the author and the publisher assume no responsibility for your actions.

Print information available on the last page.

ISBN: 978-1-5043-3196-8 (sc)
ISBN: 978-1-5043-3197-5 (hc)
ISBN: 978-1-5043-3198-2 (e)

Library of Congress Control Number: 2015906427

Balboa Press rev. date: 06/15/2015

Dedication

This book is dedicated to the rays of joy in my life:
My son, Lawson Kwia Tolbert, the fruit of
my womb, and my grandchildren.

Salute

To Lawson and my grandchildren, you are my legacy. It
is my hope that each of you will live this legacy to the
fullest, and I hope that each of you will cherish and live
your life in such a manner as to be a credit to society.

Contents

Acknowledgments

I thank Ms. Amber L. Jones sincerely for editing the full manuscript and for her detailed attention to both major items, like content and organization, and small things, like where I place my commas.

I am indebted to Dr. Marigold Linton for her moral support and insight as she critiqued the first version of the manuscript for this book. Her suggestions are sincerely appreciated.

Also, I am deeply grateful to my former undergraduate classmate, Robert Peoples, Jr., for his encouragement and suggestions for improving the first draft of this book. I truly welcomed his suggestions and critical commentary. He was especially helpful with information on the Tuskegee Institute experience.

Dr. Carrie P. Hunter contributed items of information for the section of this book that covers our trip to Ghana, adding much-needed details for clarity and enhancement. For her input, I am most grateful.

Additionally, I am grateful to Dr. Willie Pearson, Jr. His comments gave me a great deal of food for thought and led the way for the restructuring of selected sections of this book for enhanced flow of the information presented.

I appreciate the helpful suggestions from my siblings—Lee Vania Mayo Williams, Jessie Benjamin Mayo, Sr., Eleanor Olivia Mayo Minns, and Mary Lee Mayo Brown—who assisted in making the family sections of this book interesting, accurate, and fun.

My son, Lawson K. Tolbert, helped me immensely by scanning the photographs and ensuring that they were properly labeled and uploaded to my computer. His assistance in this endeavor and in overall computer operations is very much appreciated.

I offer special thanks to the team of experts at Balboa Press, a division of Hay House Publishing, Inc., for final preparations, publication, advertisement, and distribution of this book.

Finally, I offer my thanks to all who assisted in any way in the compilation of facts and the development and completion of this book.

Photograph and Logo Credits

The following individuals and agencies are recognized for their generosity in permitting the use of photographs and logos in this book.

- Painting of Mrs. Fannie Johnson Mayo—Courtesy of VA Art Expo; Artist: Hamid Choobin
- Logos of NSF sponsored Science and Technology Centers—Courtesy of Dr. S. Shankar Sastry, Director of the Team for Research in Ubiquitous Secure Technology Center led by the University of California at Berkeley; Dr. Eric Baer, Director of the Center for Layered Polymeric Systems led by Case Western Reserve University; Dr. António M. Baptista, Director of the Center for Coastal Margin Observation & Prediction led by Oregon Health and Science University; Dr. David M. Karl, Director of the Center for Microbial Oceanography led by the University of Hawaii at Manoa; Dr. David A. Randall, Director of the Center for Multi-Scale Modeling of Atmospheric Processes led by Colorado State University; and Dr. S. Prasad Gogineni, Director of the Center for Remote Sensing of Ice Sheets led by the University of Kansas
- Photographs taken in Ghana during the National Cancer Program Workshop—Courtesy of Prof. F. K. A. Allotey, Former Director of the Ghana Atomic Energy Commission
- Photographs of me (Margaret E. M. Tolbert): One included in the top center of the page titled "Photographs of Me at Various Stages of My Life" and the one in the section titled "About the Author"—Courtesy of Photographer: Calvin Austin
- Drawing of Busts of Former CRF Directors—Courtesy of Tuskegee University School of Veterinary Medicine Media Center, Artists: Bob and Robert Hagerty

- Photographs of Tuskegee University activities, including those of CRF—Courtesy of Tuskegee University School of Veterinary Medicine Media Center, Photographer: Mr. Walter Scott
- Photographs of Former USDA Secretary Lyng—Courtesy USDA and the Tuskegee University School of Veterinary Medicine Media Center, Photographer: Mr. Walter Scott
- Photographs of ANL, including the Division of Educational Programs, activities—Courtesy of Argonne National Laboratory
- Two of the photographs (the one of me—three exposures—in cap and gown and me wearing a white dress) on the page titled "Photographs of Me at Various Stages of My Life"—Courtesy of Hawkins Studio in Tuskegee Institute, AL
- Photographs containing images of key individuals—Courtesy of The Honorable Hazel O'Leary, The Honorable Bill Richardson, The Honorable Federico F. Peña, Mr. Joseph S. Mahaley, The Honorable Judge R. J. Leon, Dr. Martha Krebs, and Mr. Marvin E. Gunn, Jr.

The diligent efforts of everyone who assisted in obtaining consent statements for the use of photographs and logos in this book are acknowledged with heartfelt thanks.

Introduction

I have had good and bad times in my life. I initially began documenting them—my upbringing, my personal struggles and joys, and my professional accomplishments—to share with my son and grandchildren. I wanted to record the details of my life's journey before the "door closes," as so often happens unexpectedly. However, I soon learned that writing about oneself is a journey in itself, forcing me to reflect on long-ago decisions and their long-term impacts. I realized that, with a little more work, I could serve a broader goal: inspiring others pursuing their own journeys.

Like many people, I spent my childhood preoccupied with the family I was born into, the neighborhood, and school; and my adult years with professional accomplishments as well as family of my own.

For me, however, the path from one to the other was much longer, and harder, than for many. My path was strewn with obstacles—rocks that tripped me up and quicksand threatening to mire me down and suck the spirit right out of me.

That path began and ends at extremes: At the beginning, a poor Black girl in segregated southern Virginia, orphaned at an early age, just trying to keep my shoes patched, avoid the switch, and get enough to eat. At the other end, an accomplished African-American scholar with three degrees, credentials in science and education, jobs in which I contributed to the advancement of science and growth of the nation, and the mentoring of others pursuing similar professions.

Missing from my early years in the small town of Suffolk was the freedom to play, learn, and grow up free of fear and weighty adult responsibilities. Instead, I endured violence, segregation, discrimination, lack of educational opportunities, and premature domestic obligations. I went to schools and used drinking fountains in the downtown area designated for "Colored" people. I began working before I got to eighth grade, and assumed responsibility for my younger sisters and brother before I reached my teenage years.

Despite this rough beginning, I found the strength of will and perseverance not only to survive my home life, and take care of my siblings, but also to excel at school, make connections, and become the first in the family to pursue higher education. I attended a predominantly Black university at a historic and violent period of emerging civil rights. Through a great deal of effort, I ended up at an Ivy League university. All of this effort paid off during the following four decades, during which opportunities continued to unfold—opportunities to contribute scholarship and proud service to my country and personal support to many of its people.

In 1987, as I stood straight and tall at the Birmingham Branch of the Federal Reserve Bank of Atlanta to accept a national award for distinguished service as a director of that Branch,[1] I reflected on how far I had travelled in my thinking as well as my circumstances. That transition—and thought pattern—continued throughout the following decades, and is the theme for this book.

Though some good luck and some incredibly good samaritans were strewn along my path, I believe that my ability to achieve professional prominence against overwhelming odds was largely due to two factors. The first was an aggressive pursuit of education. The second was merely a choice—a decision to improve my prospects, and the fortitude to persevere in that choice.

When I think about the path that I took in my journey through life, at times I am filled with pride and joy at what I have achieved. I have served as researcher, scientist, university faculty member, director of national programs, director of a national laboratory, wife, mother, and grandmother. I have traveled widely. I have delivered speeches and advised governments. At other times my thoughts are filled with "what ifs." What if my parents had lived longer? What if my relatives had turned away me and my siblings? What if I had been more careful in my relationships? Sometimes I wonder where I gained the ability to find peace within myself, and the wisdom to avoid conflicts that I would have lost, people who would

---

[1]   The award was presented to me by the Branch president and vice president.

have been negative influences, and situations that would have been unproductive.

Despite my wondering, however, I realize that I never seriously doubted my ability to overcome difficult circumstances. I merely decided that's what I was going to do. Although there are always many options, it is possible to make thoughtful and informed choices. I am fortunate that most of my choices advanced my career and my life in general.

It has taken a long time to reach this point in my life, at which I recognize that my attitude and choices served me well. Despite the years, some of the memories, especially of major events and decisions, are still vivid.

Although others have written about me during my professional years, this book is about my entire life, from my perspective. It is about hardships, triumph over adversity, and successes. In the following pages, some of what you read may seem far-fetched. Could it really have happened that way? It could, and did. In my mind, the past is clear but often disturbing. I do not wish for the "good old days." I am happy to live in the much-improved "here and now." I invite readers to join me on the mental journey from past to present—a journey that for me has been most cathartic.

My hope is that readers will benefit from hearing about the way I have lived; that they will learn from my actions and decisions, and be inspired to persevere through their own trials until they, too, achieve success.

In the words of Booker T. Washington, a man I greatly admire: "I have learned that success is to be measured not so much by the position that one has reached in life as by the obstacles which he has overcome while trying to succeed."[2]

By that measure, my accomplishments should have a place at the top of the charts!

---

[2]   Booker T. Washington, Up from Slavery: An Autobiography, A. L. Burt Publisher, New York, 1901, page 32.

Here, then, is my story—about what it takes to choose a path from darkness to light, to employ the power of the human mind and the resources of community for the betterment of self, and, in the process, move from ignorance toward enlightenment.

Part One

The Early Years

Survival in Saratoga

In the early 1940s, Suffolk, Virginia, was a segregated city. I was born in Saratoga, one of the sections of Suffolk for Colored people. Saratoga was, and still is, bordered on two sides by forest. The other two sides were bordered by Wellons Street and the Norfolk and Western Railroad track. By the time I was six, I was aware that Colored people lived on one side, and White people on the other side, of Wellons Street.

There were times, during the summer months, when Whites would ride through the neighborhood in nice cars, sometimes with their children. Perhaps the adults were teaching their children about Colored people; perhaps it was just an adventure. The White children would stare and sometimes sing, "Bye, bye, black birds."[3] Or, they would chatter and point their fingers in our direction as they passed our house. My siblings and I were so accustomed to such attention that we did not react.

It was no secret that we were different. Colored people were relegated to the back of the bus and the balcony of the downtown movie theater. The outdoor drive-in theater had a separate entrance for us. This was the situation everywhere—drinking fountains, restrooms, stores—even though everyone paid the same amount for services. "Colored" signs dotted the city, and many privileges were reserved for Whites. Whites could touch the goods in stores and even try on clothes; a Colored person trying one of those actions could result in an angry look or being expelled from the store.

As a child, when I first read about a "White Sale" in the newspaper, I thought it meant that only Whites would be offered the sale prices. Only much later did I learn the true meaning of the term—sales on bed linens and other "white" items.

---

[3]   From song "Bye, Bye, Blackbird" by Mort Dixon and Ray Henderson, 1926.

Perhaps the most significant impacts, besides housing conditions, were in educational opportunities—or lack thereof. The schools for Colored students were overcrowded and poorly supplied with equipment. There were neither enough teachers nor sufficient classrooms, occasionally resulting in two grade levels being taught in the same room. To compensate for these shortcomings, students in one grade sat on one side of the room and kept quiet while those in the other grade were being taught.

As a child, I was aware, but ignorant of the impact, of these aspects of our lives. As an adult, I can begin to understand the negative effects on young minds of being shut out from mainstream services and social activities.

In the Saratoga neighborhood, however, we stuck together and supported each other. Doors and windows were unlocked, and people helped one another. Children belonged to the neighborhood. Adults, especially the older ones, served as protectors and mentors of children, whether or not they were related. Many of the adults were known as sister, cousin, uncle, and aunt—regardless of kinship. It seemed to me that every adult participated in teaching, guiding, scolding, helping, feeding, and otherwise taking care of the children. If an extra child ended up at someone's house at meal time, or homework time, it didn't matter. A lot of times, it wasn't even noticed.

We needed all the care we could get. Conditions were marginal in Saratoga—though as a child I didn't know that; I had no frame of reference for comparison. The houses had no electricity; we burned kerosene lamps. Most homes had hand pumps for water, and a place to burn trash. Streets were gravel and lined with ditches, which carried rain and wastewater from kitchens and baths to places distant from its source, perhaps to the Nansemond River, which is a part of the Chesapeake Bay ecosystem. The ditches were breeding grounds for mosquitoes and other insects. The mosquito man rode through the neighborhood periodically, spraying a fog and squirting a liquid into the ditches to kill the mosquitoes, though it was never long before they returned. My sisters, brother, and I, along with other neighborhood children, would play by running behind the truck, inhaling the chemical fog, unaware of any long-term risk to our health.

In hindsight, I can identify numerous health risks in Saratoga; I feel fortunate to have avoided a wide range of ill effects. As in many small towns and cities, there were no sewers or inside toilets. Such was the case in Suffolk's Colored neighborhoods of the 1940s. Outhouses sat out back, just far enough away from the houses to keep the odor from overwhelming us day and night. Even the outhouses were primitive—a small wooden shelter containing a stool with a hole in it, set over a hole in the ground. In addition, we had a bucket inside the house so that we did not have to go outside in the night to use the toilet. Of course, our least favorite chore was dumping and cleaning that bucket in the morning.

Houses were usually one story, and none were more than two stories high. None had basements; they would have flooded because of the high water table. Our house, two rooms and unpainted, was stacked high off the ground on bricks and cement blocks. Yards were bare, with any grass that encroached on the lawn quickly chopped up, probably to discourage snakes and rodents. For Suffolk, where I grew up, is in Virginia's tidewater region, at the edge of the Great Dismal Swamp—a vast wetland cloaked in peat, dotted with cypress, and home to deer, bears, and numerous small critters, some of which appeared on our dinner table.

Seafood and wild game were staples in my home, caught and trapped by my father and cousins or purchased in town. We grew corn, collard greens, cabbage, and snap beans in our yard. Chickens roamed free during the day, returning to the chicken coop in the backyard at night. Some people in the neighborhood raised goats, pigs, and other animals—resulting in a zoo-like pandemonium when they were all aroused from their torpor at once. Adding to the noise was our dog, Rex, who roamed free, as did most pets in the neighborhood.

Raising family members and keeping them healthy, putting food on the table, and tending the menagerie were chores which largely fell on the overburdened and long-suffering women of the community. My Mama was certainly one of those.

Raising the Family: Mama's Burden

I was the third child born to Jessie Clifford "Clifton" Mayo and Martha Taylor Artis Mayo. My Mama, who was strong, quiet, and a diligent worker, was assisted in my birth by a midwife, Miss Little. I was told that Miss Little provided her services for very little pay, and sometimes just for food. Those were the days when newborn babies had to wear stomach bands to hold their navels in place, and they wore cloth diapers held in place by safety pins. Disposable diapers were a luxury of the future.

My two older sisters, Audrey Mae and Lee Vania, helped my mother take care of me. My Mama could not go to the large hospital near the downtown area of Suffolk for any of our births, lacking both money and insurance. Or maybe Coloreds weren't allowed to be treated there; I don't know. She did not trust the White doctors who worked there, regardless. A small number of Colored doctors, pharmacists, and nurses were available in the city, but most people relied on home care.

My brother, Benjamin, was born three years later. Having a boy in the family made my Dad very proud. Two years later another sister—my "knee" baby sister Eleanor—was born, followed two years later by my baby sister Mary Lee, bringing the total to six kids. This resulted in an exceedingly crowded house on Linden Avenue, with a total of eight people living in two rooms. My two older sisters, my knee baby sister, and I slept on a large folding bed while my brother slept on a small one. My parents slept in the only real bed, often accompanied by my youngest sister. Sometimes my siblings and I would pile clothes and other items on the floor to sleep on. At meal time, we would gather at the small kitchen table, where we sat on large empty cans that had formerly contained lard. Mama kept our clothes reasonably clean, though we often went barefoot, saving our shoes to wear on special occasions.

As soon as my Mama recovered strength following the birth of each child, she returned to work as a domestic servant in the homes of White families. They liked her work, and as a result she was always employed. In addition to the monetary payments for her maid service, sometimes they gave her food to bring home. The food from my Mama's employers was appreciated. It supplemented vegetables from the garden, chickens raised in the yard, wild game that resulted from hunting by my father and cousins, and the limited amount of money available for purchases from the local store.

I do not recall ever going inside any of the houses in which my Mama worked. However, she told us stories about the beauty of the houses and how the family members acted. I could see in my mind how nice the homes were, with sheer curtains, linoleum kitchen floors, and carpeting or hardwood floors in other rooms. I imagined those people had a lot of everything. Sometimes Mama brought home used clothes, household items, and leftover food. She also told us about having to enter the homes through back doors and about how she worked hard to please her employers.

People in Saratoga called my Mama "Lil Boy," but she was no boy. She was only my Mama. Most of the time, she wore pants over her wide hips and a simple shirt over her disproportionately small upper body. Her hair was short and coarse—perhaps the reason for her nickname. People often commented that she spoke with a slight accent like that of a Geechee—a coastal population with African roots in the American southeast—and she could also speak Pig Latin. She could neither read nor write well, but she could surpass anyone when it came to cleaning houses and cooking. Although she always had a job, she could not earn enough money to do relaxing things like take vacations. She worked as a domestic for as long as I can remember. After working all day cleaning others' houses, she was usually too tired to clean our own.

I do not believe that my Dad did much to help around the house or to remedy the family's money problems. I was too young to be fully aware of family and financial matters. However, I knew that, when he was not working, my Dad was usually drunk from corn liquor he bought at local juke joints. He would buy his friends drinks with money that he should have spent on us. Many of my most vivid memories center on his disruptive influence and the fear he instilled in us.

Enduring Dad's Tantrums

My parents seemed to me to be an unusual couple, with different appearances as well as personalities, a distinct lack of affection between them, and the family burdens resting largely on my Mama of whom I have no photographs.

My Dad, Mr. Jessie Clifford "Clifton" Mayo

Dad inherited his skin and hair traits from his parents, Grandma Fannie and Granddaddy Benjamin. Granddaddy had died by the time I was born. However, people said that his skin was very dark brown, and he had straight black hair, an unusual combination. I never saw a photograph of Granddaddy, but I have one of Grandma Fannie. She was an odd sight to see in a Colored neighborhood because she looked like a White person, with silky dark brown hair and very light skin.

My Grandma, Mrs. Fannie Johnson Mayo

A few other people who lived near Grandma also had light skin and looked like White people, and they had fine homes with fences. When children in some of those families grew up, they were able to choose friends of both races. Some even moved north to begin new lives, sometimes passing for White.

Grandma Fannie lived around the corner from us on Battery Avenue, in a bigger, nicer house. Her sister and brother-in-law, Aunt Lucy and Uncle Ruel, lived on Brook Avenue, parallel to Battery Avenue, also in a larger house, made of cinder blocks. They had a large yard in which Uncle Ruel built a one-room building, which served as his barber shop. Although we occasionally were taken to their houses, I do not recall any of them ever visiting us at our two-room house. They did not seem interested in the way Dad treated Mama, my siblings, and me. Although we were all in Saratoga, seemingly we might as well have lived in two different worlds.

Granddaddy who died before I was born was about 20 years older than Grandma Fannie. Of their five children—including my dad—all are now deceased, including one of his sisters who was shot to death in the neighborhood before I was born. I have been told by several people that I look like her and that our mannerisms are similar, though I did not share the long, straight hair that came to her waist.

The gossip was that Grandma Fannie, my Dad's mother, did not like my Mama. The reasons are unknown to me. In those days, people were color conscious even within races. If Grandma Fannie or her sister were in a crowd of White people, you would not be able to distinguish them from those people. Some said that Grandma was Cherokee while Granddaddy Benjamin was part Mohawk and part Colored; however, I have been unable to find any documentation of their heritage. On the other hand, since Granddaddy had dark skin and straight black hair, it does not stand to reason that my Mama's dark complexion was the cause of her not being accepted into the Mayo family.

We never discussed Mama's roots during her lifetime. However, my youngest sister, in recent years, did some research that revealed Mama was the daughter of George Cherry and Erma Taylor. There was a gentleman in the neighborhood that we called George Cherry, to whom we spoke respectfully when we passed his house. Also, my Mama frequently visited a lady we called Grandma Equilla. I never heard any discussions about her actual relationship to us; however, I knew Mama had lived with her and her husband—Joshua—prior to meeting my Dad. Whether the two of them were our grandparents by blood remains a mystery.

My Mama and Dad met in a juke joint. When he spotted her, she was said to have been "dancing on a dime"—a sensual type of dancing involving more movement with the hips than the feet. She was very dark complexioned, and he had olive brown skin with dark wavy hair. As previously indicated, I do not have any photographs of my Mama, I have one of my Dad, proudly wearing his U.S. Army uniform, which made him popular in my section of town (see his photograph).

At some point, they moved in together, probably at Grandma Fannie's house initially. Later they moved into the two-room house on Linden Avenue. As far as I know, their marriage was never officially recorded and was likely what we know of now as a "common-law" marriage.

My Dad was handsome, and well-liked by his side of the Mayo family. He dressed well, and he seemed to care for my Mama when he was sober. There was no stopping him when he wanted to complete a task. He was a hard worker, and his boss liked his work results. Although I feel confident that I inherited my strong work ethic and values from Mama, perhaps I inherited some of my drive from Dad.

However, when he had taken a few drinks of corn liquor, he became a different person, often getting into fights. He never went looking for trouble, but it always seemed to find him. Many of the men in Saratoga carried knives and other objects of defense, and fighting was a common weekend pastime. Dad seemed to fight with people for the sheer heck of it. When he fought, he used his switch-blade or anything he could get his hands on.

I never saw my Mama and Dad have an affectionate moment. They usually sat in silence, or he would argue or sleep in her presence. When he was sober, Dad was ill-tempered but relatively quiet. Until he began drinking, that is. When he had consumed a small amount of whiskey, he was still reasonably calm. But when he drank a great deal, which he did often on weekends, our home was rocked with violence. He would come home from a local juke joint and tear up the house, throwing the small, wood-burning heater across the room or tossing chairs here and there. If anyone got in his way, they would get hurt. When he came home drunk, my sisters, brother, and I would hide under the house or in the bushes. On occasion, Mama would take us to a neighbor's house to wait until Dad calmed down. Fortunately, he was away from home a good deal of the time.

Dad worked as a landscaper in the yards of White people, working for the R.W. Askew Landscaping Company. He did not use his skills on our yard; our vegetable garden was tended by Mama, my siblings, and me. My Dad's spare time was spent in the neighborhood juke joints, socializing with his friends.

Some say Dad became violent after serving in World War II; others say that he inherited "a bad seed." The Army may have left him shell-shocked—the condition now known as post-traumatic stress disorder. When he was discharged from the Army, into which he enlisted voluntarily, the war in his head never stopped. His World War II scars were both physical and mental. He could sleep standing up with his eyes open—perhaps another wartime trait. When he stood still, we did not know whether he was asleep or awake.

In addition to being able to sleep with his eyes open, Dad could eat a live chicken and enjoy it. He could survive off the land. He feared no one.

However, his khaki Army uniform was his pride and joy. He sometimes wore parts of it with regular clothes. His handsome and youthful face, combined with the uniform, attracted many women.

Mama continued to love him, and stood by him, even when he cheated on her and beat her. She endured numerous beatings and never returned a blow. When he ransacked the house during a temper tantrum, we helped her clean up the mess he left behind. Mama always welcomed him back home whether he was drunk or sober, verbally or physically abusive, or penniless. As I watched their often-violent interactions with fear and trepidation, in that tiny house, even at that young age I knew that I wanted a better life. I vowed that I would never settle for a husband who abused me. I yearned for the perfect family—though at that stage of my life, good role models were scarce, so I didn't know how to achieve such a goal.

On a warm fall day when I was still a young child, I heard my sister scream "Run, run!" We did not waste any time. The tone of her voice indicated a dangerous situation: Dad was on the loose. I never understood the reasons for his anger. However, we knew the score, and this time he had a rope in his hand. So we ran like crazy. On most occasions, we ran to get out of the way of his beating Mama. This time, the focus was on us.

One of my sisters ran to the neighbor's house to hide. Another sister and I hid in a filthy ditch, from which we peered warily as he hunted for us. When my dad was on a rampage, my brother would hide under the house. That hiding place was easy to find, since our house was stacked off the ground on bricks and cement blocks.

We were scared stiff, watching our Dad prowl the yard for us. Finally, my Mama appeared in the street, on her way home from a hard day's work. "Lil Boy!" yelled one of the neighbors. "Cliff is trying to kill your children!" Mama accelerated to running speed, screaming as she came. I knew that my Mama could holler, since she would often call my oldest sister by her nickname, in a voice loud enough to "wake the dead." She would place one hand on her hip while standing in the door of our two-room house, yelling "Augie Mae, come here, girl!" This day, she did not have to call us. She was our savior, and our refuge. When we saw her, we ran to the comfort of her arms, and she reached out to us, still trembling in our knees and crying.

That was the only time that I saw my Mama stand up to my Dad. She used some choice words as she told him off for frightening us so badly. The incident surprised us, since she had never resisted before, even when he was beating her savagely. Finally, he went away, probably to meet some of his friends or indulge in more corn liquor. Although we were temporarily safe in the comfort of Mama's arms, we feared that Dad would return to complete the job that he started before she rescued us.

Making Our House a Home

O ur house had a small kitchen and a large attached room that served the combined functions of bedroom and living room. The house was made of unpainted wood, and a roof of tin. A window and the front door of the house faced Linden Avenue, a quiet street. The house also had a kitchen window that faced the backyard. The kitchen door and a front room window faced Brook Avenue, a busy street where people talked and walked past our house. Outside, an outhouse sat several feet behind the house, and, not far from that, the chicken coop. The vegetable garden was at the side near the corner of Brook and Linden; the rest of the lawn was hard dirt.

The kitchen contained a wood- and coal-burning stove, a table, and some homemade stools—some of which were large cans in which lard was purchased from the local grocery store. This was the gathering place for meals. The boards on the kitchen floor were bare. The floor of the front room was covered with linoleum that had large holes in several areas. A small tin heater with a chimney to vent the smoke kept the front room warm in the winter. Pots that were used for cooking were placed on the floor to catch the rain that seeped through holes in the rusted parts of the tin roof. The noise of the rain dropping into the pots sounded like music to me.

Our other furniture consisted of a bed and two cots for sleeping, a dresser with a mirror, and a couple of wooden chairs. An iron Mama used for pressing clothes was kept near the heater, and clothes were hung on nails in the wall with wire hangers. Clothes were washed by hand or with the aid of a washing board. We used Clorox to bleach the white clothes and bluing to give them a hint of blue. Shirts and blouses were then dipped into an Argo starch solution to give them body. The wet clothes were hung up to dry with wooden clothespins on a wire line in the backyard—solar drying was used by everyone in the neighborhood. Since we had no clothing made of permanent-press material, Mama had to heat the iron on the heater or kitchen stove and press the clothes on a wooden board covered with an old sheet. For support, each end of the board was balanced on a large can. We were always proud of our crisply pressed skirts and blouses, shirts, and pants.

While Mama worked hard, taking care of every little thing around the house, we were expected to pay attention and learn for ourselves so we could help as we got older.

I remember some very pleasant times, too. Mama would take time to teach us proper posture by having us walk with books on our heads, and she would show us dance steps and exercise routines, like jumping jacks. She even taught us how to do the limbo using the broom handle as the bar to dance under. She also showed us how to pat ourselves on our heads while simultaneously rubbing our stomachs—a feat of coordination that I can still do. We learned to stand upside down on our heads with our butts and feet against the wall. Being with Mama was fun!

I can only imagine what it must have been like for Benjamin, the only boy, growing up with five sisters. He was never our "baby brother," to be coddled and guided. From an early age, he was independent, full of mischief, and always willing to get my sisters and me in trouble. We learned to hide our transgressions from Benjamin, lest he tattle to our parents, which could result in getting the switch against our legs.

I spent a great deal of time playing when I was little, skipping rope to tunes like "Mary Mack"[4] or playing jacks with sisters or friends. My brother spent many hours under the house playing with fishing worms, small snakes, and our dog, Rex. Other times, he would play kickball, marbles, or some other game in the yard of the house. When my brother was very young, his hair was kept in long plaits. He wasn't given his first haircut until he was ready to attend school for the first time. At that time, a plait of his hair was placed

---

[4] "Miss Mary Mack," children's rhyme used in jumping rope and hand-clapping games. Recorded by Ella Jenkins on the album "You'll Sing a Song and I'll Sing a Song," Smithsonian Folkways Recordings, 1992.

in the Bible, which we believed conferred blessings on the child. This was the case for all boys in our family, including our cousins and other relatives.

I often fought with my brother for a kid-size rocking chair that we had gotten for Christmas one year. Rocking in that chair was comforting to me, and he seemed to always want to use it at the same time that I did. I always won the battles because I was older and stronger than he was.

Most of the time, we had to share our toys. One Christmas, my two older sisters and I were filled with joy because Santa had left a Black doll and a White doll. But there were three of us. I grabbed the Black doll, and a tug-of-war began, resulting in a lot of fighting and crying. Mama intervened and told us to share our play time with the dolls. We always obeyed Mama, so there was no more fighting. We knew that if we fought again, we risked a whipping.

Another Christmas present was a toy into which I would push one finger of each hand into each end and then try to pull them out. The harder I pulled, the tighter the object became—and my fingers were stuck. When I relaxed, my fingers could be removed easily. Each year there was a new checker board, for which the checkers were lost after a few days. We would substitute Coca Cola bottle caps. One opponent would use the caps turned upside down and the other would use them right side up. I loved to play that game— because it required the use of brain power to outsmart an opponent. A spinning top, a metal slinky, and yo-yos were also among our favorite Christmas toys.

We sighed with relief whenever we awoke on Christmas and found toys. If we had been bad, only a bucket of ashes and some switches from trees would have been placed under the tree. When the toys were all broken or lost, my sisters and brother and I would go back to playing in the mud—making mud cakes and playing with earthworms. Sometimes we did nothing more than watch blimps fly slowly across the sky and small airplanes dropping leaflets of information. Since none of us had learned to read, we had no idea what was written on those leaflets. Perhaps it was information on the war.

At times, Mama would sing gospel songs such as "Sometimes I Feel Like a Motherless Child,"[5] "The Lord Will Make a Way Somehow,"[6] and "What Are They Doing in Heaven Today?"[7] We would join her in singing. Mama would dance more than usual during the Christmas season, and we would join her in singing and keeping the clapping and stomping rhythm.

We cherished these times with Mama—respites in an otherwise difficult and stressful childhood. She bore the brunt of our upbringing, and kept the family safe, clothed and fed as long as she was able.

---

[5] Traditional Negro spiritual.

[6] Gospel song written and popularized by Thomas A. Dorsey, about 1942. One of his recordings is on the album, "Precious Lord Recordings of The Great Gospel Songs of Thomas A. Dorsey," released 1994 by Legacy/Columbia.

[7] Hymn written by Charles Albert Tindley, first published in 1901.

Growing Bodies, Growing Minds

—————————————

None of the food in our home went to waste. One day my Mama brought home a ham with tiny white worms in it. She was always resourceful in keeping us well-fed. She may have gotten it from one of the families for whom she worked, or she may have seen someone throw it out and decided to claim it. The worms appeared to jump when they came out of various parts of the ham. We called them "skippers." We were not going to let that ham go to waste! It was placed outdoors for several days to allow the skippers to jump out; my older sisters and I were given the task of keeping dogs away from getting the ham as it lay in the sunlight. When no more skippers appeared to be coming out, my mom boiled the ham for a long time. Of course, I ate some of it when it was served for supper.

I was young and hungry, and ignorant of things like proper cooking and food storage. In our neighborhood, we said, "What don't kill me, sure will fatten me." What we ate did not kill us, and quantities were seldom large enough to make much difference in our weights.

We relied heavily on lard, purchased in large cans from the grocery store, to make biscuits and cakes, for frying, and for other facets of cooking. It was an important staple, and it would be decades before the impact on health of consuming large quantities would become widely known.

One of my hardest lessons about life was how Mama kept the family fed. Most of the chickens we raised were for eggs and, later, for eating. However, Mama let me have one chicken as my pet. Playing outside with my pet chicken, "Twenty," was special to me. Although other toys were fun, nothing kept me fascinated like Twenty did, with her beautiful, shiny black feathers and red comb. Twenty would be let out of the chicken coop fencing to scratch in other areas of the yard. When the mosquito man sprayed DDT into the ditches and into the air, I kept my pet away from the bugs that died from the potent chemical.

I was very protective of my pet. I would pick her up and stroke her gently, which she seemed to like. We would play around the yard, and she would follow me from place to place. Whenever I came out of our two-room house, Twenty would run to meet me. I always thought that she recognized me, but perhaps it was because I always gave her some old bread from the table. Twenty could cluck with a rhythm that, to me, could not be matched by other chickens. I would put her back into the coop at nightfall.

One day, Mama sent Audrey Mae and me to the store. When we returned home, I looked everywhere but could not find Twenty. I had not been gone long; a trip to Mrs. Hurdle's store only took a few minutes, since it was just around the corner near Grandma Fannie's house. I had bought some Mary Janes and Tootsie Rolls with money I found in the street—tasty treats that only cost one cent for two pieces of candy. Audrey Mae bought some BC Headache Powder for Mama and a gallon of kerosene for the lamps. I did not tell Mama about the Coca Cola that Audrey Mae had bought with some of the change, drinking it while waiting for Mrs. Hurdle to pump the kerosene into the jug. Mama would never miss the five cents used to pay for it.

Besides, I was preoccupied with finding Twenty. She wasn't in the coop, under the house, in the vegetable garden, in the barren front yard, or inside the house. In fact, she was never allowed in the house anyway. I gave my brother Benjamin a dirty look and accused him of letting the dog eat Twenty. He denied it and crawled from under the house, where he was playing with worms in the dirt, and went into the house crying. Rex, the dog, followed him. Lee Vania was visiting one of her friends; therefore, I could not accuse her of doing anything to my pet chicken. Eleanor, the youngest child at that time, was too little to understand what was wrong.

The day moved very slowly into dusk. I was miserable. As night fell, Mama called for us to come into the house for supper. Everybody else moved fast because they were hungry. Besides, when an adult—especially my parents—gave an order, it was to be obeyed immediately. If one chose not to do this, it was at the risk of punishment. Sometimes a slap with the nasty wet dish rag was just as painful. So I reluctantly responded to the call to supper.

We gathered in the kitchen, taking our respective places around the wooden table. I observed the usual things. Mama wiped the table with a rag that she dipped into the dishwater. The Oxygen-brand soap made the water turbid, as did the grease and soot from the wood/coal burning stove. The walls of the kitchen suffered from too much soot and too many fly specks.

This evening, Mama took a large black pot from the top of the stove and put it on the table. Whatever it was smelled delicious. She commented that we would eat well that night and grow strong. The pot was opened, and I could see that it was chicken. My goodness! Could it be Twenty that was covered in white sauce and hiding among the dumplings? No, it could not be! I could not eat, but I could not leave the table. I had managed to be good all of my life and avoid whippings. I could not risk it now. Besides, I had an excuse for not being hungry. Not long ago, I had eaten candy while at the store with Audrey Mae.

I could hardly wait for everyone to finish eating supper. There would be no saving some for me later because the ice in the ice box had melted. The food would spoil if kept on the stove, or flies might get into it and lay eggs that would become maggots. Instead, the remaining food was divided among my sisters and brother. Later that evening I accompanied Audrey Mae and Lee Vania to the toilet, as usual. When we were young we never went to the outhouse alone. One of us would stand outside in case assistance was needed, such as chasing away a snake or rat, or fetching personal hygiene items. Our house sat on a corner; therefore, with the light of the moon, I could clearly see everything in the backyard as we headed for the toilet.

Something caught my eye in the distance, near the wood chopping block. The ax was still sticking in a log. When I got closer, I could see black chicken feathers and blood on the log near the ax. I concluded that what I had suspected was true: Twenty, my pet chicken, had been served for supper! I was very upset, but did not dare show it or ask about it. Children were expected to mind their manners and not question the actions of the adults. For weeks I felt sick. When I went to bed, I could not stay still. The thought of Twenty being killed and eaten by my own family was sickening. How could they do that to me and to Twenty?

The cot that was my shared bed was covered with an old blanket and some old coats. Often when I awakened, the blankets and coats would be on the floor, and I would be on the bare springs of the cot. This night, I dreamed about Twenty as I tossed and turned in bed. It wasn't long before my joints got stiff from the extreme tension, and I could not lift my legs to go up or down the three steps of our house. I had to crawl. I refused to let the others know the reason, or how hurt I was to have my pet chicken served for supper.

While everyone else had enjoyed that unforgettable meal and went about their lives as usual, my world had stopped, and it took me a long time to restart it. Life went on around me as I gradually pulled out of my negative state. After several days, I resumed interacting with my sisters and brother—playing and fighting with my brother for the rocking chair. Since I had always been quiet, they didn't even notice the difference.

I know now that keeping us fed and clothed was always a challenge for the family. We did not have a car, so walking was our sole means of travel. When my sisters and brother and I went for a walk, we seldom went across the part of Wellons Street where the White neighborhood was. However, we had to go through that area to visit family friends in another Colored section of Suffolk, the neighborhood of South Suffolk. We walked in groups when going through White sections of town because dogs would attack us. When we visited family friends in other Colored sections, such as Philadelphia and Norfolk Road, we were able to go a different way. Life was not much better in those other sections than in Saratoga.

And walking took its toll on our shoes. When holes appeared in the soles of our shoes, we would cut pieces of cardboard box in the shape of our shoes and put them inside the shoes. The cardboard became uncomfortable when the shoes were old and worn, or when the ground was wet and the moisture seeped into the cardboard. When this happened, new pieces had to be cut. When the sole of a shoe came loose, we used chewing gum to glue it back on, except for the rare times that glue was available. If the sole of the shoe was thick enough, very small nails were used to reattach the loosened part.

Mama's requirement was that we all stick together. When one of us went anywhere, the others went too. We were to protect each other, even if it meant fighting. Dad told us that whenever we decided to fight, we must completely destroy the enemy. If we failed to do that, the enemy could return for revenge. We were not involved in many fights because we had safety in our numbers. I was the pacifist, avoiding conflict when I could, and running away when a situation seemed to be developing into a fight. My oldest sister, Audrey Mae, however, was a fighter who would bite her opponents, often drawing blood. Once a big mean girl that she bit went home crying and came back with her cursing mama. Her mama threatened to put chicken droppings on the bite wound to make Audrey Mae's teeth rot out. Audrey Mae was afraid for a long time because she believed that her teeth would really fall out. She stopped biting people after that incident.

Mama had methods for dealing with most of the trouble that came our way. Among the visitors to my neighborhood were insurance men, rent collectors, health nurses, vegetable and seafood salesmen, and the ice man. The insurance men, who were White, would go door-to-door collecting insurance money. When it was time to file a claim, though, often the insurance men could not be found, or the amount was so small that it was an insult. Nevertheless, people continued to pay the insurance men or hid from them when they did not have any money.

One time while we were still living with our Mama, an insurance man came to our house. Mama hid behind the door and told Audrey Mae to tell him that she was gone. When she told him that, he pushed the front door wide open as if he owned the house. Mama's feet could be seen under the door. So, the insurance man said angrily, "Tell her to take her feet with her the next time that she goes somewhere!" His face turned red, and he walked hurriedly to his car. My siblings and I laughed about that incident for a long time. Our insurance plan was canceled after Mama could not keep up the payments.

Mama never stopped caring for my siblings and me, and she never stopped teaching us how to behave. Despite the hardships and abuse from our father, she worked endlessly, both in and out of the house, trying her best to raise us properly and make our house a home. Alas, however, our up-and-down, yet familiar, existence was not to last for the rest of my childhood.

The End of Life as We Knew It

Mama's last baby, Mary Lee, was delivered with the help of a midwife—just like her other five children. I saw and heard it all through the skeleton-key hole, since the children were sent out of the room when the exciting part began.

I remember that the midwife requested some newspapers that were folded to make spit cups for Mama, during and shortly after the birthing period. Some of the paper was placed on the floor to catch the water, blood, and afterbirth matter resulting from the birth process. Boiled water was used to sterilize the surgical equipment, which was in the midwife's black bag that resembled a doctor's bag.

The midwife reached into her bag several times during Mary Lee's birth, to get medicine, scissors, or other items. The metal items were dipped into the boiling water prior to use. The baby was covered with white stuff at birth. The adults said that the white stuff was probably the Argo starch that Mama ate regularly during her pregnancy.

Just before the baby came out of my Mama, there was a lot of noise in the room. Mama was screaming in pain. The midwife urged her to push hard, while other adults in the room tapped her forehead with a towel to remove the sweat and to comfort her. Often they were in my line of sight through the key hole, or my older sisters pushed me aside so that they could peep too. Therefore, I could not see everything that I wanted to see. Where did that baby come from? I wondered. No stork was anywhere near that room. My sister moved away from the key hole just in time for me to see the midwife tie some string in two places around the long rope that connected the baby to Mama. She then grabbed her scissors and cut between her two ties.

I know that the tying and cutting hurt because the baby was crying very loud. The midwife covered the baby's navel area and put a cloth band around the baby's midsection. Cotton bands were normally worn around the baby's midsection until the navel healed; they could be purchased from various stores. If the navel poked out, a coin covered in Vaseline was placed over the navel and held in place with the band.

Mama named the baby Mary Lee. Once again, Mama recovered her strength and went on with her busy life. However, things were about to change.

Despite her outer calm demeanor, we soon learned that Mama was finally getting tired of the abuse from Dad. One day, she simply got up and went away. She confessed that she was afraid she might "wake up one day and find herself dead." The first time she left Dad, she stayed away for only a short while. Some say that Dad "put the roots on her" to force her return. This was not an unusual sentiment for a number of people to have in those days; belief in witchcraft was thought to be widespread in the various neighborhoods. Items owned by the person were given to the root doctor, who served up incantations. Then the items were buried near the steps of the person's home, supposedly forcing that person to do what was desired.

I never believed in witchcraft. Instead, I believed that my Mama loved my Dad. He could be charming at times. She liked that, and she would fall for his wooing every time. Having observed the drama and trauma that typified their life together, however, I decided at an early age that, for myself, I would never marry or remain with a man who beat me. I have always believed that life is too short to endure that kind of treatment.

When Mama finally left my Dad for good, she moved to another neighborhood, the Pleasant Hill section of Suffolk. She took all six of us children (Audrey Mae, Lee Vania, Benjamin, Eleanor, Mary Lee, and me) with her. Immediately after the move, we lived in a large two-story house, but we had only a few pieces of old furniture. Eventually, we moved into a place that had a small kitchen and a bedroom. Those two rooms were attached to a white, run-down building. We had a front porch and a tiny yard. It was the early 1950s and my baby sister, Mary Lee, was only a few months old.

The crushing blow came shortly after moving out of the house we grew up in. Mama became sick.

Mama stayed sick for weeks and was eventually sent to the community hospital for Colored people in Suffolk. Maybe Mama just didn't have enough money or insurance to pay for care in the larger, well-staffed hospital downtown. I believe that hospital may have been a segregated facility. Some Colored people worked there as house cleaners, launderers, cooks, and gardeners; however, I do not know if any Colored doctors or registered nurses were allowed to work there.

As a matter of fact, those kinds of medical facts were not discussed in my part of town. This may have been a result of a lack of health education. For example, no consideration was given to the fact that Dad's corn liquor might cause liver damage or another ailment, or that childbirth at home could result in extra risk. During my early years, no one seemed to care about medical concerns in the modern sense of the term. Old people had home remedies for everything. What they could not heal, witch doctors or midwives could handle.

The community hospital for Colored people that were too sick to be treated at home was a big, old yellow house with large windows that were often opened for fresh air. The floors were wooden and bare. There were many metal-framed beds with white sheets and pillowcases in each room. Bed pans were placed near the beds for use by patients who could not walk to the room that contained a slop jar; as far as I know, there were no flush toilets.

Mama's bed was near a window. She seemed so sad and often stared into "space." Once she asked for an orange, but she was never given one. For a long time, I wondered if she would have lived if she had received an orange. On August 13, 1951, she was pronounced dead, and my life changed forever. I was almost eight years old.

After Mama's death, a wreath of flowers was hung on the front door of the place where we lived, to remind everyone of what had happened. At the funeral, Mama appeared to be sleeping in the casket—resting, finally, after approximately 30 years of living in pain and hardship. She had on a cotton dress that was off-white with a big flower on the skirt. It was neither tight nor flared, but sort of A-lined. Her kinky short hair had been hot pressed and curled back from her face, the way she wore it when she was alive. The makeup that had been applied to her face at the funeral home made her face appear ashy and gray. I heard that one of the White people for whom she worked paid tribute to her by paying the funeral expenses.

At the funeral, my sisters and I were dressed in our best white dresses, and our brother wore his blue pants and a white shirt. People were crying and singing. Everyone was sad. The funeral home was scary—it was dark and smelled of death—and I wanted to get out of there. Finally, the funeral service ended. Someone made photographs of Mama in the casket and gave copies to my siblings and me. In time, those photographs were lost.

Mama had lived her adult life serving and taking care of others, and she died poor in terms of money and helpless in terms of being able to receive adequate medical attention. However, she was rich in terms of having left a legacy of children who will love her forever. She instilled strong work ethics in my siblings and me, and we used what we learned from her to survive. Although she was not formally educated, she was smart and caring, and she was a hard worker. She did what she could to teach us various skills that would continue to support us.

Often I imagine what my life would have been like if Mama had lived to see us become adults. Many years later, I recall my oldest sister saying that Mama would have been proud of all of our accomplishments. Yes, I agree she would have been proud of each of us. Her grave in Oaklawn Cemetery in Suffolk was marked by a simple wooden cross. The site was near a wooded area that seemed peaceful, a good place to serve as her final resting place. I felt then, and I still do, that she deserved to rest after such a hard life. My sister Eleanor later wrote the following tribute to Mama:

Mama[8]

In the graveyard, there is no headstone to visit.

There is no marker for your grave,
But we know how you unselfishly gave.

---

[8] Poem adapted from one written by Eleanor Olivia Mayo Minns in 2010.

Although without anything in return,
Heavenly rewards, you did earn.

What was due you in this life,
As a mama, server, cook, and wife,
Will be bestowed upon you in the next life.

You will continue to live in our hearts,
From which the memory of you never departs.

Mama, we love you, and we will never forget you.

Grandma Fannie Takes Us in

When the death and funeral service of my Mama took place, my Dad and Grandma Fannie still lived in Saratoga.

With Mama's death, however, my siblings and I were left without a home, family, or someone to take care of us. We did not hear from my Dad, who still lived in our house on Linden Avenue, about giving us any help with our living arrangements. It is likely we would have tried to avoid living with him anyway.

My oldest sister, Audrey Mae, was only about eleven years old, and Lee Vania was only nine or ten. I had not reached my eighth birthday. Benjamin, my brother, was about five. Eleanor and Mary Lee were three and almost one, respectively.

Given our predicament, we thought that we were headed for the orphan home, which in those days was viewed as the juvenile detention center. We had heard the gossip and teasing of the neighborhood children. However, Mama's wish was for us to stay together, and we decided that we would find an adult to take us in and make Mama's wish a reality. We were lucky; the good deeds of our neighbors made it possible. Shortly after Mama's death, my siblings and I lived in five or six different homes, in the same neighborhood where we had lived prior to Mama becoming ill. We stayed in one home after another, each for only a short period. The important thing is that we were all together just as our Mama wished.

Each of our temporary adoptive families did its best to care for us, and my siblings and I are very grateful for their assistance and the sacrifices they made to keep us together. I would thank those families in person, but I do not remember their names.

Although we were treated well in the different homes, the sudden presence of six small children was undoubtedly too big a burden for the host families. We probably ate too much, and broke toys or dishes. Heaven forbid that we would break anything deliberately, but we were only children. We surely made too much noise and needed too much time and attention from the adults of the house.

In each home, we slept in one room, and we ate meals after the host family had finished eating, since the table was never large enough to seat all of them plus the six of us at the same time. We were not abused in ways that orphans often complained about, then and now. In return, we tried our best to be obedient and respectful "orphans." We tried to be helpful; however, we just did not know many useful things. We were too young. Usually, our home had been cluttered and messy because, when Mama was alive, she was usually very tired after working all day cleaning someone else's house. Although Mama had tried to teach us how to take care of our house, she was not a strict person, and discipline had been somewhat lax.

Although Granddaddy Benjamin had died long before I was born, Grandma Fannie—my Dad's mother—was still alive and living in Saratoga, with some of our cousins, when my Mama died. During the time that our community was passing us around every few weeks and taking care of us, someone contacted Grandma Fannie about our situation. By that time, we had already lived with five or six different families in our neighborhood.

Grandma Fannie came to our house in somebody's car and took us to live in her house on Battery Avenue, in the Saratoga section of Suffolk—around the corner from where we had grown up with Mama and Dad. It was a nice two-story, unpainted house with three or four bedrooms upstairs. There was a large kitchen with a large walk-in pantry, a dining room, a living room, a big hallway upstairs and one downstairs, a front porch, and a porch, called the back porch, on the side of the house. The back porch had a water pump—our only source of good water. Grandma Fannie had flowers, including hydrangeas (which we called "snowballs") and gladiolas, in her front yard and a walnut tree in the back yard—a welcome change from our previous barren lawn. Of course, the outhouse and clothesline for drying clothes were in the backyard, too.

Grandma Fannie had many beautiful glasses, cups, and saucers. Some were green, and others were pink. She also had several clear glass items. Some of this was hand-blown glass, which I can only imagine might have been valuable. In the backyard, she kept a pig in an enclosed area, some chickens that ran free (which today would be known as "free-range" chickens), and a small garden. Our former dog, Rex, had been moved there after being left at our old house on Linden Avenue, and a cat lived there, too. There were plenty of flies—so many that the downstairs walls of the house were covered with fly specks. These specks could be seen even among the soot from the wood stove and heater—just like in our former home.

There were a number of other fancy things in my Grandma's house. She had a manual Singer sewing machine as well as pots and pans made of cast iron. But the glassware was the most beautiful. Some of the clear glass saucers had been prizes from boxes of oatmeal. Some of the glassware was Depression glass, a type that years later was prized by antique shops.

After being at Grandma Fannie's home for a while, we accidently broke all of her fancy pink and green depression glasses and clear glass saucers. I must admit that my siblings and I were a destructive force. Within a few months, there were only mayonnaise and mason jars from which to drink water, lemonade, and tea since all of the glasses had been sacrificed to the romping and rough-housing of young children.

When the six of us moved into the house, the dining room was converted into a bedroom in which four of my siblings and I slept. Mary Lee, the baby, slept in Grandma Fannie's bedroom, which was the converted living room. Thus all of the rooms in the house became bedrooms, except the kitchen. I did my homework by the light of a kerosene lamp, since electricity still had not reached the Saratoga neighborhood.

As always, the kerosene was purchased from Mrs. Hurdle's store, which was near my Grandma's house. Whenever my sisters and I went to that store, we bought whatever our Grandma sent us to buy, plus some ginger snaps and penny candy. When we did not have any money of our own—which was usually the case—we would take some from the bag of coins that Grandma kept under her bed. This meant that we had to eat anything purchased with the stolen coins before returning home.

Sometimes Audrey Mae just took a few coins and headed straight to Mrs. Hurdle's store. There she bought candy and five-cent sodas in tinted glass bottles. She would open each soda with the metal bottle opener that was nailed onto the door frame of the store. She ate and drank before reaching home, or hid in the house until she had drunk and eaten all that she had bought. She took enough coins to buy goodies for us, too.

In time, the bag was only half full and, later, almost empty. Grandma Fannie may not have noticed that some coins were missing. She never said anything about the missing coins, and my siblings and I did not say anything either. There were benefits for not telling on our sister. Whenever Audrey Mae was sent to the store with a glass jug to purchase kerosene for the lamps—or when she just headed there on her own—she always shared the goodies with us.

The following year, 1952, electricity was installed in Grandma's house and in the entire neighborhood. A light hung by a cord from the ceiling of each room. There was a string attached to each light to turn it on and off. At last, we could put away our candles and kerosene lamps, and reading was much easier. I could travel to many lands in my imagination by reading books I brought home from the Ida V. Easter Grade School. The ice box remained the same, requiring blocks of ice for cooling food. Each week, the ice man rode through the neighborhood in a truck and sold ice to Grandma Fannie, as well as other adults.

Since Grandma Fannie lived around the corner from where we once lived in Saratoga, we were very comfortable in the neighborhood, and we knew many of the people. Of course, people gossiped about each other, as always. We heard rumors that in earlier years Grandma Fannie had passed for White while teaching at a school in another county. When she found out that the school officials had learned she was Colored, she left that job, since Colored people were not permitted to teach in schools for Whites. If she had stayed, she would have been fired anyway. By the time my siblings and I began living in her home, she was employed at the Planters peanut factory—owned by Planters Nut and Chocolate Company—the largest employer in Suffolk. While we were still living with her, she retired, giving her more time to work around the house instead of at the factory.

With our arrival, the total number of people living in Grandma Fannie's house rose to about a dozen. One of my cousins, Joe Louis Bullock, was older than my oldest sister. He had a trumpet and a motorcycle, and I spent a lot of time helping him with his trumpet playing by turning the pages of sheet music at his command. He took me riding on his motorcycle, and my siblings and I had many hours of play time with him. As children in Grandma's home, we considered all of us to be brothers and sisters, although, in fact, most of those who already lived there were our cousins. Our other cousins—the sons of our great aunt Lucy and great uncle Ruel Myrick—who lived on Brook Avenue visited on occasion.

When Grandma was away from home, my sisters and I played with her sewing machine. It was the most intriguing machine that I had ever seen, and I wanted to operate it. One day as I sat in the chair at the sewing machine and worked the foot paddle as if I were sewing, my sister yelled that Grandma was coming down the street. She had finished her work day at the Planters factory and was returning home. As I turned to look toward my sister, the foot of the machine that holds fabric in place landed on a finger of my right hand, and the needle of the machine penetrated the finger. My finger bled profusely, and my fingernail was distorted permanently.

I did not tell my Grandma about what had happened, however, because of the fear of being punished for misbehaving. My sisters kept it a secret, as I did about bad things that they had done in the past. My brother, Benjamin, did not see what happened since he was outside playing with one of his friends. Some of their choices for playtime were rolling in old car or truck tires or inner tubes, walking around on stilts, and kite flying. I was relieved to know that he was preoccupied with whatever games he was playing that day because, surely, he would have told on me.

Our neighbor, whom we called Sis' Arie, bought a TV just after electricity was installed in her house. Although my Grandma would not permit us to go inside Sis' Arie's house to watch TV, we watched it through her window as we stood in our yard. It was the most exciting thing that I had ever seen. There was Mickey Mouse Club, American Bandstand, the Little Rascals, the I Love Lucy Show, the Ed Sullivan Show, Amos and Andy, dramas with cowboys and Indians, and much more. We would stand in our yard watching TV through the window for hours. Sis' Arie didn't object.

Sometimes Cous' Lessie, who lived with Sis' Arie, would be in the room watching it, too. That was amazing to us, since she was a deaf mute. Sometimes watching her was even more fun than watching the TV. We communicated with her using a made-up sign language. When other residents of the house, Mr. Thurman and Mr. Cutie, were watching TV, they would close the curtains so that we could not watch through the window. We assumed that Mr. Thurman was tired from working at his cleaners all day. We knew that he worked hard because we stopped by there to sell wire coat hangers to him. We did not know why Mr. Cutie needed peace and quiet, since we never actually saw him working. When they closed the curtains, we would listen to the sound of the TV and be just as satisfied. Sometimes we could hear that TV even while we were in our beds. The windows were not closed and doors were kept unlocked, even when no one was home—at their house as well as ours.

Sis' Arie had a bad dog named "Black Diamond" in her backyard. Black Diamond was big, shiny black, and ferocious. He was kept chained to a tree in the fenced yard. Sometimes, however, he broke loose and ran like a wild animal across our yard and into the streets of the neighborhood. When he was loose, everyone would run into their houses and close their doors until he was caught by Mr. Cutie and a few other men. Black Diamond never bit anyone, but he would attack other dogs and the goat that was kept on the trash heap around the corner. Black Diamond acted crazily whenever he was not chained. One thing was clear: no stranger ever went into

Sis' Arie's backyard while Black Diamond was there. I think this was what kept her from being robbed of all of the pretty and expensive things she had in her house.

Grandma Fannie and Sis' Arie were good friends and were thought to be related. They often talked to each other. The latter was true of Mrs. Hurdle as well, whose store was beside Sis' Arie's house. Grandma Fannie and Sis' Arie would go to Mrs. Hurdle's store and buy Coca Cola and BC or Stanback headache powder. There they would sit and talk for a while, take their headache powder, and wash it down with Coca Cola. Then they would return to their homes and prepare family meals or complete other tasks.

Across the street from Grandma's house was the home of the Barnes family, and across from Mrs. Hurdle's store was the home of the Green family. Most people sat on their front porches to relax. Everyone knew each other, and everyone spoke politely when passing. On the other side of Grandma's house was a large single-level house that sat on the corner of Linden Avenue and Battery Avenue. The Darden family that lived in that house owned a garden that separated their house from ours. They grew a variety of vegetables and shared them with us. A sweet scuppernong grapevine separated the side of our house from their garden. In the summertime, I would swing on the large wooden swing that was hung on the front porch and eat grapes or another fruit or nuts. Near the grapevine was a pear tree from which we snatched many delicious pears. Grandma even made pear preserve, which we ate during the winters.

From another neighbor's fig tree, Grandma made fig preserve. She pickled watermelon rind, too. Very little was wasted. Even the swill from garbage was fed to our pig (we never kept more than one pig at a time) and chickens. There was no garbage man to pick up the garbage; therefore, anything that was not recycled was burned in the backyard, and the ashes were scattered around the yard.

Grandma Fannie did not grow melons in our small garden. She bought watermelons and cantaloupes from the watermelon man. He would ride through the neighborhood with watermelons and other melons on his truck, singing: "Watermelon man; come get 'um if you can. Nice and juicy and sweet as can be!" When Grandma went to his truck, he would give her a plug of watermelon as a sample. That way she would know the quality of his watermelons.

He would try to convince her to buy other vegetables and fruits as well. He would point to his berries and say, "The blacker the berry, the sweeter the juice." She would walk away. What money she had left was needed to buy a block of ice from the ice man for the ice box. Sometimes she would buy a whole fish from the fisherman who would ride through the neighborhood with a large fish on ice in the back of his truck. The ice would melt and mix with fish juices and drip onto the street made of packed small rocks. In the hot summer, the odor was awful, but the fish was good.

We never bought much fish from the fisherman, since Grandma often purchased fish from the Harding family's shop. The supply of food was excellent in Grandma's home. The only dish that she prepared that I did not like was turtle. It had muscle contractions while being cooked in the frying pan. My imagination went wild. I imagined the turtle contracting as I swallowed it, and I could see it shaking all down in my stomach. No, that was not for me!

The health of my siblings and me was addressed on a regular basis by Nurse Betty Davis. Nurse Davis picked us up in her car and took my siblings and me to the Suffolk Health Clinic for x-rays, required vaccinations, and other medical services. This was done for several years after the death of my mother in 1951. We were frequently tested for tuberculosis (TB). In the process, I learned that my mother had died from miliary TB,[9] a form of the disease in which the highly contagious bacteria spread to multiple organs in the body. If left untreated, miliary TB is fatal. Unfortunately, my Mama had not received any treatments for miliary TB.

Fortunately, our examinations at the Suffolk Health Clinic did not result in the identification of any health problems in my siblings

[9]   Virginia Certificate of Death #18016 issued for Martha Artis Mayo, wife of Clifton Mayo, on August 13, 1951; changed on December 9, 1952 to Martha Artis (her last name and Clifton Mayo are crossed out by hand) at the request of the Veteran's Administration.

and me. We did not have any health insurance coverage. Primarily, my siblings and I survived from Grandma Fannie's home remedies. I remember having to take castor oil, Black Draught (a laxative), and cod-liver oil for different aliments. When we had worms, each of us had to swallow a spoonful of sugar spiked with turpentine. Then my Grandma would make a circle around the navel with turpentine and draw a cross under it with turpentine. When we had chest colds, our chests were rubbed with an ointment from the store or a substance prepared by her. Alcohol or tincture of iodine was poured on sores and cuts to disinfect them and facilitate healing. Most of us sustained cuts from glass, since we walked barefoot most of the time. Grandma's treatments sometime hurt, but they always worked.

On occasion, we ate oatmeal in the morning. Other times, we ate Grandma Fannie's homemade biscuits with preserves or store-bought molasses. On other occasions we ate meat and bread or whatever was left over from supper. Sometimes we had leftover biscuits that we dipped into weak coffee containing Carnation milk from a can. I never developed a taste for coffee, but the combination helped to keep away hunger sensations until lunch time. With the exception of coffee, I found the food at Grandma Fannie's delicious—except when we had to take medicine with it, of course.

While living with Grandma Fannie, my two older sisters attended Ida V. Easter Graded School, and I attended Miss Estelle's kindergarten until I began attending grade school three months prior to my seventh birthday. This kindergarten was located on the corner of Battery Avenue and Linden Avenue. It was not even a block from where my family lived at the time. Attending kindergarten was a great deal of fun, and my fellow classmates and I learned a tremendous amount—the alphabet and many other things that kids should know by the time they reached first grade. I enjoyed the time spent in kindergarten with Miss Estelle teaching me and other kids in the neighborhood. I felt comfortable there.

Once I began attending Ida V. Easter Graded School, I had to overcome my fear of being there and of walking in certain areas of the neighborhood to get there. The school was a few blocks from home, but I was afraid of dogs in the yards of homes that I had to pass as I walked to and from school. There were no animal laws; therefore, dogs were seldom kept on leashes.

At school, I was in the company of a number of relatives and friends—I particularly remember Caroline Perkins, Geraldine Williams, Yvonne Boone, Ruth Harding, Ruby Smallwood, and James Grant. I recall sitting in the classroom full of students and refusing to speak because I was frightened of the teachers, who, unlike the students, were strangers to me—but I overcame that fear. I already knew quite a bit but did not communicate it well. One very important thing that I learned at school was—with the exception of Benjamin—the other males who lived in my Grandma's home were not my brothers. They were cousins with different last names. I also learned that my birthday was not November 6, the date on which my Grandma would have a birthday party for all of us. She would make a yellow cake with apple or grape jelly between the layers. Then she would cover the cake with chocolate icing—delicious! Candles were added, and all of us would blow them out together. Then we would sing the happy birthday song and play while eating cake and homemade ice cream.

Early in the school year the beginning students had to get vaccinations. My vaccination made a large scar on my left upper arm. The pain of the injection caused me to cry, as did other children. Some cried even before they received their injections. Then my classmates and I practiced saying the alphabet, which I already knew, having learned it at Miss Estelle's kindergarten. Learning to spell my full name and learning that my birth date was not November 6 were major feats. I did not want to learn a new birth date; I liked having cake and homemade ice cream with my family members on our special birthday. However, it was mandatory to learn and use the correct birth date and name in school.

As I learned to interact with the children at school, I became more relaxed. Prior to entering first grade, most of my time had been spent with relatives in my home and with the students who attended kindergarten with me. We played hide and seek, hopscotch, jump rope, spinning around until dizzy, spinning tops, bob jacks, and ring around the roses. I was not good at riding my light green bicycle and roller skates, so I did not try that often. On occasion at Ida V. Easter Graded School, teachers had students sell candy to earn funds for school supplies and activities. Although I accepted boxes of Hershey candy bars, I did not sell them. I ate the candy and had to earn money to pay for each box. I loved sweets, and I still do, especially chocolate candy.

For my first job, when I was less than 12 years old, I worked as a maid for Mrs. Welch, who lived on the same street as we did in Saratoga. To earn money, I scrubbed and waxed hardwood floors and washed wooden window blinds. Sometimes I helped her pick and snap beans from her backyard garden. On other occasions, I helped her with other chores. She paid me for all that I did. By present-day standards, it was not much—fifty cents for scrubbing and waxing the wooden floor. A dollar here and there was great for me, though.

Mrs. Welch was a well-off person who did not have to work outside of her home. Her house was beautiful, and I enjoyed working for her. When she prepared to go out of the house, she would fix her hair in a special way and cover the gray using a special coloring stick. She would ask me if she had covered all of her gray before she left the house. I often wondered why she did that, since gray hair suited her well. I used the money from the job to buy needed personal and school items and to pay for the school candy that I had eaten instead of sold.

Another person for whom I worked as a maid was Mrs. Jones, whom we called Miss Pearl. She was a teacher at Ida V. Easter Graded School. Her house was loaded with expensive things, such as real silverware that had to be polished, a caged bird that was messy, hardwood floors to be kept clean, and heavy furniture made of real wood that had to be polished with an oil. Rewards for my work included money, gifts, and food. I recall receiving from her a beautiful light blue set of "Baby Doll" sleepwear and other clothes. I really appreciated all that Mrs. Welch, Mrs. Jones and Mr. and Mrs. Cook—my later employers—did for me. I was such a diligent worker that one of my cousins was occasionally brought to our house by her mother to watch me work. Perhaps it would have been better if she had worked along with me, but that never happened.

On some summer days, Audrey Mae, Lee Vania, and I would stand on the corner in our neighborhood early in the morning to wait for a truck to pick us up. In our jeans, old blouses, and tennis shoes we would join others in the truck, which took us to a farm to work. We never knew to which farm we would be taken on a given day. Once at the farm we picked strawberries, vegetables, or cotton. The work day was long, and the payment was small. I hated picking cotton, and I was lucky that I only went to the cotton field once. While the cotton was soft, the part of the plant that held it was hard and scratched my fingers. It was difficult to pull the bag of cotton when it was filled. It was sometimes very hot in the fields, and usually there were no nearby outhouses. I just wanted to go home. A major problem in some of the fields was snakes, the thought of which was frightening.

One time when we stopped for lunch in the field, Audrey Mae and Lee Vania asked for some of my lunch. I knew that they had brought their lunches with them, as I had. They were sure that I had some tasty sandwiches and that I would share my lunch with them; therefore, they gave away theirs before lunchtime. Since I am a soft-hearted person, I gave each of them one of my sandwiches. They were disappointed when they found out that my sandwiches were made of bananas, mayonnaise, and bread. I laughed at their reaction to what I considered to be a delicious lunch. After that incident, they never begged for my lunch again, and they fixed their own.

During the academic year, I worked after school on some days and on Saturdays. I had other tasks to complete at home at night, including studying.

Living at Grandma Fannie's House

Eventually, Uncle Ruel, my great uncle, died, and the last of his children moved out-of-state to begin their families. Aunt Lucy was lonesome, and she asked for and received Grandma Fannie's permission for me to stay at her house during the night on several occasions. The presence of someone else in the house made her feel more comfortable. In my neighborhood, there were no assisted-living or senior-citizen homes for elderly Colored people. Most people continued to live in their own homes even after they became elderly, or family members moved them into their homes and took care of them.

Uncle Ruel and Aunt Lucy had four children. Their oldest son became a lawyer and lived with his wife and children in the Washington, DC, metro area. Their youngest son joined the Coast Guard. When he came home for visits, I would wash his white gloves for him. I had never seen a man wear gloves until then, but white cotton gloves were a part of his Coast Guard uniform. Their other children had good positions in other states.

In the late 1940s and early 1950s in Saratoga, I recall being cautioned about the dangers of being caught out of my section of town and about the racism that existed. While we were busy at home, the world outside was a different place. The Saratoga section of town had the reputation of being somewhat violent. Seldom did anyone leave there without physical or mental scars. There were reminders everywhere: persons with knife scars, one eye, missing teeth, and missing limbs. However, these things did not have any direct impact on me, because I rarely went out, and almost never alone. I was too busy working for other families and doing my chores at home—chopping wood with a large ax, washing clothes on a washboard in a large tin tub, hanging clothes on the line in the backyard, and picking walnuts from the tree in our backyard.

My siblings, also, were busy with different home chores. Under the guidance of Grandma Fannie, my oldest sister did some of the cooking for the family. Grandma could make the most delicious biscuits in the world, and she explained the recipe to my oldest sister, Audrey Mae. Those biscuits were even more delicious with the fig or other preserves made by Grandma. As a matter of fact, my Grandma was an excellent cook, and she taught Audrey Mae well.

Sunday dinners were special. Lee Vania, my second oldest sister, helped cook some of those dinners. On Sundays we would have dessert (such as sweet potato pie, sweet potato jacks, bread pudding, rice pudding with raisins, cake, jello, apple jacks, or strawberry short cake) and tea or lemonade. We ate chicken, pork, and other meats too. Bear meat was very good, but venison was the best. We ate chicken legs cooked with dumplings, and navy beans with dumplings. There was very little that we needed from Mr. Smith's Grocery Store located at the edge of the White section near Saratoga. There, Grandma bought the few items she needed to purchase from a store: flour, sugar, bologna, molasses, franks, and lard.

Dressing for school in the mornings was a hassle because most of our clothes were stacked in the hallway of the house and had to be sorted daily. I had to find my clothes and make sure that they were in order for me to wear. Sometimes my socks did not get dry during the night, and I would dry them in the oven of the wood-burning stove in the kitchen, which was warm as a result of my Grandma's breakfast cooking. Usually she or Audrey Mae cooked oatmeal for us. Sometimes the oven was too hot, and the socks would scorch, but that did not matter since the imperfection would be inside my black-and-white saddle oxford shoes. Paying for a new pair of those shoes was not easy. Often the shoe soles would have a hole in them from long wear, which was remedied by inserting a piece of corrugated cardboard into the shoes, as explained earlier. We outgrew them, too—but wore them anyway. If we received a donation of a pair of shoes that was too large, one of us would wear them after pushing some paper into the toe parts of the shoes. This made the shoes fit better. My siblings and I brushed our teeth using Arm and Hammer

Baking Soda and rinsed our mouths with water from the pump on the back porch.

Getting my hair done was another task. For regular school days, either one of my sisters or I would braid it. Lard was used if no Royal Crown hair dressing was available. On special occasions, my hair was pressed with a hot comb. When I had to be on a school or church program, Mrs. Olivia, our local hairdresser, would shampoo, press, and curl it for a small amount of money. She did such a great job of straightening and curling my hair that I could feel the heat of the comb and curlers as they occasionally nicked my scalp. Bangs and a row curl in the back was my style; that was common for a kid my age.

Me wearing my favorite hair style

On special occasions, I would wear a blue or white ribbon in my hair, tied in a bow. To make the curls last a long time, pieces of brown paper bag were twisted and used as hair rollers at night. The top of a stocking was cut, and the cut part was tied so that the large part of the stocking could be used as a night cap to cover the rolled hair overnight. That kept it in place while I slept. When my hair was combed the next day, it looked great for a while, but as soon as moisture was in the air, my hair reverted to its natural state. In its natural state, I would wear it in beautiful braids. I loved the variety of hair styles that I could achieve with my hair, whether it was natural or pressed.

At school, some of the girls had pierced ears and wore beautiful earrings attached through the holes in their ears. For some, gouges on the ear lobes were prominent, but it was said that those resulted from the way ear piercing was done—with a needle that had been "sterilized" by burning the tip with a lit match and then used to pierce the ear lobe. Vaseline was rubbed on the ear lobe, and a straw from the broom used to sweep floors was burned on both ends and pushed into each hole made with the needle. The straw covered with Vaseline was kept in the hole in the ear lobe until the area healed. Each straw was pushed back and forth on a daily basis. When and if the area around the hole healed, earrings were worn. I chose not to have my ears pierced. Never did I want to have the problems associated with ear piercing.

At home, there was always something exciting happening in our neighborhood. A very important salesman who came through the neighborhood after we moved to Grandma's house was the ice man. Most homes were still equipped with ice boxes that required blocks of ice to cool the food. The ice man drove up and down the streets of Saratoga yelling, "Ice for sale!" He would chisel any size of block using an ice pick—a dangerous-looking item that anyone could purchase. Ice picks had multiple purposes. Some people used them in their weekend fights when whiskey flowed freely, tempers got hot, and emotions became uncontrollable. Some of the fights were over cheating lovers and other unreasonable things. Even though this happened often, policemen were seldom seen in our neighborhood. However, the rescue squad was seen in the neighborhood on numerous occasions. This was due to accidents, fires, animal attacks, water rescues, outhouse rescues, snake bites, the results of knife and gunshot fights, and attempted suicides, all of which would usually require emergency personnel to provide assistance.

The Raleigh cigarette man never stopped in the neighborhood. However, he would drive slowly through the neighborhood and throw snuff and other tobacco samples out of his car window.

My two older sisters ran to retrieve the samples before the adults noticed them. The two of them would keep the tobacco samples for themselves. Any products that I found I turned over gladly to my older sisters. Audrey Mae would put a dip of the snuff between her lower lip and gum and periodically spit brown spittle for hours. Lee Vania would smoke the cigarettes. Of course, no adults knew this, and they told me not to tell. I didn't tell anyone because I knew my sisters might beat me up if I did.

When we needed groceries, Grandma sent or took us to Mr. Smith's Grocery Store, a White-owned store. It was common practice in the South of the 1950s and 1960s for Whites to own stores in or near Colored communities. Such stores extended credit to Colored people in the area. Both White and Colored People frequented Mr. Smith's store, and he even had some Colored employees. Grandma Fannie knew Mr. Smith, the owner, and she had a grocery credit account with him. He would cash her paychecks and let her have food until her check was received. She only bought a few items of food from the store. Most of the meat she needed was provided by relatives and neighbors, who sold meat from their houses, or by salesmen who sold meat from trucks. Vegetables were grown in the garden or bought from other salesmen who rode through the neighborhood. Dan Doodles, a pork mixture that family members made for seasoning the salad and collard greens, seemed to last forever. The same was true of meats that were smoked by my relatives in their smoke house in Courtland, Virginia, and brought to Grandma Fannie by our cousins. Those cousins were the children of Aunt Armeania and Uncle Phil who lived on a large farm. They, like other family members, shared their resources.

My family members liked the different seasons, but they liked the hunting season best. They also liked fishing and crabbing. Those who went hunting or fishing would wear high boots with paper stuffed into them. That paper provided a limited amount of protection from the bites of snakes, and the rubber boots provided protection from water. After a successful hunting or fishing trip, they would bring wild game, fresh farm animal meat, fish, and crabs to share at Grandma Fannie's home.

When the food was ready, the amount seemed to have multiplied. There were pots and pans full of meat. Grandma added other food items (e.g., cornbread, navy beans, some of which were cooked with dumplings to make the soup heavy and delicious, cabbage, collards, corn, and other vegetables) to complete the meal. For treats, we often ate peanuts that had been roasted in the oven of our kitchen stove, and desserts.

Adults ate first. Perhaps this was due to the large number of relatives who sat at the round table in Grandma Fannie's kitchen. There were lively conversations among those around the table and in the yard. After the adults had finished eating, children were permitted to eat at the table. Sometimes we would make fun of the adults or repeat jokes that we had heard them tell as we waited for our chance to sit at the table. The mood was lively, and this was a fun time.

Fishing and crabbing were not the only means by which my family obtained seafood. As mentioned earlier, fresh fish was bought from the Harding family, who lived in the neighborhood, and from a man who sold seafood from his truck. Living near the ocean and the muddy Nansemond River proved advantageous. These were ready sources of crabs and fish that I love to eat. Although I never went hunting, I did go crabbing. For me, this was a challenge since I had to wake up very early in the morning and sit by the river with my relatives as they did the fishing or crabbing. The sounds of the early morning hours were frightening. I was told to be careful as I watched for snakes and large frogs. The rumor was that the Nansemond River had a number of sinkholes in it. Anyone who fell into one might be pulled underwater and drowned. This happened to a boy from my neighborhood who tried swimming in the river. That incident was sad, and his grandmother with whom he lived was traumatized by the incident, as were other family members and neighbors.

The yard of Grandma's home was stripped bare of grass, but the flowers made it look nice in the summertime. In the backyard, there were two clotheslines on which washed clothes were hung to dry with wooden clothespins. These wire clotheslines served double duty. When one of the chickens kept in the yard was needed for supper, its feet were tied to the clothesline. Then its head was grasped and the neck pulled while a sharp butcher's knife was used to cut its neck. The chicken would flutter, flinging blood everywhere, but it did not get messed up by fluttering in the dirt, since it was tied on the clothesline. After it stopped fluttering and the blood had drained out, Grandma would untie its feet and put it into a pan of scalding hot water. This would make it easy to remove the feathers. Once the feathers were removed, the chicken's guts were removed and discarded and its body cut up. We used all parts—gizzards, heart, liver—except the head and guts in our meals. We even had chicken-feet soup. None of the children wanted to eat the "last thing that came over the fence"—the chicken's tail.

Some Northern parents sent their children to live with relatives in Saratoga for the summer. My siblings and I would watch some of them out of curiosity. One day, we heard about a girl who visited her grandmother in my neighborhood. We had seen her several times, but we never said anything to her except to speak politely. When we heard the siren of the rescue squad and saw where it stopped to provide service, we ran to the scene. We learned that the girl from up North who lived in that house had swallowed some lye. Perhaps she did not know how dangerous it was, or perhaps she was unhappy with the strict way she was treated in her relatives' home. I think that she wanted to kill herself.

The girl was called "fast," a negative term usually used to indicate premature mental and physical maturation and sexual involvement with many males at a premature age. She wanted to have many boys around her, but by local unwritten standards, she was too young for that. On the day that she swallowed the lye, her grandmother forced her to swallow some lard. That stopped the burning a little. By the time the rescue squad arrived, she was still screaming from pain. She was treated on the spot and restricted to bed rest with prescribed medication. Her actions seemed ridiculous to me and other young girls who lived in the neighborhood. We knew that most people in our neighborhood bought cans of lye in powder form to sprinkle in their outhouses. The lye facilitated fecal decay and the killing of pests. Neighborhood children knew its dangers.

In addition to this type of case, the rescue squad was summoned to provide other emergency care. The siren of the rescue squad vehicle was loud, and it struck a sense of horror in me. I remember the response to provide assistance to a person who had fallen through weak floor boards of an outhouse. As the person was pulled out of the hole, the odor was awful. Water was poured over him, and he was checked for physical responses. Special efforts were made to ensure that he could breathe correctly and talk. On another occasion, a lady tied her cheating and abusive husband in a sheet after he went to sleep. She poured hot water on him and ran out of the house. The rescue squad responded to that tragedy, too. It was clear that the rescue squad was needed and valued in my neighborhood.

My siblings and I were church-goers. Lakeview Baptist Church located on Brook Avenue was our home church. There we did much singing and speech making for years. I was the giver of welcome speeches, but at home I was the cleaner, wood chopper, and water pumper. Lee Vania was the singer in the family. She also helped with the house cleaning, the washing of clothes, and other chores. My oldest sister was the cook. My two other sisters and brother were too young to do anything of significance except play and make noise. Many hours were spent listening to the pastor, Reverend Daughtry, preach fire and brimstone.

We watched elderly ladies shout and make testimony to God at key moments in the church service. After special services, church members participated in a feast, each dish of which had been prepared by different members of the church. I do not remember my Grandma, Dad, or Mama going to Sunday school or church, but my sisters, brother, and I attended regularly. A gentleman in the neighborhood held meetings one day each week for Bible study and discipline discussions. With his guidance, we named our club IAH, which stood for I Am HIS. The "HIS" referred to God.

I liked attending school, but it had an undesirable feature. During my years at Ida V. Easter Graded School, a teacher could discipline students by beating them. I guess child abuse was not recognized in those days. Audrey Mae received many such beatings by a teacher using a piece of stove wood or a switch from a tree. Seemingly, this happened because Audrey Mae had difficulty learning. Finally, she quit before finishing grade school. Even though she could neither read nor write well, she could cook and carry on a conversation with anyone. Her cooking was that down-home type that tasted as if she had "put her foot into it." Another thing that she could do well was count money. Perhaps this is a capability that develops in people who do not have much money to count. With limited resources, people learn to value each penny.

Even though there were approximately a dozen people living in Grandma's house at one time, no one went hungry. Even some of the neighborhood people came by for food. Hog-killing day was an exciting one that our neighbors enjoyed as much as we did. The hog was let loose in the yard, and the children (including me) would chase it to try to make it run toward our cousin so that he could hit it in the head with the ax. Sometimes it would run under the house where we had to go to flush it out. When the hog was killed, the men would cut the big pieces of meat into smaller parts—ham, pork chops, ham hocks, pork ribs, and neck bones. The women would salt down certain cuts of meat or prepare them for immediate cooking or slow smoking in the smoke house. Hog brains were used as a breakfast food after being fried. For many Sundays we would have ham to eat. It was delicious when eaten in a biscuit with mustard.

The hog's stomach or large intestines sack was cleaned and all scraps that were left from other edible parts of the hog were cooked, seasoned, cut into small pieces, and stuffed into it. The resulting sack full of meat was placed into a smoke house for several days. A sign of its readiness was the change in its color to mahogany. This was the making of the Dan Doodle that was used to season greens and other vegetables or sliced and fried for eating. Ham hocks were used to season vegetables, too. The intestines of the hog were cleaned.

This was a stinky task. Once cleaned, they were boiled in a large pot on the wood stove. White potatoes were added to absorb some of the odor, but nothing could completely eliminate the odor, which lingered for days. When this gray mass of chitterlings was served, some used vinegar to enhance the taste.

Often the potatoes used were from the potato flat—a conveyor belt where potatoes were being sorted—near the railroad that separated downtown Suffolk from the ball park, junkyard, and other areas. My siblings and I would pick up the potatoes that fell from the potato flat as people sorted the rotten ones from the good ones. One day, as my sisters and I were picking up potatoes near the potato flat, the White foreman yelled to us to give him the bag of potatoes that we had collected. We looked at each other. As we began running, he threatened to call the police. With that, we dropped the potatoes and continued running like mad. After that incident we did not go back to the area. Rumor had it that the foreman thought that some of the workers were throwing good potatoes to us. Maybe so! Maybe not!

Desserts were served on Sundays. Cakes were the specialty of our house. Grandma would make them from scratch. My oldest sister could make delicious cakes, too. Also, she could make some great-tasting sweet potato pies. On some summer days, when we had a lot of strawberries, they were washed and allowed to sit with sugar sprinkled on them. When the sugar dissolved, that sweet combination was served over a piece of cake. I loved all of the desserts, and I could hardly wait until Sunday to have some. My siblings and I ate many sweet potatoes, some of which were grated and baked after the addition of butter, nutmeg, cinnamon, vanilla extract, and sugar to make a pudding. Other whole sweet potatoes were baked in the oven until soft. These were served as a side dish for a Sunday meal of kale or collards seasoned with bacon or ham hocks. Also, chicken, homemade biscuits, and beans seasoned with fatback were served. Sometime we had bread pudding or rice pudding made with sugar, raisins, and cinnamon.

On several days of the week other children would come over to play. If they were there at mealtime, they would stay to eat. That was perfectly acceptable to my Grandma, who never objected to their presence. It could be that she never noticed that there were additional children at the table.

Whenever there was a thunderstorm, however, no one came to visit. People in the neighborhood would stop whatever they were doing and be quiet—a courtesy to God. Grandma said that "God was doing his work. When he does his work, we are to keep quiet." There were other odd sayings about the weather. One of them was: "When the sun is shining while rain is falling, the devil is beating his wife." I did not know that the devil had a wife, and I thought that men in my neighborhood learned from the devil how to beat their wives, since some of them did it so often.

Mrs. Barnes, who lived across the street from Grandma Fannie, was a very pleasant and generous person. Her son, Bennie, and my brother were very good friends. They appeared to be the same age. Her daughter was also friendly. Whenever Mrs. Barnes went shopping downtown and found a bargain, she would buy items and give those new items to Grandma Fannie for us. Mrs. Barnes never accepted anything except a "thank you" in return. Through her and a number of other people, we ended up with a lot of clothing and household items. Most people gave us old clothes, which were also useful. However, we did not have storage space for all of the clothing; it ended up being stacked in the downstairs hallway. I never understood why my Grandma did not give some of those items to someone else, since it was impossible for us to use all of them. Whenever she had a free moment, she would use her sewing machine to repair or alter some of the clothes so that we could wear them.

When we lived in Grandma Fannie's house, we were never dirty. There were large tin tubs and small basins for bathing or washing up. These were the same tubs used for washing clothes. Water was heated on the wood-burning stove in the kitchen and poured into the tin tubs. When enough water had been added, a bar of soap was provided, and the bathing began. Sometimes all of the small children bathed in the same tub of water.

When our hair had to be washed, my sisters and I would do that at the pump in the summertime so that rinsing would be easy. After washing it, all the girls in the house would sit around braiding each other's hair or straightening it with a hot comb. This was a great time for conversation.

In addition to bathing on Saturdays, we washed clothes and hung them on the line to dry, and we cleaned the house. If we did not complete those tasks on Saturday, we risked having to do rush jobs like washing our socks and underwear during the week, using precious time that we needed for studying. We were not permitted to do chores like washing or sewing on Sundays because that was considered to be a sin.

One day, Grandma Fannie took me with her to the Post Office, where she paid the rent. She met with the postmaster, who seemed very pleased with her presence. They chatted for a while in a low tone. I could not hear what they were saying. We then went to Mr. Smith's store, where she introduced me to him as the one who would be coming by to purchase groceries and cash the monthly checks. It was years later before I understood what was happening with these visits. She was setting me up to take over the responsibilities of the home. I wondered: why was she doing this, when I was not even in my teens? At the time, I didn't know. It became clear only later, when my older sisters got married and left home.

My Grandma did not provide any of us with allowances, and we did not object to that since we did not know what that was. Instead, all of the children in her house had innovative ways of earning spending money for the movie theater and other recreational activities. The movie and drive-in theaters were popular places to visit on weekends. When my cousin, Joe Louis Bullock, bought a car, he used it to drive us to the drive-in theater. A whole carload of people could go to the drive-in theater together for one low entry fee, which was cheaper than for us to go individually to the movie theater downtown.

With funds that I earned as a maid cleaning homes, I was able to pay for the theater, the school candy that I was eating instead of selling, and small items that I needed. Also, I was able to make deposits into my bank savings account. The savings account was set up after a White lady from one of the downtown Suffolk banks came to Ida V. Easter Graded School and explained the importance of banking. She guided me and my schoolmates in the banking process, and we were grateful. There were times in which we deposited less than a quarter per week, but we were all proud to have banking accounts. This was a tremendous lesson in responsibility.

My lessons in life continued in earnest when I met the Cook family.

Mr. and Mrs. S. A. Cook

As if I were not already involved in enough activities, I wanted to be a Girl Scout. I had attended the meetings on several occasions with two of my classmates. Therefore, I knew that the Scouts had cookies and milk at each meeting. I have a sweet tooth, and those treats helped to satisfy it. One day while attending a meeting of a Colored Girl Scout troop at my school, Ida V. Easter Graded School, I was asked by the Scout mother, Delia Darden Cook, if I wanted to join. I said yes but had no idea that it was so costly. After the meeting, the Scout mother explained the organization to me and gave me information on the costs for a uniform as well as for activities such as trips and dues.

Wow! I could not afford those costs with the small amount that I was earning by scrubbing floors, washing blinds, and working on farms. However, I really wanted to be a Girl Scout. During the meetings the Scouts did arts and crafts, sang songs, and read books in addition to having milk and cookies. They said a pledge and did a number of things of which I had never heard. For example, they earned badges, attended religious and educational programs, and went camping on the church grounds, since it was too dangerous to go into the woods.

As the Scout mother continued to talk to me, she found that I lived with my Grandma and had several sisters and a brother. She knew that my family could not afford to sponsor my membership in the organization. She asked if I wanted to work for her. I gave an enthusiastic "yes" without thinking about it. However, she insisted that I ask my Grandma's permission, which I did.

The following Saturday, I went to work at the home of S. A. Cook and his wife, Delia Darden Cook, on Boat Street. When I arrived at their two-story white house, almost at the end of Boat Street, I rang the doorbell—something that was rare in my neighborhood. I was still in the city of Suffolk but outside of Saratoga. As I entered the house I stopped and looked around in awe. There was carpet on the floors, linoleum on the kitchen floor, and beautiful, expensive furniture. The Cooks had an indoor bathroom, a separate living room and dining room, and lots of books and magazines. The bedrooms were upstairs. There were light switches on the walls and beautiful lamps on tables in each room. Even the corners of the living and dining rooms had shelves that held real china items such as decorative plates, cups, saucers, and objects that had been collected during the family's many vacation trips.

The house had storm doors and windows with screens on them. Also, there were locks on each exterior door. The place seemed already clean to me, but I was there as the maid. So I began working: scrubbing the kitchen floor and vacuuming the carpets. When my brother, Benjamin, got a little older, he sometimes joined me in doing other tasks, but he only worked for a short amount of time. I dusted the furniture all over the house and pressed Mr. Cook's light blue shirts that he wore as a U.S. postman, a job he had following his service in the U.S. Navy. Mrs. Cook was an elementary school teacher. Both were college graduates.

Before I finished work the first day, I was told I could pick a book from the bookcase and read it, something I did with joy and continued to do while I worked at the Cook's home. There were books about Colored people and their great deeds as well as about colleges and universities for Colored people. *Jet* and *Ebony* magazines were prominently displayed on the coffee table. I read them, too. Every month new ones were received in the mail. Week after week, I did my cleaning chores and read.

With the money I earned, I could more than adequately afford the fees needed to be a Girl Scout. However, Mrs. Cook paid the fees for me anyway, and even bought me a uniform. I was deeply grateful. She and Mr. Cook treated me as if I were their daughter rather than their maid. They took me on trips to Virginia State University. We toured the campus, attended football games, and visited with their relatives who worked at the university. I also went with them on their vacations. At that time I had never traveled outside of Virginia.

The most traveling that I had done was to Norfolk, Petersburg, Courtland, and Portsmouth to visit family friends and relatives and to go to the beach. With the Cooks, I toured parts of New York and Canada. I was fascinated by Niagara Falls.

One day, as I sat at the table for dinner with Mr. and Mrs. Cook, the conversation took a turn that surprised and delighted me: they asked if I would live with them on a permanent basis. I did not know how to respond to that question! They went on to talk about the possibility of adopting me. I enjoyed the attention that they bestowed upon me. I was already treated as if I were their daughter, and I felt that it would be great to be a part of that family. However, it wasn't to be.

One day when Mrs. Cook drove me home from a Girl Scout meeting, Grandma Fannie was on the porch of her house. As I exited the car, Mrs. Cook did, too. She politely greeted Grandma Fannie and held a conversation with her. She asked if she and Mr. Cook could adopt me. Grandma Fannie responded angrily, "As soon as one of these kids gets old enough to do some work, people want to adopt them. No, you cannot adopt Margaret." With that, Mrs. Cook left the porch in a hurry.

When I went to work at the Cook's house the following weekend, the mood was solemn. However, the family continued to treat me well. In addition to cleaning house for Mr. and Mrs. Cook, I served as babysitter for their son, Alfred, upon of his arrival as a baby in their home. He was taught to call me "Big Sister." As he grew older, he called me "Aunt Margaret." When he became an adult, he referred to me as his sister. This has caused confusion in some settings, among people who knew my real brother and sisters. Even today, he and I communicate and occasionally visit each other.

During some of the Saturdays while I was at their house, Mr. and Mrs. Cook talked with me about the importance of a good education and life in general. I usually ate Saturday lunches and suppers with them. It was during those times that they taught me proper etiquette and other valuable life lessons. An example of a change that they made in my table etiquette is their instruction on how to eat fish at the supper table. At home, I ate fish and cornbread with my hands. The cornbread was thought to cushion any fish bones that might accidently pass down the throat. Using my hands to pick up pieces of the fish enabled me to feel the fish bones and discard them. At Mr. and Mrs. Cook's home, fish was eaten with a knife and fork. Cornbread was not a part of the meal. Grandma, and my parents before her, did not teach me the same kinds of lessons, and the ones they did teach were imparted to all of us children as a group, whereas the Cook family's teachings were specifically for me.

Eventually, Mr. and Mrs. Cook told me to call them Mama and Daddy Cook. They would continue to play an important role in my life, as I left grade school for high school, and later, as I made the decision to seek even higher education.

A New School Environment

I studied diligently and graduated from the sixth grade, the highest grade of Ida V. Easter Graded School. I had dreamed of graduating, and when the time was near, I remembered clearly many of my early years at school. I was unresponsive in the first grade. As I was promoted to higher grades, however, I became more relaxed in the classroom and made friends with many of my classmates. When I was in the fifth grade, my classes were held in the same room with sixth graders. The fifth graders would keep their heads on their desks as the teacher taught the sixth graders their lessons. Although my head was at rest, my mind was fully alert. I learned the sixth-grade material along with the sixth graders, but I still had to complete the sixth grade the following year.

I sometimes helped other students with their homework. By the time I reached higher grades, all of us interacted well, and we looked after each other as if we were blood relatives.

For the sixth-grade graduation program, my female classmates and I wore white dresses and socks and black patent leather shoes. The boys wore white or light-blue shirts and dark pants. The folding doors that separated classrooms during the day were folded back so that the room was twice its normal size. Additional chairs from other classrooms were placed to accommodate the large number of guests who attended the program. It was strange to see our relatives and other neighborhood people sitting in our school chairs listening to us recite poetry and sing the songs that we had been rehearsing for months.

Finally, one by one, my fellow classmates and I walked across the small stage and received our graduation certificates from the principal. Everyone seemed to enjoy the program, as indicated by their applause.

My classmates and I felt very special during the graduation, but we were somewhat apprehensive about going to high school. We thought that everyone there was older than we were, and they were from other neighborhoods. Most of us had to walk about two miles to get to East Suffolk High School, and then we had to walk back home at the end of the school day. I walked it alone, usually wearing my black and white oxfords with white cotton socks. On numerous occasions, I wore a pleated skirt with a white blouse. My hair was usually fixed in a single row curl or two pony tails in the back and bangs in the front, a style that I gradually changed as I grew older.

As I walked out of Saratoga and began the walk to school each day, I had to pass between the junkyard and the ball park—the most unnerving part of the journey. I turned down the street beside the railroad tracks, where the potato flat was located, and walked past the Planters peanut factory with peanut man—"Mr. Peanut"—statues on the fence posts. It was during this part of the journey that peanut dust would accumulate in my hair, which was greasy from the use of Royal Crown hair dressing or lard bought from Mr. Smith's Store. After passing the peanut factory, I passed through a section called "the block" where there was a drug store owned and operated by a Colored family. "The block" was also the area where men hung out most of the day, going in and out of bars. As I turned the corner to begin the part of the journey that took me down Norfolk Road, I was more at ease since that road had many homes on both sides of the street. I could see the crossing guard, Mrs. Backus, in her neat black uniform, stopping traffic so that students could cross the street.

At 6th Street, I turned the corner to walk the last leg of the trip to the school. The atmosphere changed drastically. I could see many students heading in the same direction in which I was going. On the school grounds, other students seemed to know which students were from Saratoga. Perhaps, it was because we had peanut dust in our hair. There was another high school that was closer to my section of town, but I could not attend it because it was for Whites only.

In addition to going to high school, I periodically went to the movies and to sports games played by high-school students at the park near Saratoga. The East Suffolk High School football team, the Wolverines, played some of its games there. It was always nice to see my school mates dressed in their black and gold outfits, chanting songs to promote school spirit. To attend movies such as Tarzan and Woody Woodpecker, I only had to pay fifteen cents. Since I looked younger than my actual age, I was able to take advantage of that privilege for years beyond the age limit at which the price changed to forty cents. As was the law in those days, Colored people sat in the balcony while Whites sat on the main level of the movie theater.

I never went outside of my neighborhood alone except to attend East Suffolk High School. On occasions when I had to go to social activities outside of Saratoga—as I increasingly did as I reached my high-school years—my siblings or cousins accompanied me. When the county fair came to town, my siblings and I went by bus to see the shows, animals, and food displays. On the bus, my siblings and I sat in the back section, the part for Colored people. At the fair, cotton candy was our favorite treat. We would walk around the fairgrounds eating cotton candy, looking at domestic and wild animals, and petting some of the domestic animals. I always won when I played the guessing game on age and weight. The attendant was usually wrong by several years and pounds. Peeping into the tent where the hoochie-coochie woman was dancing was also fun. The rides that I liked were hoppy horse and other slow ones. When we returned home from the fair our shoes were always muddy, and we were tired.

Another fun activity was going to Seaview Beach on the shores of the Chesapeake Bay. There was a division between the parts of the beach for White and Colored people, and no one ever broke the rule. We were always careful to watch the time to ensure that we returned to the bus on schedule for the departure for home.

Also during the summertime, a man from New York came into town with his son to hold talent shows. We participated in those shows, as did several of our neighborhood friends. My sisters, especially Lee Vania, sang beautifully during the shows, but I did not have musical talent. Nervously, I tried to sing once, but the attempt was a disaster. Gracie Lee, a friend from Saratoga, sang better than any of the other participants in the talent shows, and she received a lot of applause along with the top prize at each show.

Eventually, Audrey Mae received Grandma's permission to go to New York City to work for a short period. She was not even 15 years old, yet she got a job in a café with a relative who lived there. I was surprised, since Grandma normally did not allow us to go unsupervised even to Norfolk, which was less than 20 miles from Suffolk, probably because there were too many military men there. As a child, I did not understand the reason for this rule, since military men who returned to Saratoga were honored and sought by women. They were the ones with regular sources of income, and they were impressive in their military uniforms. Mothers sent their sons to war to help support families. Wives waited for their return. At least some did, and some did not.

Anyway, I yearned to visit Audrey Mae in New York City, the Big Apple, and to see the city itself. She sent photographs of herself at wonderful-looking places like the Empire State Building and other skyscrapers. I could not wait to visit her. So, one day Grandma Fannie gave me that long-awaited permission to take the trip.

The bus ride seemed to take forever. When I arrived at the bus station in New York City, I went into the restroom, for which—to my surprise—there was an entry fee. I put my purse on the floor of the toilet stall to enable better maneuvering in the small area. Suddenly, I saw a hand reach under the side wall of the stall in the direction of my purse. Rapidly, I snatched it out of the reach of the hand. The event sent a chill down my back. I had been warned to keep my purse near me, but the hook in the stall was broken. For that reason I thought that it was acceptable—even necessary—to put my purse on the floor. Never again!

When I exited the toilet, I saw no one. After getting my nerves back together and summoning my courage, I took the city bus to 125th Street and Amsterdam Avenue, where my sister's apartment was located. I was in Harlem.

You cannot imagine the excitement of it all! There I was in New York, the Big Apple, feeling very alone and having no unaccompanied travel experience. Whenever I went to Courtland—only a few miles away from Suffolk—to visit relatives, other relatives went with me.

I wondered why Grandma permitted Audrey Mae to live in the Big Apple and why she had allowed me to visit her. Initially, most of what I saw in the city was unnerving. There was activity everywhere both day and night, lights galore, a lot of noise, very tall buildings, and more people than I had ever seen.

There were far more people on the streets in Harlem than the number that attended the county fair in Suffolk. Some of them looked sick, very sick. They lay on the sidewalk and in the alleys. They drank liquor on the streets, and there were women signaling men in cars. They were poorly dressed. Some wore hot pants and tops that covered very little. They wore too much makeup and smoked cigarettes. This place was wild! It was difficult to take it all in.

I hurried to the building in which Audrey Mae lived. She answered the door with a buzzer when I pressed the doorbell. That is the way city folks did it, I had been told. As I entered the building, I had to walk up a staircase to the door, which had the apartment number on it. As my sister showed me around, I thought that the bedroom she showed me was the one in which I would sleep, alone. Since there were additional closed doors inside what I thought was her apartment, I assumed that she had another room in which she slept. The bedroom she showed me was only large enough for a twin-sized bed, but she had a larger one in there, and she had pushed it against two walls to leave room for squeezing past it to get to the window, near the small night stand. With the closet on the left and the night stand on the right, I could squeeze my way to the window. From that window, I could look out onto the streets that were always full of amazingly activities.

The first night, I learned that my sister and I would share the bed, and the other doors in the apartment were entrances to the rooms of other people. For example, a West Indian lady occupied one of the rooms there. She was very kind. She would watch for me to come home and remind me to lock my door whenever I got inside the little room that Audrey Mae and I shared.

One day the street activities took on a special significance, as Adam Clayton Powell, Jr., stopped along the street in his white convertible with a red interior. He, an African-American pastor and politician, was campaigning for a Congressional re-election. There had been much excitement in Harlem when he first won the Congressional seat in 1945—a seat he lost to Charles B. Rangel in the 1970 primary election. In his time in Congress, Powell was a controversial figure and fighter for civil rights.[10] I had learned about Congress in school, but this experience brought home to me the reality of what I had learned. I had never seen anything like a campaign in my life, or the kind of excitement it generated.

Audrey Mae was often out late, so I would stay up late looking out the window, absorbing all that I could. One day I summoned the courage to go to the pool that was near our apartment building. I took my one-piece, pea-green bathing suit and thick, white rubber swimming cap and went to the area where I had seen other girls my age swimming. Although I could not swim, I waded into the water. I soon learned that I was not in the same league with those girls. From their talk, I realized they were into sex, illegal drug use, and many other activities that did not appeal to me. After talking to me for a short period, they ignored me. I think that they considered me to be too much of a country girl for their taste. Maybe I was, and probably I was scared, too. When things got rough around the pool, I would run to my apartment.

The numbers racket was in full swing on the streets, seemingly in full view of everyone. The openness of this activity would lead anyone to believe that it was legal. People would bet on numbers, and if they were correct, their bets, which were supported with money, would be increased several fold. If the numbers that they played were incorrect, they lost all of the money they placed on the bets. There were men on the streets who accepted bets on the numbers without writing them down. They could calculate the winning amounts in their heads. I thought that they were geniuses. I wondered for a long

---

[10] Charles V. Hamilton, Adam Clayton Powell, Jr.: The Political Biography of an American Dilemma, Atheneum, New York, 1991, pages 139-487; and Wil Haygood, King of the Cats: The Life and Times of Adam Clayton Powell, Jr., Houghton Mifflin Company, New York, 1993, pages 381-415.

time how they remembered the numbers and the people who bet on them, and how they did those calculations so fast and accurately.

Eventually, I stopped thinking about those activities because they were illegal and none of my business. My observations were very educational, though. I was excellent in mathematics, but I could not do what they did, especially while under the type of pressure that they experienced. I could not help but wonder at the time what type of life those individuals might have had if their efforts had been applied to getting a formal education and living decent and productive lives.

After staying in New York for a few weeks of the summer, I decided it was time for me to go back to Suffolk. The summer was almost over, and I had to go back to school. It was too lonely in New York, anyway. Audrey Mae had to work long hours, and I had no friends. The West Indian lady who lived down the hallway gave me a bra, a beautiful beige silk slip with lace around the top and bottom, and some silky panties as farewell gifts. I had never received such beautiful gifts before. I thanked her again and again. She told me to take care of myself and to finish my education. Since that time I have not seen her, but I remember her words – "finish my education." I promised to do that because I did not want to end up like the people I saw on the streets of Harlem.

Audrey Mae stayed in New York a little longer. When she returned to Suffolk, people seemed to regard her highly because she had been to the Big Apple. Oh, if they only knew! People who visited Suffolk from New York City always spoke differently. They called it "proper talk." However, I thought it was strange that I had not met anyone in New York City who actually talked that way. I thought that it was best not to reveal to people in Suffolk that people in New York City did not talk that way. I was happy to get back to Suffolk after my visit. My relatively quiet hometown was a relief. I did not like the crowds, the hustle and bustle, and the never-ending noise of the big city with its tall buildings. People had not been friendly, and I had felt quite uncomfortable. I eagerly resumed my work on

Saturdays at the home of the Cook family, my classes, and my after-school activities.

Although both Audrey Mae and I left New York City that year, in later years, my other siblings lived there. On one occasion when I visited them, we went to the Apollo Theater in Harlem. There we saw a number of performances by African Americans, as Blacks were becoming known by then. One of the performers was Moms Mabley, the comedian. Part of her captivation was her stage appearance: an elderly-looking woman who was toothless and dressed in a floppy hat and an ugly house dress. Her voice was interesting; it was not like I expected a grandmother's voice to sound. Nevertheless, her jokes were funny. Other performers sang, played music, and danced in front of a tough audience to satisfy.

At another time, in a smaller entertainment room of the Apollo Theater, my sister Eleanor competed for a beauty title and won. All of us attended the program, in which she displayed her modeling talent as she strutted across the stage and her intellect as she responded to questions posed by the master of ceremony. For that show, the audience sat at tables and snacked on tidbits of food. Audrey Mae brought to our table some fish cakes that she had prepared. This upset Eleanor, because the odor of fish was not what she had in mind for the family's table at her special event, but we enjoyed the dish anyway. We left the theater in good spirits.

Taking Over as Head of the Family

One day during my high-school years, there was excitement at home. It was focused on Audrey Mae, who had been promised in marriage by Grandma Fannie. I assumed that Grandma also had the consent of our Dad. The decision had been made that Audrey Mae would get married to the man chosen for her, even though she was only 15 years old. In about a month, she would have celebrated her 16th birthday. The marriage took place on July 2, 1955.

Lee Vania was also 15 when she was given into marriage to Andrew "Bay" Williams, Jr. It seemed to me that as soon as my sisters had shown an interest in boys, they were forced into marriage, with someone they hadn't even chosen on their own. That frightened me. To avoid getting into the same bind, I decided not to show interest—at least not openly—in boys and courtship. I did not want to have to marry a man whom I did not choose and live in Suffolk for the rest of my life. I especially did not want someone else to choose my mate for me; I wanted to do that myself.

I was thrifty and a hard worker. Even when I was in my teens, I worked diligently on my school work as well as my jobs. I did not wear makeup (e.g., powder, rouge, and lipstick) like other girls did. Grandma Fannie did not approve of wearing makeup. Besides, it was impossible to purchase makeup that matched my skin tone. The white or pink powder used by older women made them look unusual, but they liked it. It was a time of high heels and pointed-toe shoes that hurt my feet when I tried them. So I remained a conservative dresser. I did not wear shoes while at home, continuing to prefer going barefoot, but I wore them to work, school, and church. Black and white saddle oxfords were the shoes of choice for wearing to school. On Sundays, I wore either black or white patent leather shoes to Sunday school and church. Even though I dressed well and had an overall attractive appearance, I did not try to date anyone until after Grandma Fannie died.

After both of my older sisters were married in civil ceremonies and moved into their new homes, I assumed a new role as the oldest child among my siblings in Grandma Fannie's house. Our cousins continued to live there as well.

About seven years after the death of my Mama, my Dad's health began to fail. I rarely saw him. One day in the late 1950s, though, I learned that Dad was on his "last legs." In November of 1958, he died of lobar pneumonia,[11] which is a form of pneumonia that affects a large area of the lung. Prior to his death, because he had served in World War II, he was treated at the Veterans Administration (VA) Hospital in Kecoughtan, Virginia. Although it was not noted on his death certificate, Dad was buried with a full military ceremony at the Carver Cemetery in Suffolk. At the time of his death, he was 41 years old. An interesting note is that his death certificate indicates that he was never married. In addition, Mama's death certificate[12] showed her name as Mrs. Martha Artis Mayo, but someone had crossed out "Mrs.," "Mayo," the word "married," and the husband's name, "Clifton Mayo."

A handwritten note indicates that those changes were made to Mama's Certificate of Death and other records on file in response to a request from the Veterans Administration. However, rumor has it that the changes were actually prompted by Grandma Fannie. The change was dated December 9, 1952. Now, that was most interesting! On the date of Dad's death, in 1958, I was a few weeks from my 15th birthday, and it was clear that my siblings and I were now real orphans. However, no one ever used the word "orphans" around us.

Although my siblings and I saw and experienced a number of negative mental and physical actions by our Dad, I have no ill feelings

---

[11]   Virginia Certificate of Death #26914 for Clifton J. Mayo. (His name appears as Jessie Clifford Mayo on his birth certificate #23640.) Dad lived May 13, 1917, to November 5, 1958. According to his death certificate, the attending doctor was H. T. Haden, MD, and the funeral home used was the Lawrence B. Wood Funeral Home in Hampton, Virginia.

[12]   Virginia Certificate of Death #18016 for Martha Artis Mayo; see footnote 8 for more information.

toward him. I am convinced that the trials and tribulations in his life, including his service in the military, made him what he was. During that time no one spoke of post-traumatic stress or counseling to address problems of the type he had. No one spoke of treatment for alcoholism. Most people had no knowledge of those types of services. We simply lived with the problems as best we could. My family, in fact, had continued to live from day to day in survival mode, even after we moved in with Grandma Fannie.

There was always someone living in or visiting Grandma Fannie's home where my siblings and I lived. When he was alive, Dad visited Grandma Fannie often. He had continued to live in the house we grew up in on Linden Avenue, and he had a new companion we called Miss Geneva. I never knew her last name. My Dad's sisters and brothers visited Grandma Fannie, too; they included Aunt Maebell Mayo Artis of Portsmouth, Virginia, whom we called Aunt C; Aunt Armeania Mayo Rawlings and her husband, Uncle Phil, of Courtland, Virginia; and Uncle John Mayo and his wife, Aunt Marie, of Philadelphia, Pennsylvania. Aunt Margaret Ellen Mayo had died before I was born.

Sometimes Uncle John and Aunt Marie's two children accompanied them on visits to Grandma Fannie's home. They never came empty-handed. Their gifts, whether old or new, were appreciated. Aunt Margaret Ellen's son, Joe Louis Bullock, lived with us at Grandma Fannie's house. His father lived somewhere else in Suffolk.

Age and the burdens of taking care of so many family members took its toll. After several years of Grandma Fannie taking care of all of us, in addition to our cousins, she became ill. Aunt Maebell (Aunt C), Aunt Armeania, Uncle John, and Dad came to visit her, as did other relatives. As her illness worsened, she became bedridden. Finally, Aunt C took her to Portsmouth, Virginia, to live with her. I thought that Grandma would recover and return home, but she never did. Our cousins took us in their cars to see her on several occasions.

My three younger siblings and I would stand side-by-side by her bed so that she could see all of us. On our last visit to Aunt C's house prior to Grandma's death, Grandma looked me straight in the eyes and said, "Margaret, you are the strongest of the bunch; so, take care of your brother and sisters, and don't let anyone harm them." In her weak voice, she told me that checks would be delivered in the mail each month. I knew that those checks resulted from my father's military service. I was instructed to take those checks to Mr. Smith's Store and buy food for my siblings and me. She told me also to use some of the money to pay the rent.

I felt weighed down. How could I take care of my two younger sisters and my brother at my young age? I was only a teenager, but I rose to the challenge. When checks came in the mail, I took them to the corner store as I was told. I put the food into Benjamin's little red wagon and walked home. It wasn't far, and all I had to do along the way was watch out for dogs that ran loose. When I got home, the butter was placed into the ice box along with the franks. Canned goods were placed in the large walk-in pantry in the kitchen. The butter was white and had to be colored with the small reddish ball in the center. This was fun to do, since the butter was in a pouch that could be mashed around and manipulated until the color of the butter was uniformly yellow.

I had learned from Grandma how to make biscuits, too. I used lard from the large can that we used as a seat in the kitchen. To get the wood-burning stove ready to bake the bread, Benjamin had to chop some wood, a job that I had before becoming head of household. If he did not chop the wood, I would have to do it. I could handle the ax easily by flinging it into the air and bringing it down on the wood block with fierce force, leaving the wood block split into pieces. Eleanor had to pump the water as best she could, since she was small and so was Mary Lee. For dinner, the peas had to be shelled and the corn shucked. Seasoning them with fatback and the grease from fried bacon was the best way to make the meal appealing and tasty. The peas and corn would be eaten with pig feet, pig tails, or slices of Dan Doodle sausage and biscuits or cornbread. Kool Aid was our prized drink. When it was not available, sweetened water or lemonade was prepared and drunk with the meal. I knew that, occasionally, my older sisters had spiked their glasses of sweetened water with a spoonful of vinegar, for a different taste. Therefore, occasionally, I did likewise.

Easy tasks included preparing my younger sisters and brother for school and seeing to it that they arrived home safely and did their homework. They obeyed me. If they had not done so, I would have given them the spanking of their lives. My two older sisters were no longer living in Grandma Fannie's house; they were married and had their own lives to live. It was up to me to make our house a home, as best I could.

Living in Grandma Fannie's house after she went to live with Aunt C were two cousins, Joe Louis Bullock and Ennis Rawlings. Ennis had a girlfriend with whom he sometimes had arguments. Of course, they had good times, too, when both were laughing and joking. As we eavesdropped on them during their arguments, we could hear that our cousin accused his girlfriend of various wrongdoings. Sometimes the accusations were reversed, and she would accuse him of not giving her enough money to do what needed to be done or something else. The arguments were nerve-wracking for me. This type of behavior reinforced my earlier decision to never marry anyone, or keep company with anyone, who would beat me or yell and scream at me.

Unfortunately, Grandma Fannie never returned to her home on Battery Avenue in Saratoga. She died in Portsmouth on May 12, 1962. As time passed, rumors surfaced that people in our community were talking about having us adopted. The thought of being adopted and staying with strange families again was not appealing. As a matter of fact, it was downright frightening.

One day, I put as many of our belongings into the wagon as I could and walked with my two sisters and brother to Audrey Mae's house on Norfolk Road. This was a very long walk. We walked past the ball park that was across the street from the junkyard, past the potato flat and the Planters peanut factory. We walked past the area where there was a drug store owned by a Colored person and some bars and other businesses. We passed nice houses and churches along the way. We walked past the credit union, gas stations, the Elks Lodge, and the house where one of my former teachers lived, and where I had once worked. We also passed other large houses that sat gracefully on Norfolk Road.

Before we got to the tunnel under the railroad track—it was really just an overpass—we arrived at Audrey Mae's house. It was farther than walking to my high school from the Saratoga area. But we made it! There was no way to warn her or ask for permission, since she did not have a telephone and neither did we. So, we just showed up one day at her house with our meager possessions.

Moving in with My Oldest Sister

Overnight, Audrey Mae's family increased from three to seven. She already had a baby son. He had a big head like his daddy. We played with the baby many times. I quickly knew that it had been a good decision to choose Audrey Mae's house rather than Lee Vania's. Audrey Mae could cook. We really liked being in her house because she always had something good available to eat. We knew that we would never be hungry. I could cook some, but not like Audrey Mae. She could season grass and make it taste like collards; or at least I imagined that to be the case.

It seemed to me that her husband did not like the fact that we were living with them, which, in hindsight, doesn't surprise me, since we seriously disrupted his life. The house was certainly big enough. Audrey Mae and her family had lots of room and not much furniture. They had a small rocking chair, which I really liked. It looked like the one over which my brother and I used to fight. In the evenings when I returned from school, I would rock in it. Whenever Benjamin came inside the house and saw me rocking, he would try to pull me out of the chair, just like earlier times. Of course, I would not permit him to take the chair from me, and a fight would ensue. I would always win and go back to rocking. Sometimes, I would give him a final punch with my fist to assure that he hurt enough to keep out of my way. That never stopped him from fighting for the chair on other days, but it stopped him for a while as he cried.

Mostly, sibling rivalry was not a major problem in our new home. Audrey Mae seemed to enjoy our presence in her home, but I am not sure how her husband felt about our living there. However, we did not focus on his feelings. We knew that when we arrived home from school Audrey Mae would be cooking, and we knew that we would eat well and be all right.

One day while returning from school, as I neared my home, the neighbors warned me that a violent incident was in progress.

I raced to the house and began protecting my oldest sister from a vicious attack. Audrey Mae avoided serious injury, though I sustained some permanent scars—both physical and mental. The incident demonstrated what a world of violent men I came from, and strengthened my desire for a different kind of life.

When I went to work the following Saturday, Mama and Daddy Cook were very much concerned that I had been in a fight and was hurt. I had never seen them fight or even raise their voices at each other. I knew that they would not understand the situation. However, I shared the details of the incident with them.

The relationship that Mama and Daddy Cook had was ideal. It was the only ideal one that I had the opportunity to observe on a first-hand basis. The relationships of my relatives with their loved ones were very different and sometimes not at all pleasant.

My sister and her husband often disagreed, but they never got a divorce. In time, they stopped living together, and he moved away from Suffolk. As time went on, I wondered if the presence of my younger siblings and me in their home of was the sole cause of their marital problems. That thought saddened me. I was not aware of any alternatives for us, though.

Eventually, I gave the money from the government check to Audrey Mae, since she was trying to make ends meet as she took care of her instant family. In addition to her son, Roy Lee, she had suddenly inherited her three sisters and brother without any prior warning. We had caused significant strain for her family. She rose to the challenge of keeping us together, and to this day I am grateful for Audrey Mae for fighting for the opportunity to keep the family—her siblings—together. She was our heroine and deserving of our highest compliments.

We moved from house to house a number of times while living with Audrey Mae. The houses were never furnished well, and bed bugs in the mattresses were a persistent problem, even though we sprayed often. I am convinced that our oldest sister did the best that she could with what she had.

As time passed, another problem developed in the family. My knee baby sister, Eleanor, wanted her share of our government check given to her. That did not happen. The amount of each check was so small that dividing it among my siblings and me would have caused a problem. It was the combined funds that enabled our family to afford what we needed to keep us fed and clothed, and perhaps Eleanor did not understand that. The fact that she did not get her share of the money directly caused animosity for a number of years.

My personal life was full of such family problems. The primary issue, for me, was survival, and an ambition to make the problems go away someday. I was convinced the solution lay in education and earning a lot of money. So I studied with a passion and continued to work for Mama and Daddy Cook on Saturdays. My high-school years were especially demanding, since I was enrolled in advanced courses in science and mathematics. With Audrey Mae running most of the household, however, I managed to put in a lot of time on schoolwork.

My studying paid off. I completed my regular curriculum as well as upper level science and mathematics courses, which prepared me for college. My extracurricular activities were limited by the fact that I had to help with chores at home and work on weekends. However, during my high-school years, I took the time to keep company with a very nice young man a few times. When my special friend enrolled at Virginia State College, I visited him on one occasion. He was in the Reserve Officers Training Corps (ROTC) and was studying for his bachelor's degree in bacteriology. I had no means of making regular trips to the campus to see him, since I had neither a car nor a driver's license. His home, where he spent his time away from campus, was in a different section of Suffolk than the one in which I lived. It was not long before he found another girlfriend, and we did not see each other again.

During two summers of my high-school years, I got a job as a chambermaid at Sally Walker's White Horse Lodge and Paradise Resort in Cuddybackville, New York, through a referral by a schoolmate—a guy named Shirley. This part of New York was very different from the part that I saw when I visited Audrey Mae in Harlem. The trip to Cuddybackville by bus up the winding roads of the Catskill Mountains was scary, but I was determined to earn money to help pay for college and to help care for my family.

My primary role at the lodge was to clean 15 guest rooms per day. Being the diligent worker that I have always been, I usually completed my chores quickly. Then I had time to rest before calling guests to meals using the paging system at the resort. Everyone had the same menu, which Mrs. Walker prepared with minimal assistance. She was a Colored lady and a hard worker. She cooked for more than a hundred guests, especially on weekends and holidays. She was the owner and top managing executive for the entire resort.

When I returned to Suffolk at the end of summer, I continued to live with Audrey Mae, her son, and my young sisters and brother. I also resumed my work at the home of Mama and Daddy Cook during the school year. Their son and I got along extremely well as he got older, and we stayed in touch even after we both reached adulthood.

At East Suffolk High School, I was elected president of the National Honor Society and of the Student Participation Association. Also, I was selected to represent my school at the District Science and Math Conference Testing Program and won several certificates in science and math over the years. As my siblings got older and more independent, I was able to expand my extracurricular activities and stay out later in the afternoons to participate in them. I became a member of the Modern Dance Club, as well as the Science and Math Club. In my senior year, I served as a member of the annual yearbook staff. By then, my brother Benjamin was in tenth grade, and my sister Eleanor was in the eighth grade at the same school.

Me wearing my high-school prom gown on prom night

I attended the senior prom in my high-school senior year, and was also privileged to participate in the local Debutante Ball, with Mama and Daddy Cook as my sponsors. They bought me a beautiful white gown and a pair of black formal shoes. Mama Cook took me to Petersburg, where my hair was done by one of the employees in Aunt Susie's hair salon. Aunt Susie was the wife of Mama Cook's brother, Kenneth Darden, whom I called Uncle Ken. Alfred, the son of Mama and Daddy Cook, always accompanied us on trips.

Shown here are Mr. & Mrs. S. A. Cook
(Mama and Daddy Cook) and their son, Alfred.

I had to find an escort for the Debutante Ball, and my close
school mates helped me find a date. He lived near East Suffolk High
School. When he agreed to take me to the ball, I was very happy but
nervous. Mama and Daddy Cook drove us to the ball and served as
chaperones, which was proper since they presented me to society at
the ball. When the ball ended, they gave a breakfast party at their
home for me, my date, and a few friends.

During my high-school years, Principal W. Lovell Turner provided a great deal of academic advice to me and others who showed potential for college. The counselor and teachers encouraged me and my classmates to prepare, by making the required courses available and by providing tutoring as well as classroom instruction. Mr. Turner joined with Mama and Daddy Cook in recommending that I choose Tuskegee Institute (now Tuskegee University), a historically Black university, out of the three universities to which I applied for admission. I valued their opinions. Mr. Turner knew Tuskegee Institute well, since he had participated in a teachers' training institute there.

At the end of my senior year at East Suffolk High School, my academic diligence paid off. In addition to earning high marks in regular and advanced science and mathematics courses, I also completed courses in typing, home economics, and physical education. I learned to type on a manual typewriter; word processors and computers were still a distant fantasy. I was pleased that I had found time to participate in extracurricular activities as well. I had made many new friends and kept the ones from my neighborhood of Saratoga.

Altogether, my high-school years were a satisfying experience, and a very welcome one, thanks largely to the generosity of Mama and Daddy Cook as well as my oldest sister, Audrey Mae. To top it off, in 1963, I found myself at the top of the class, as number one— valedictorian—in a class of 99 graduating students of East Suffolk High School.

Part Two

Higher Education
and Marriages

Chemistry and Civil Rights at Tuskegee

By the time of my high-school graduation in 1963, I was ready for college life. My fellow classmates had listed me in the Yearbook Hall of Fame as "Most Likely to Succeed."

Principal Turner, my teachers, school counselor, and Mama and Daddy Cook—all had provided guidance and support in preparing me for my launch into the academic world outside of Suffolk. My family provided support too, but most were not focused on formal education.

I wanted to become a doctor. More specifically, I wanted to become a physician like Dr. Margaret Reid of Suffolk—the only female doctor I had ever known, and she was very knowledgeable about medicine. This profession, I thought, would allow me to help people around me, which I thought was my calling—as well as to make money.

Several of my high-school teachers had given me advice on how to survive college, especially the many years and obstacles involved in preparing for my chosen career in medicine. A few felt that I should adopt a tougher attitude and not be so kind to everyone. They believed that people would take advantage of me. Although I appreciated their thoughtfulness, I managed to survive my first college experience well without changing much in the way of personality. As indicated by messages written in my senior high-school yearbook, a few classmates thought that I was already mean! Others described me as kind and serious-minded.

People in my neighborhood and in other sections of town gave me numerous high-school graduation and college-enrollment gifts, which gave me a head start in leaving "home." Aunt Lucy, my great aunt, gave me a radio. Mama and Daddy Cook bought a trunk and filled it with new dresses, dishes, curtains, and many other items. Mama Cook's brother, Uncle Ken who was a tailor, made a beautiful purple coat for me. A neighbor of the Cook's, who often waved from her porch, also contributed clothing. The congregation of Mama and Daddy Cook's church even chipped in with a monetary gift, as did a number of civic organizations, including clubs, societies, and even a local beauticians group.[13] I was both surprised and pleased with the outpouring of congratulations on my rank in the graduating class as well as my plan to attend college. I greatly appreciated every gift as well as the verbal and written greetings.

I received acceptance letters from all three universities to which I applied. I accepted the offer from Tuskegee Institute, the only predominantly Black university to which I had applied, even though one of the other universities offered me a full scholarship for the entire four years of study. Shortly after receiving my acceptance from Tuskegee Institute, I received another letter containing a list of items that I would need on campus. The list included items from a black dress, a white dress, and a girdle to tennis shoes and dress-up shoes. Between the gifts I had received and a few shopping trips with Mama Cook, I acquired all of the items on the list and more.

When it was time for me to report to college, Mama and Daddy Cook drove me from Suffolk, Virginia, to Tuskegee Institute in Tuskegee, Alabama. The trip was long and tiring. It seemed surprisingly safe, however, along Highway 29, the truck route we had to use as we got farther south. It was 1963, and racial tensions were in full bloom in the Deep South, and civil rights activities were gaining prominence. However, that did not deter me; I was determined to pave the road to my dreams with a college education. I had lived my whole life in a segregated society, and I felt that I could survive anything that the Deep South would bring.

Although tired from the long trip to Tuskegee Institute, I was very excited to arrive in both a new city and a real college environment,

---

[13]   I received monetary gifts from the Alphabets, the Ladies Auxiliary, Suffolk Chapter of the National Honor Society, the Parent Teachers Association of East Suffolk High School, the Suffolk Beauticians Chapter of Suffolk, and the FAHOCHA Club of Suffolk. Additionally, I received the Lambs Good Attitude Award in the form of a certificate and a monetary gift. Several additional organizations and individuals gave me gifts and greeting cards.

where I hoped to transition to the new life I had wished for and dreamed about. We arrived a few days early and spent the first night in the home of the Howells, friends of Mama and Daddy Cook. They worked on the campus and lived nearby. Getting to know someone involved with campus life was quite comforting. They told me about the history of Tuskegee Institute, even though I had immersed myself in research and knew most of it already. They told me about life on and off campus. Most important, they invited me to come to them with any problems that I might have while on campus. In the Howells, I had a much-appreciated surrogate family in Tuskegee.

With monetary gifts from various individuals and organizations and with a four-year Newton Scholarship for part of my tuition, I entered Tuskegee Institute in September 1963, secure in my ability to finance the tuition as well as room and board. I declared my major in chemistry in the College of Arts and Sciences, and got ready to buckle down to my studies.

I had moved to Alabama during troubling times, however. Tuskegee Institute was less than 50 miles from Montgomery, which was at the heart of several major civil rights actions. In 1955, Rosa Parks, who was born in Tuskegee, defied the rules of segregation when she would not give up her seat to a White person on a Montgomery bus.[14] By the time of my arrival in the state in 1963, protests for basic human rights were at a high level. The status of Colored people—still listed as "Negroes" in the U.S. Census and soon to be known more commonly as Blacks—was on the cusp of change, but the transition would be difficult and long. The Tuskegee Syphilis Study, an experiment on impoverished males begun by the federal government and sanctioned by Tuskegee Institute in 1932, was still in progress. That study did not end until 1972. Freedom Riders had begun actions in 1961 to check compliance with federal rulings to desegregate buses, and the Southern Christian Leadership

---

[14] Fred D. Gray, Bus Ride to Justice: Changing the System by the System—The Life and Works of Fred Gray, Preacher, Attorney, Politician, Black Belt Press, Montgomery, Alabama, 1995, page 50.

Conference was on the rise, soon to be joined by the Black Panther Party.

Organizations such as the National Association for the Advancement of Colored People were actively addressing critical issues of Black people. The problems were numerous, including a lack of compliance by Whites with federal rulings, the continuation of segregation, the lack of quality education for Black people, and mistreatment and abuse of Blacks.

Three years before my arrival, the city of Tuskegee had won a U.S. Supreme Court decision, which ruled that a redrawing of the city's boundaries to favor White candidates had been unconstitutional.[15] The lead plaintiff, Dr. Charles A. Gomillion, was dean of students and chair of the Social Sciences Division at Tuskegee Institute. He had also been instrumental in facilitating voter registration of Black people in the city. The case heightened the institute's visibility in the fight for the rights of Black people, but it made it difficult for the institution to obtain state support. It was abundantly clear to me that a large number of Whites did not welcome Dr. Gomillion's presence on campus or even in the State of Alabama. The same was true for other civil rights activists at the institute.

Confrontations and clashes between Whites and Blacks took place in the streets, in restaurants where sit-ins were occurring, and at educational institutions like my own. The radio and burgeoning television newscasts were full of stories. A person whose name still instills fear in some people is Eugene "Bull" Connor, who as a public official in the early 1960s had ordered the use of high-pressure water hoses and attack dogs on civil rights demonstrators in Birmingham. A few weeks after my arrival in Tuskegee, Birmingham's Sixteenth Street Baptist Church was bombed (September 15, 1963) by Ku Klux Klan members, taking the lives of four young girls. Segregation was

---

[15]   Ibid., pages 4-5 and 155-132. The *Gomillion vs. Lightfoot* case challenged "… the Alabama Legislature's gerrymandering of Tuskegee for the purpose of denying blacks the right to move. The case is recognized today as one of the landmarks in U.S. voting rights law."

a way of life in the region, and, unfortunately, so were acts of terror against those who protested it.

George Wallace, Alabama's governor while I attended Tuskegee Institute, was a notorious racist. He proclaimed his position in his 1963 inaugural speech: "Segregation now, segregation tomorrow, segregation forever."[16] He demonstrated his position by literally standing in a doorway at the University of Alabama to prevent the court-ordered admission of Black students. It was clear to me that my people would need to remain organized and fight for our rights. The Tuskegee Institute faculty and staff were deeply involved in that fight, in the streets and in board rooms. I decided that, once I entered the job market on a full-time basis, I would take up the fighting in board rooms. Dr. Luther H. Foster, Tuskegee Institute's president at the time, made it clear that both strategies were needed. He honored Dr. Gomillion's efforts, and led the faculty and staff in outlining strategies to keep students and staff safe.

Those strategies included rules and regulations that required students to get written permission to leave the campus, and discouraged travel outside the city due to the dangers associated with racial tension. Even trips home required permission. Although some students regarded the rules as too restrictive, I had no argument with them. In fact, I breathed a sigh of relief when Mama and Daddy Cook accompanied me safely to Tuskegee without any trouble along the way.

When it was time to check in at the dormitory, Mama and Daddy Cook helped me unpack and decorate my room—a new and exhilarating experience for me. We hung curtains over the large window. My black dress, my white one, and other outfits were hung in the closet, and my required girdle was put in its proper place. My toothbrush and toothpaste were kept in a glass on my dormitory desk, since the bathroom was down the hall.

---

[16] Alabama Dept. of Archives and History, Montgomery, Alabama. "In the name of the greatest people that have ever trod this earth, I draw the line in the dust and toss the gauntlet before the feet of tyranny...and I say... segregation now...segregation tomorrow...segregation forever." Excerpt from January 14, 1963, inaugural address of Governor George C. Wallace.

I was anxious to attend classes, especially the chemistry classes held in Armstrong Hall. Other classes were held in Huntington Hall, and athletics in the gymnasium. As weeks passed, I met my instructors and classmates and settled in.

I noticed that my dormitory mates did not attend any of the same classes as me. One day, I received a message that the dean of nursing wanted to meet me. I soon learned that the dormitory to which I had been assigned was the Nurses Home, restricted to nursing students. Although surprised, I nevertheless followed the dean's instructions to move out of that dormitory. The housing director assigned me to the basement of White Hall, where a number of other young ladies were living together in a large area while awaiting room assignments. Eventually, I was assigned to a room of my own in White Hall, a stately residence hall dating from 1910. Although it was an excellent room with a central location, I will never forget the loud bells of the large clock on the roof. The chimes could be heard throughout the campus. The clock's mechanisms could be heard in my room as they moved; therefore, I knew when the chimes were going to ring to indicate the hour.

Each dormitory for females had a "house mother" who made sure that students followed the rules. Male students who called on females were required to be properly dressed and remain in the lobby. Female students had curfews, as well as bed checks by the house mother or her assistant. Attendance at Sunday chapel and vespers on Wednesdays were checked for all students. On occasion, some patients and staff members from the Tuskegee Veterans Administration Hospital were in the audience.

As my first academic year progressed, I found myself in the midst of a number of fellow students (most of whom were chemistry or engineering majors, the latter being easily distinguished by the large slide ruler hanging from their belts) who became good friends.[17] We

17 Including James A. Bennett, James Bryant, Benjamin Goff, Leverne Green, Garfield Grimmett Jr., W. T. Hall Jr., Jefferson D. Herring, Louis Jackson, Calvin Lee Jeffers (Cee Lee), Tiny L. Laster, Willie C. Nevilles, Robert Peoples Jr., Gregory Pritchett, Earnestine Psalmonds, Leonard Scott, William Stallings, and Maceo Woolard.

made use of the advice and tutoring of upper-class students, especially those majoring in chemistry.[18] Chemistry students studied together primarily under the instruction of Dr. Courtney J. Smith and Dr. Lawrence F. Koons (see their photographs). We were enrolled in German classes together, too, which I enjoyed. Most of my male classmates were in the ROTC, and it was due to their support that I was selected to serve a one-year term as "Miss ROTC." However, I rarely had time to fulfill all of the social obligations it entailed.

Here I am at Tuskegee Institute wearing formal attire
as I prepare to attend the ROTC Ball.

---

[18] Including Bessie McDowell and John Stephens.

At Tuskegee, I was able to continue the pattern of academic performance begun in high school, and was soon accepted into the honors program directed by Dr. Stanley Smith. There, I came into contact with other honor students and faculty members and participated in joint programs with the University of Michigan at Ann Arbor. As part of those programs, I once was interviewed by a University of Michigan representative about my future plans and reasons for pursuing a college degree. My response—naturally, I thought—was that I wanted to earn a lot of money. I explained my reasons: overcoming a history of never having enough money, enough food, and enough medical care; and wanting to be able to fully take care of myself and family members. In the duration of the interview, however, the interviewer suggested that I consider other reasons for earning a degree.

What a surprise! I was young and had not thoroughly thought through what I wanted out of life, with the exception of my partially formed desire to become a doctor. Under the guidance of Mama and Daddy Cook and high-school personnel, I had begun to think about pursuing a career even before leaving my hometown. Participating in the honors program and interacting with faculty members, staff, and fellow students, however, encouraged me to devote considerably more thought to the topic.

In participating in the honors program, I also experienced my first airplane ride, from Montgomery, Alabama, to Ann Arbor, Michigan, home of the University of Michigan. This was also my first visit to a predominantly White university. With the anxiety involved in the airplane ride, my fellow honor students and I did not have much time to think about the differences and issues we might encounter on that campus. Once on the campus, we participated in group and individual discussions with Michigan faculty members and students. We discussed good study habits, career choices and advancement, cultural enrichment, and the importance of a formal education. We also played in the snow, sliding down hills on cafeteria trays and anything else that was handy at the time. It never snowed in Tuskegee! Being in a white wintry wonderland was new and exciting.

Once I experienced the Ann Arbor weather, however, I knew that I did not want to live in a cold climate for long periods of time.

On the Tuskegee campus, my chemistry classmates called me "Mayo" rather than "Margaret." Together, we attended required activities—chapel on Sundays, vespers on Wednesday evenings of each week, and special events such as honors and awards ceremonies. The Tuskegee education program was designed to ensure that students were culturally enriched in addition to well-educated. The social, emotional, physical, and educational needs of students were addressed. On numerous occasions, President Foster gave us pep talks to encourage us in our academic pursuits. We also enjoyed speakers at chemistry seminars and performances by the Tuskegee Institute choir. Often we heard singing and saw other activities on campus by students who were pledging sororities and fraternities. They always put on eye-catching performances.

To broaden our scope, we were introduced to great leaders and entertainers from around the world. Among the guests were foreign officials, such as the president of the United Nations General Assembly, political leaders such as Malcolm X, famed professional boxers such as Cassius Clay (later known as Mohammed Ali), and entertainers such as Dionne Warwick. During the program with Malcolm X, President Foster made a disclaimer statement that the opinions expressed by Malcolm X did not represent those of Tuskegee Institute—a new and surprising concept for me, but one that made sense, given the racial climate in Alabama.

Tuskegee Institute was already a target for racial tension, and Dr. Foster almost certainly wanted to appease state officials and board members, not to mention avoiding antagonizing the Ku Klux Klan. In 1923, the Ku Klux Klan had marched past the campus to protest the role of a former Tuskegee Institute president in the hiring of Negroes into important positions at the new Veterans Hospital for Negroes.[19]

---

[19]   W. H. Hughes and F. D. Patterson, eds., Robert Russa Moton of Hampton and Tuskegee, University of North Carolina Press, Chapel Hill, NC, 1956,

In the midst of all of this excitement, I had not forgotten my siblings. At the beginning of a week-long university break, I took a 24-hour bus ride home—my second trip home for the academic year. Upon my arrival in Suffolk, I had one of the greatest shocks of my young life. The house in which Audrey Mae and my younger siblings lived prior to my departure for Tuskegee was empty! I knew that I was approaching the right house because I had stayed there during my first holiday break from Tuskegee. In fact, a dear male friend and fellow classmate had accompanied me on that first trip back to Suffolk. Upon traveling back to Suffolk the second time, though, I was alone, and I could not find my family, leaving me sad and discouraged. I had no idea why my sisters and brother had not written to me about the move. I had written home several times and, therefore, was confident that they had my address.

I walked slowly from the bus stop to the area where my family had been living. As I approached the house down the long walkway, the next-door neighbor, who did not recognize me, asked where I was going. I told her that I had come to spend my university break period with my sisters and brother. She told me that no one lived in that house, which shocked and frightened me. She did not know where they had gone.

I asked several other people if they knew where my siblings were and was eventually directed to another section of Suffolk. I searched that section but could not find my sisters and brother. The only public facility in the area was a juke joint, which I entered to use the telephone. From there, I called Mama Cook. I did not know what else to do. I gave her my location, and within a short time, she and Daddy Cook showed up. They took me to their home, where I stayed until returning to Tuskegee Institute.

While staying in their home during that university break, we took short trips and participated in a number of social activities. Daddy Cook was a member of the Alpha Phi Alpha Fraternity as

---

pages 128-139; "TRT play to celebrate opening of VA Hospital," *The Tuskegee News*, January 23, 2014, page 1.

well as a number of other organizations. Mama Cook, also, was a member of the Ladies Auxiliary and other organizations—groups that kept them busy and socially involved. I was very comfortable in their home, but the thought that my family had moved without telling me where they were weighed heavily on my mind.

Finally, it was time for me to return to the institute.

Upon returning to the campus, I felt an urgency to develop a new plan of action, and to do it fast. I gradually reestablished contact with each member of my family, starting with my brother, but after what I had experienced upon my return home from campus, I knew I did not want to go home to Suffolk again anytime soon. I made up my mind to become fully independent.

By the end of my freshman year, I worked for another summer as a chambermaid at Sally Walker's White Horse Lodge and Paradise Resort in Cuddybackville, New York. My brother, Benjamin, also worked there that summer. He did general work under the supervision of Mrs. Walker's husband. After that, on holidays and other campus breaks—except the summers—during my sophomore, junior, and senior years, I remained on campus.

While attending Tuskegee Institute, I kept busy by completely immersing myself in various activities, yet thoughts of my siblings and their welfare weighed heavily on my mind. I tried placing those thoughts on the "back burner," but they would not stay there. It seemed like every time I had a moment when I was not immersed in work, those thoughts returned.

I forced myself to focus on my academic work. I was now conducting research, under the guidance of my chemistry professors and mentors, Dr. Courtney J. Smith and Dr. Lawrence F. Koons.

Shown here are Dr. L. Smith, Mr. Brinkley, and
Research Interns at Central State College. I am the
first person on the left in this photograph.

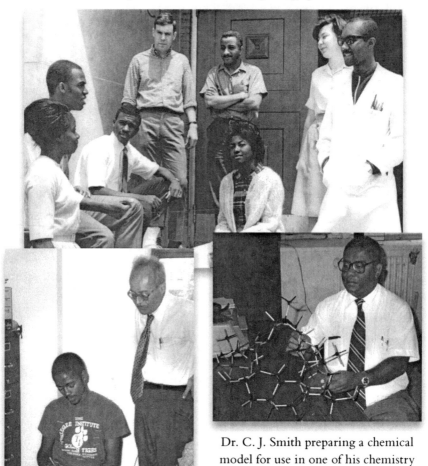

Dr. C. J. Smith preparing a chemical
model for use in one of his chemistry
lectures at Tuskegee Institute

Dr. L. F. Koons and student
discussing a chemistry assignment
at Tuskegee Institute

My primary on-campus research project was a study of the mechanisms of the photo-oxidation of water at semiconductor electrodes, at various temperatures. Even to me, the project seemed complex, but it was an important subject in the world of chemistry. So I was willing to learn. In response to a recommendation of Dr. Courtney J. Smith, I accepted an appointment in the Summer Research Program at Central State College in Ohio, under the mentorship of Dr. L. S. Smith. I wanted to expand my knowledge as broadly as possible to prepare for a future career. Besides, I had never been to Ohio.

This was the summer at the end of my sophomore year, and the program was sponsored by the National Science Foundation, a federal government agency. Each student worked on a major research project under the guidance of Dr. L. S. Smith and his assistant. I learned a lot about various chemicals and their interactions.

Upon returning to the Tuskegee Institute campus at the end of the summer, I continued to take on more student responsibilities, serving as a counselor of freshmen, as vice president of the university chapter of the Berzelius Chemical Society, and as a member of several committees. Although this was a heavy load, consuming many hours of each day, I loved interacting with faculty and other ambitious students. I had finally found a niche in life in which I felt comfortable and fulfilled. Over time, concentration on academic life began to replace the focus on family that had filled my mind in previous years.

At the end of my junior year, I was awarded the I. S. Derbigny Award for having maintained the highest scholastic average in chemistry for three years, as well as the Luther H. Foster Award for three accomplishments: excellent work performance, superior scholastic average, and outstanding service to a student organization. By then I was a member of Beta Kappa Chi Scientific Honor Society. I had been working hard and smart, and continuing to enjoy academic life. I knew that, if I wanted a different life from the one I had been headed toward, no one else was going to make that happen for me. I had to do it myself. I was reminded of this mindset years later when I heard a speech (see the insert) by Senator Barack Obama who later became President of the United States.[20] In my mind, studying chemistry instead of medicine was becoming a possible alternate path to achieving my goals, which still centered primarily around home and family.

> "Change will not come if we wait for some other person or some other time. We are the ones we've been waiting for. We are the change that we seek."

At the end of my junior year, in 1966, I again took advantage of a summer research program. This time, it was at Argonne National Laboratory (ANL) in Argonne, Illinois. In addition to offering a challenging opportunity to advance my future career, I would have the opportunity to travel to another large, vibrant city, Chicago. My appointment was in the Analytical Chemistry Laboratory—an amazingly well-equipped wonderland of science with experiments being conducted by experienced chemists.

ANL was, and is, a prestigious government-owned laboratory, solving energy-related problems for the nation. I felt honored to be part of such an important endeavor.

Dr. Lawrence F. Koons at Tuskegee facilitated that appointment for me. Alice Essling of ANL served as my research advisor. My project involved analyzing uranium compounds containing tungsten, arsenic, rare earths, and the like. I felt very comfortable in the laboratory setting. Ms. Essling and her co-workers made sure that I learned and practiced safety in handling radioactive materials. They included me in sessions in which we discussed published scientific articles, as well as the actual unpublished research of the laboratory. They also took me to restaurants to acquaint me with the community of researchers at ANL. I loved this camaraderie of the research environment. I felt truly accepted as a member of the research team. In the process of getting to know people, I also became a close friend of a young man, who was a researcher at the laboratory.

---

[20] A quote from a speech given in 2008 by Senator Barack Obama who became the 44th President of the United States.

After my exposure to this diverse group of people with a variety of careers and degrees, I once again mulled over what I wanted for my future career. Shortly after my experience at Argonne, I made a momentous decision: instead of becoming a physician, I now wanted to become a doctoral-level researcher and teacher. That meant pursuing a PhD research program rather than eight years of medical school. I was ready for that, and I looked forward to it.

While participating in the summer program at ANL, I lived in Chicago at the home of Hattie Fields, a graduate of Tuskegee Institute, class of 1950. She was so kind to me that I call her my "Other Mom." I enjoyed living with Mrs. Fields and her two daughters. We attended Tuskegee Institute alumni club meetings in Chicago, and we participated in other social activities together. I got to see the sights of Chicago, including the waterfront, the many shopping areas, and ethnic communities. I recall preparing a dinner for the entire Fields family one weekend, and I was surprised at the successful outcome. At that point in my life, I did not consider myself to be a good cook.

Mrs. Fields and I posed for this photograph in the late nineties in Chicago.

Although my stay in Mrs. Fields' home occurred in the 1960s, she and I still keep in contact. From her house, I rode the Argonne shuttle bus to and from the laboratory. The 25-mile trip from Chicago to Argonne enabled me to become acquainted with a number of other

ANL employees and to gain useful insight on careers. I made a few friends that I would meet again later, as my career developed. As I have gone through life I have continued to make a number of friends, and I have kept them while continuing to make new ones. I treasure memories of all of them.

When the summer program at ANL ended, I returned to Tuskegee Institute to complete my senior year. The young man who lived in Chicago and worked in the ANL Chemistry Division—the one with whom I had become a good friend—came with his brother to Tuskegee Institute to visit me. However, campus restrictions prevented me from going offsite or riding in their car with them. During those days, female students could not ride in vehicles or leave the campus unless they had written permission from their parents or guardians. I knew that I would not be able to obtain permission, since the sister who served as my guardian of record never responded to my letters or to correspondence from Tuskegee Institute. This was puzzling. Even though Audrey Mae could not read or write, I felt that she could have found someone else to write for her.

While I was a student at Tuskegee, parents or guardians were responsible for students; therefore, they had to review and sign their grade reports and return them to the appropriate university official. Initially, Audrey Mae was the responsible person for me, but because of our difficulty with communicating, I asked Mama Cook to take over as my guardian of record on campus. She accepted that responsibility, and everything went smoothly after that.

Years later, I realized the importance of the safety and security rules of campus. Even going into the downtown part of the City of Tuskegee could be dangerous. This point was well illustrated when a Tuskegee student, Sammye Young, Jr.,[21] was shot while at a gas station in downtown Tuskegee in 1966. Although he was shot in the back, the White shooter was acquitted of the crime. Students protested

---

[21]   Additional details on the Sammye Young, Jr., incident can be found in the Tuskegee Human and Civil Rights Multicultural Center in Tuskegee, Alabama.

in response to the murder. We marched downtown pass that gas station and held rallies on campus. I was nervous and angry about this situation. Other murders and violent incidents occurred in the city in an atmosphere of racial tension, and often no one was identified to pay for those crimes. Montgomery, Alabama, was still ablaze with racial activities—restaurant sit-ins, police brutality, and protest marches. It was a dangerous time in the South, but in the sheltered campus setting, my fellow classmates and I felt safe and protected. We were able to focus on studying diligently to better ourselves and the lives of others.

As a student on the campus, I had numerous resources and helpful persons at my disposal. Among the most helpful individuals were Dr. Andew P. Torrence who was then the dean of academic affairs and Mrs. Benson, a counselor. House mothers in each dormitory for females were important parts of the safety structure of the campus. Faculty members were eager to address issues pertinent to the students' whole experience as opposed to just the academic facets of their lives. I made use of most of the available support services.

Health issues of students were addressed at the John A. Andrew Hospital, which was located on the campus. Long before my time on the campus, Dr. George Washington Carver worked with a medical doctor in a wing of that hospital. It was there that Dr. Carver massaged the limbs of polio patients with an oil that he developed in his laboratory. In my time on the campus, incoming students, including me, received health examinations and treatments for various ailments at that hospital.

Staying on campus during the holiday and academic breaks enabled me to have time to study and socialize with Tuskegee employees who lived in the community around the campus, as well as with foreign students. During an international social event on campus, I was introduced to a handsome young man from Monrovia, Liberia, and later he and I began dating. He had a large social circle of foreign students, and I fit into it well, within the limited amount of time that I had to socialize.

While at Tuskegee, I became well rounded—socially and culturally as well as professionally—something for which the institute was well known. I listened to music, including that of several artists in particular. Among the music I liked were the gospel songs of Mahalia Jackson, the popular music of Johnny Mathis, the soft baritone voice of Nat King Cole, the pop/classical/gospel music and sassy style of Nina Simone, the African music of Mariam Makeba, the folk music/blues/jazz/spirituals of Odetta who was considered to be the voice of the civil rights movement, the Caribbean-American music of Harry Belafonte, and the gospel/pop/jazz music of Della Reese. On the TV were several actors whom I enjoyed. Among them were Sidney Poitier, Eartha Kitt, and Redd Foxx. In later years, my tastes continued to evolve; currently, my favorite celebrities are Denzel Washington, Morgan Freeman, Oprah Winfrey, and Tyler Perry.

In addition to listening to music and watching television, I participated in a limited number of campus activities, although much of my time was spent in the chemistry laboratory, conducting experiments. I did not have much appreciation for the sports-oriented training to which I was exposed; however, the completion of several physical education courses was mandatory. I had some bad times in a couple of those courses. One day, I was trying to learn to swim when I found myself in the deep part of the pool. I panicked. It was Tiny Laster, a chemistry major, who pulled me to safety. In return, I assisted him with his master's thesis. Thankfully, there were many more positive things that happened to me than bad ones. I was positive in attitude, and I felt confident that I had made excellent use of my time as a student.

My social life at Tuskegee Institute did not detract from my academic performance. I made the honor roll each year. I continued my involvement with the families to whom Mama and Daddy Cook had introduced to me. Among the most generous families was the Howells. Dr. Elva Howell, who earned her doctorate degree later in life, often invited me and a few other students to her home for Sunday dinner. In addition to having dinner, we took the time to talk about our progress in classes and about other matters. I always enjoyed those gatherings. After I graduated and began working on campus, Dr. Howell reminded me of one dinner during which she served green beans along with other delicious food. As I sat with others around the table, I said "Please pass me the snaps." She recalled that the reactions of the other guests were interesting, since they did not call them "snaps"; the usual term was "green beans." This reminded me that there were a number of ways in which I had learned to refer to food and other items based on how they were named in my hometown. I slowly began to refine my pronunciations and adopt the names used in the area in which I lived at that time.

My May 29, 1967, graduation was held on the lawn of the Tuskegee Institute campus and was attended by a large crowd of people. Mama and Daddy Cook and Lee Vania were there for me. It was a proud time to "walk the water." This was a term given to the part of the graduation exercise in which we walked across the stage to accept a graduation certificate and shook the hands of university leaders and other high-ranking officials. The stage was a covered reflecting fountain that was dedicated to students in 1965. So in a sense, graduates did indeed "walk across water."

I graduated with high honors with a major in chemistry and a minor in mathematics—the only female who graduated at that time with that major and minor. The other female who was initially in my chemistry class changed her major and did not graduate when I did. Studies in chemistry held special significance since Tuskegee's Chemistry Department was accredited by the American Chemical Society. My male classmates and I were very proud of ourselves. To complete requirements for graduation, I had used scholarships, a student loan, work/study hours, and awards. My name and accomplishments were included in Who's Who in American Universities and Colleges. I participated in campus balls and parades. I had studied hard and smart, and as a result, I won academic awards, served as a member of the Honor Society, lived in Honors Dorm, conducted research, and participated in internships at a college in Ohio and at a national research laboratory in Illinois. Throughout my years at Tuskegee Institute, the completion of my formal education was my top priority. I always tried to keep my priorities in appropriate order, even as they changed in later years.

Wedding Bells: Pursuing the Dream of Marriage

In writing this book, I spent long hours thinking about how I met the love of my life and about my wedding day. Although I had a few gentlemen callers while on campus, I eventually chose to keep company with one young man exclusively—the Liberian to whom I had been introduced earlier. He was majoring in economics. It was 1966, and focusing on African customs was in vogue. A large number of students wore their hair in natural styles that were popular at the time and dressed in dashikis. Having African friends was not unusual. Some female students wanted (or already had) African husbands, and they wanted to visit the Motherland as African wives. It was an exciting time, a time for identifying with people of Africa while fighting segregation and inhuman acts in the Deep South.

According to my future husband, his father had served as Liberia's Minister of Finance during the presidency of the Honorable V. S. Tubman. Before we got married, I received permission from Mama and Daddy Cook, and he received permission from his parents in Liberia. His parents and my guardians did not attend the ceremony because of the distances involved, but Mama and Daddy Cook promised to give a reception for us when we arrived in Suffolk. This was a promise that they later fulfilled in grand style. In addition to receiving my official guardians' permission for marriage, I sought and received advice from one of Tuskegee's counselors for foreign students, who told me about African customs of which I was not aware.

To my surprise, the counselor asked me if my husband-to-be had been promised in marriage to anyone else. The surprises continued. When I asked him about this, his response was "yes." However, he advised me that he was not interested in the young lady chosen for him by his parents. Thus, we continued with our wedding plans.

My husband-to-be and I got married a few weeks after my graduation, in a private ceremony in the church located near the Carver Research Foundation building, at the edge of the Tuskegee Institute campus. It was the summer of 1967, and we were both 23 years old. I wore a white wedding gown that was loaned to me by a Tuskegee Institute staff member, whose daughter had worn it in her wedding. The lady who loaned me the gown told me that she would be honored to have me wear it. She said that it had been in storage for years following her daughter's wedding. The gown was a perfect fit.

I remember each incident in my marriage as if it happened yesterday. They are ingrained into my mind and for many years affected my very soul. When I met with the minister of the Episcopalian church where my wedding was to take place, we talked for a while. Then he asked me go to my dormitory and think about what I was about to do. He advised that I return the following day and let him know if I still wanted to marry my chosen one. The campus counselor for foreign students advised me to learn more about my husband-to-be before marrying him. These were interesting requests from people who were trying to help me, but I wanted to marry him and have a family. Other than the question about whether he was promised to anyone else, I did not pursue this advice.

Our wedding was simple—no guests except a couple of the groom's African friends, no flowers to decorate the church, no rice to throw, and no honeymoon. Our wedding bands were simple gold-plated rings with a minimum amount of design around the edges. I did not care about jewelry. I was pleased with what I received and the fact that my marriage and rings were blessed. My thoughts were focused on how to make the transition from being single to being married. What I did know is that I needed to end my solitary life— no more dormitory living, no more cafeteria food, no more trips to Suffolk where my family had forgotten me, and no more loneliness. I would now have my own family.

After the wedding, my husband and I rented a small house on a small, one-block street that runs parallel to Old Montgomery Road in Tuskegee. The rented house was among those owned by Mr.

and Mrs. Walker, whose huge brick house was in the same block. However, their house faced Old Montgomery Road. Our home had a bedroom, bathroom, kitchen, living room, and a small screened-in porch. Although it was small, it was large enough for the two of us, and I went about the business of keeping house for me and my new husband.

I soon learned more about my husband's culture. Several of his African friends visited almost every day, especially around supper time. Some came to cook large pots of rice and other food for themselves, even when my husband was not home. All were friendly and respectful toward me. I enjoyed hearing them talk about their countries and family members. In addition, I learned a number of recipes for cooking with an African flair.

After living in the house for a while, we converted the living room into a bedroom and rented it to a student to help with paying the bills. The logistics were inconvenient—we had to pass through her bedroom to get to the bathroom—and she did not stay long. After that, to assist with paying the bills, I did odd jobs—typing the master's thesis for a graduate chemistry student and working as a tutor. For a few weeks of the summer, I worked as a laboratory instructor for a summer program at Tuskegee Institute.

Finally, I felt like I had achieved some of the goals I had been dreaming about since I was a child. I had a husband, a house, and an education. At Tuskegee, I had left Saratoga in the dust and was living the life I envisioned, as a wife and a member of the real labor force. Or so it seemed.

There were still obstacles to overcome, which took me even further in the right direction. I hired a gentleman to teach me to drive, and I bought a used car for me and my husband. Having a car gave us more freedom. Since Tuskegee did not have any central transportation services except a few cabs, I was now able to get to the supermarket and to my job. Occasionally I went to Montgomery and Auburn to shop—always being careful to return to Tuskegee before dark and to "stay in my place" while in those cities. I had heard many stories about negative racial incidents in those cities, and I did not want to become a statistic.

Another very important action that I took while we lived in Tuskegee, Alabama, was to register to vote. I walked into the downtown courthouse, where two elderly White women were in a small room, taking registrations. When my turn came, I supplied most of the pertinent information, but one question had me stumped: I had forgotten the name of the county in which I was born, and that item was required on the voter's registration application form. I called my sister Mary Lee, who reminded me that the county of my birth and upbringing was Nansemond County, Virginia.[22] How could I have forgotten that fact; did I deliberately try to block it out, along with the memories of all that transpired there? When election time came, I took great pride in voting for the first time and every election thereafter.

I had graduated from Tuskegee University, and Mama and Daddy Cook and my sister, Lee Vania, had honored me with their presence at the graduation ceremony. Although I could have pursued a job in the field of chemistry at this point, by then I considered my experience at Tuskegee as only the first phase of my plan to distance myself from my early circumstances and get ahead in life. After much thought and discussion with my husband and professors, as well as with the Cook family, I made the commitment to continue pursuing higher education, by planning to enroll in graduate school to earn a master's degree.

---

[22] Nansemond County no longer exists, having merged with Suffolk.

My Graduate Years

With my acceptance into the master's degree program in analytical chemistry at Wayne State University (WSU) in 1967, I headed for a new venue—Detroit, Michigan. My husband stayed in Tuskegee to complete the coursework he needed for his undergraduate degree. Our plan was to get back together when he completed his requirements.

In Detroit, I initially stayed in a campus dormitory, and later I moved into a one-bedroom apartment in a quiet building. This enabled me to study in my apartment rather than risking my safety on the downtown campus at night. For a while, I held a job selling coats at one of the downtown stores; however, that work schedule interfered with my academic responsibilities. I quit the job and decided to spend more time in my research laboratory.

Around that time, my major professor, Dr. Richard Hahn, assigned me to serve as a teaching assistant, which provided some income but required many hours, teaching and coaching undergraduate students enrolled in chemistry courses. While serving as my major professor, Dr. Hahn died, and I was assigned to another chemistry professor, Dr. George Schenk, for academic advice and the final processing of my master's thesis. Prior to his death, Dr. Hahn had approved my thesis.

After a year and a half, I successfully completed my research, which is reported in my master's thesis, titled "Determination of Certain Cations by Precipitation as Double Salts with Various Amine Phosphates." The title was a mouthful! For me, it was an exciting project, since no scientific literature had yet reported on the uses of phosphate salts of amines as precipitants. These precipitants would later prove to be useful in laboratory research. Explaining my work to my family and non-chemistry friends was never easy. My husband showed little interest in my work, which I assumed was because his concentration was in a different field.

My husband and I were able to handle the separation wonderfully; or at least, I thought so. I did not concern myself with his social activities, especially his involvement with a woman back at Tuskegee whom I considered to be my best friend. With hindsight, I realize how very naïve I was.

I progressed rapidly through the master's degree program at WSU. I had hoped that my husband would have completed his bachelor's degree in economics before I completed my master's degree, but that did not happen. He and I visited each other several times while I was at WSU. On occasion one of his fellow countrymen came with him to Detroit. The presence of his friends from Liberia took away from our time together, but I never expressed any concern about it. I imagined that we would have a lot of time together after we completed our academic studies. When we were not together, we kept in touch by telephone and the postal service. Newer technologies such as electronic mail and video conference were not available in those days.

A number of incidents occurred while I was living in Detroit and attending Wayne State University. Dr. Martin Luther King, Jr., was murdered, triggering unrest in many cities. That was extremely upsetting not only to me, but to huge numbers of people of all races. Also, it was during that period that student unrest occurred on the Tuskegee Institute campus. That appeared to be highly unusual to many people, since Tuskegee students were viewed as pacifists. That is not my opinion of them, however. During my time as a student there, several students were very active in civil rights activities. In fact, the campus was ablaze with protest activities in response to racial injustices.

While at WSU, surprising news reached me about Tuskegee Institute students having locked members of the Board of Trustees in the campus building in which they were holding a meeting. The students would not allow any of the trustees to leave until their demands were met. Seemingly, the students wanted reforms that would have a positive impact on academic programs and faculty. The lock-down action showed that Tuskegee students were not truly pacifists. The university president and trustees were able to negotiate with the students, and the confrontation ended admirably on all sides, or at least I think so.

After completing my master's degree in analytical chemistry, I returned to Tuskegee to be with my husband. I could not handle staying at home alone all day while he continued his classwork; therefore, I went job hunting on the Tuskegee Institute campus. This did not take long. Fortunately, I found a position as laboratory technician in the School of Agriculture on campus. My work there was supervised by Dr. Ronald Chung and Dr. John Lu. I was primarily responsible for conducting research on enzymes from chicken livers. I also planned and implemented a science training program for high-school teachers nationwide.

During the period that I was serving as a technician, I became pregnant. My husband and I had been married for two years, and we were proud of the pregnancy. I continued to work until the week before our baby boy was born. Actually, I would have worked longer, but Dr. Chung advised that I stop coming to work for fear that I would deliver the baby while alone in the laboratory. I was not concerned. I just wanted to earn a little money, so that I could pay bills and support my new habit of eating banana splits and lots of other food—indulgences related mostly to my pregnancy.

Most of my salary was used to pay for rent and utilities and to buy gas for our car. One day as I went for an evening walk, I felt a pain in my stomach. I hurried home and up the exterior stairs to the apartment that was a part of the house in which my husband and I lived at that time. This apartment was nearer to the campus than the one in which we lived earlier. When it became clear that I was in labor, my husband took me to John A. Andrew Hospital for the delivery. While he was talking to the receptionist, he did not hear me say that I needed to go to the restroom. I walked slowed across the lobby into the restroom. He was very much engrossed in his conversation with the receptionist.

One thing I had noticed about my husband: whenever he tried to impress a woman, his accent became more pronounced. I never complained when he flirted with women in my presence. My way of handling it was usually to focus on something else. In this instance, I focused on going to the restroom. I had not been in the restroom more than a minute when a nurse rushed in and led me out. She told me that I was about to deliver my baby in the restroom, and she took me to a room of the hospital where I was prepared for the delivery. Dr. Henry Foster, Jr., my gynecologist, arrived and led the delivery procedure with the assistance of several nurses. My husband and I named our baby boy Lawson Kwia. Kwia is the middle name of my husband's father.

My husband and I doted on our son. We bought him lots of toys and clothes, and we played with him continuously. We showed him off to friends, and read and sang to him, even though he was too young to know what was being said.

Following my workaholic instincts, however, I returned to my laboratory technician job on the Tuskegee campus just two weeks after my son was born, leaving him with a babysitter. While serving in that capacity, the head of Tuskegee's Mathematics Department offered me a position as an instructor of mathematics. After thinking about how this offer might influence my future prospects, I accepted it. I could manage the workload, since my son had an exceptional babysitter, Mrs. Campbell, who lived nearby and loved to keep him even during late hours and overnight. Although I could not pay her what her services were worth, she never complained. She thought that I did not know much about taking care of a baby. Admittedly, I knew scientific research and how to teach mathematics and chemistry far better than taking care of a baby. I am deeply grateful to her for what she did for me and my son.

By the time of my employment as a mathematics teacher, my husband and I were having major problems. I was slowly learning from fellow students about instances of infidelity by my husband, with both women who were close to me and some whom I did not know. In addition, his constant refusal to explain his nocturnal activities kept me upset. He seemed to be lying frequently, even about little things, when there was no need to do so. I worked long hours to help take away the emotional pain as well as to address our financial needs. Although I felt mistreated, I stayed in the marriage and tried to make it work for both of us.

On a hot and humid day, as most days seemed to be in Alabama, I felt like staying home and doing some housework with my husband. The sky was clear, and people walked in large numbers up and down the streets to and from the campus among the trees that afforded relief from the direct sunlight. The scent of freshly cut grass lingered in the air, spiked by the odor of barbeque ribs and chicken, hot rolls, collard greens, and sweet potato pie. My husband and I were at home together with our son. Our son, making baby noises in the bedroom, was the picture of health, with a head full of hair and a body strong enough to lift his head up when he was placed on his stomach to rest. He had begun to have cereal in his milk. Each day he seemed to want more cereal in it. Soon he would be ready to be given small pieces of solid food. He didn't have any teeth because he wasn't quite eight months old. His father loved him, and so did I. Often I looked at him and wondered how I had managed to be so fortunate to have such a beautiful baby boy, who was quiet and peaceful in temperament.

On this day, we cleaned the apartment and opened the windows wide, the way my husband always positioned them when he did the cleaning. Oh yes, he could clean house and cook African meals quite well. The sheer curtains bellowed in the soft, hot and humid breeze. We were a family—mother, father, and son! My dream had been realized. Together my husband and I were preparing supper on this weekend day. We had to eat early, since he planned to meet with his African friends, whom he referred to as his "Home Boys." This was his daily routine. I suppose that it was their custom. Maybe I was, as he proudly said, "a Colored woman, not a pure-blooded African" as he was; therefore, I did not interact with my friends "properly." I didn't mind those kinds of statements. I was confident in my blackness, whether pure-blooded or not.

When we were together, we did not talk much. We just enjoyed each other's company. On this day, however, the silence in our apartment was broken by the ringing of the telephone on the bookcase in the living room. He ran from the kitchen to answer it. He said very little that I could hear—not that I was eavesdropping. When he returned to the kitchen, he looked upset. I asked, "Who was that on the telephone?" In his Liberian accent he said, "No one; it's not important." In those few words, he spoke clearly, but the mood of my home had gone from complete bliss to uneasiness and unhappiness with that telephone call.

I felt a compelling urge to know what was wrong and how I could help. I really wanted to know how I could restore harmony in my home. I moved cautiously closer to him and touched him gently, and asked, "What's wrong?" He moved away. His mood was getting worse, and I became very much concerned. Were any of his relatives in Liberia ill? Even worse, maybe it was a problem with his mother or his father. I felt bad for him, since he was so far from home and family. I knew the feeling, for I had been alone and lonely for years before he came into my life. In his presence, I could tolerate being away from my siblings.

As he moved away from me, the telephone rang again. We both raced to the telephone this time, but I was the first to reach it. My effort was to protect my interest, my husband's emotions. I said hello. The voice on the telephone was that of my good friend. She was crying and sounded frightened. As she sobbed, I continued to ask, my voice becoming increasingly more intense, "What's wrong?" Before she could respond, I heard a loud thump, and the telephone went dead.

In that one moment, I had two people who were very dear to me experiencing unhappiness. How could I help both of them? I had always been the strong support they needed, but heretofore I had addressed problems that they brought to me in isolation, without one knowing that I was helping the other. As I turned to refocus on my husband, the telephone rang again. He said, "Don't answer it." By the time his words reached my ears, I had already picked up the telephone and head a familiar male voice with an accent. He said, "Did your husband tell you that he has been f*****g my wife?" "Let me speak to him," the male caller snapped rudely.

The words struck me like a knife, straight down my chest and into my heart. With my chest seemingly split wide open, I searched my brain for the right words to say. My brain would not function properly, and the words did not come. I felt very dumb as I said, "What did you say?" He repeated the words that cut even deeper into my chest, ripping my heart out of its peaceful place within me. In the background, I could hear my best friend screaming and crying. I began screaming at the caller, insisting that he "let me speak to her."

Finally, she was on the telephone, sobbing and apologizing. All of a sudden, there was a crash that sounded like someone hitting someone else, and the telephone went dead again. I imagined that he was beating her unmercifully. I turned and looked at my husband, who had the strangest look on his face.

At first, I did not feel anger. I was simply hurt. I wanted to know when he had found time to see her, whom I considered one of my best friends. According to her husband, a Tuskegee Institute student who had been working temporarily in one of the northern states, the relationship was long term. As the story unfolded over the following hours, I learned that on the nights that my husband was to have been at the campus library studying, he was actually at her house, making love to her.

The conversation between me and my husband was not going well. He seemed to blame me for asking questions. As I listened to his explanations, things began to click. One of my college mates had told me that my husband was seen often with other women in "my" car. I had disregarded that information. I trusted my husband. Although I bought the car, it was "OURS," not just mine. I was a married woman, whose property belonged to both my husband and me.

When I questioned him about whether he was studying in the library on the nights that my classmate mentioned, he simply withdrew and said, "Forget it!" What a fool I had been! Didn't I have any sense? Why didn't I know that he was having an affair with the person whom I considered to be my best female friend?

My mind was whirling out of control. I had been told that he was seen with women, but I dismissed that information even though

I had seen evidence that supported it. All of the pieces were falling apart and reassembling. Of course, at first I blamed myself, as women often do. Maybe I was not good enough for him. Maybe he wanted her because I worked long hours. Maybe I was away from home too much. Could that be true? No! The truth was slapping me in the face and ripping out my heart, and I refused to believe it. He was a womanizer, and I had been warned of that. I walked to the door and opened it slowly. I knew that everything outside had stopped dead in its tracks. To my surprise, everything outside was normal. People out there hadn't a clue of what was happening inside my apartment. I wanted to scream, but no sound came out of my mouth.

I walked back to my husband, who was still standing near the telephone. I asked him about his infidelity. The funny thing is that he screamed, "Yes, I was with her! Her old dumb husband does not have good sense! He does not take care of her." As the emotions intensified in the room and the volume of our two voices reached an angry pitch, our son began to cry. When I went to pick him up to comfort him, my husband went out the door. I screamed at the top of my voice, "Don't come back!" At that time, I really meant it. My sincere love for him had evaporated, within a few short hours, leaving only anger and the feeling of betrayal by the two people whom I had most trusted. As smart as I thought I was, I did not have a clue what was going on right under my nose. Being academically smart, I was learning, was not enough to get through my personal life.

As I walked around the apartment trying to comfort my son in my arms, I began to cry uncontrollably. I felt angry, and I felt as if a weight was pressing down on me with more intensity as the minutes passed. I thought of the times that my best friend had come to my house in the morning, after my husband left home to attend his classes on campus. He usually arrived home in the wee hours of the morning, complaining about the load of classroom assignments on which he had to work. It never occurred to me that the library closed before midnight.

Often my best friend would ask for intimate details on my husband's relationship with me. Usually, she wanted to know if I knew where he was the previous night. Now I know that she simply wanted to know if I knew that he was not in the library or with his male friends at the neighborhood big house, and that he was with her. I never suspected that they were meeting during those times that he was supposed to have been studying in the library. The news of their affair hit me harder than any of my previous experiences, all the way back to my childhood with my abusive father. I thought of the many times that I had chauffeured her around town free of charge, had loaned her money to make ends meet, and had helped her with one task or another. I thought of the many times that she and I had talked about our relationships with our husbands, who were both Africans. We were like sisters, sharing and caring—at least I had thought so.

I looked at myself in the mirror to see if I was more attractive than she was. I won by a wide margin. I had been a campus beauty queen, Miss ROTC. I was clean and dressed well. I had a job and was carrying the weight of most of the family expenses. I did not mind that, since I thought my husband would graduate soon and would assume at least half of the financial responsibilities of our household. He was in economics and surely would know more than I did about financial matters.

All of my assumptions were turning out to be wrong. As the day progressed and darkness drew closer, signifying the coming of night, I realized the extent of my devastation. No one would come through the door to soothe me, even if it were the wee hours of the morning. I already missed my cheating husband. I wanted him back. Why should I let her have him? I thought. I cried quietly all through that first night. My active mind would not let me be. Had I done something wrong? What had I done? I cried softly so that I would not disturb my son, who was peacefully sleeping in his bassinet at the side of the bed. Also, I didn't want to disturb either the neighbors in the adjacent apartment or the landlord who lived in the apartment below mine. I was truly miserable, and I was truly alone.

At the same time I was thinking such negative thoughts, however, I also began thinking positive thoughts. I wanted to get back at my friend for disrupting my marriage, for doing things for my husband that he enjoyed more than he enjoyed my company. I wanted him back! I wanted him out of my life for good! I was confused. I wanted my son to have an ideal family. I wanted to love and be loved. Questions continued to flow through my mind. Mostly, I wished that the pain in my chest would stop.

As I thought through the situation, I began focusing on my son. I did not want him to have to struggle as I did in my early years. The rumor was that male children of an African man belonged to his side of the family. That struck fear in me. The thought of losing my son to a family on unfamiliar land horrified me. My family had no interest in me or what I was enduring. Seemingly, no one cared. Then I realized: yes, there was someone who cared. Mama and Daddy Cook cared about me. I could not tell them that my marriage was unsuccessful. I did not even know the reasons.

With the passing of a few days, I managed to get out of bed and force myself to go to work after taking my son to the babysitter. On that day, my task of killing chickens to get their livers for my research was therapeutic. I was brutal to the chickens, showing them no mercy. They had pecked me in the past, and this day I got my revenge. Of course, I was really using them as stand-ins for my husband and best friend, who had betrayed me, even though I was a good person. I kept the house clean. I kept the car clean. I kept the baby clean and fed. I paid the bills. I did not overeat or drink alcoholic beverages. I never showed anger to my husband until that fateful day. I had, however, become upset when women called our home asking for him. When I answered, they would sometimes ask if I were his mother. That irked me.

When I brought those calls to his attention, he would comfort me with his smooth talking: "Those are girls from my class who probably want to know the class assignments." Sometimes he would say something like "That was just a poor girl who needed a ride to class." He would comfort me with his smooth talk. All lies! After hearing his explanation, I would block it out of my mind, relax, and go on with life, happy in my ignorance. Whenever I began to worry, I would sometimes call Mama Cook. However, I never told her that anything was wrong. She had cautioned me about him, and I could not let her be right.

With the passing of a few days, two of my husband's friends visited me. After sitting for a while and appearing not to be ready to leave anytime soon, I offered to prepare a meal for them. After eating, one left, leaving the second fellow to make conversation with me. At first, I was pleased to have someone visit me. No one had been to my home since my husband left. Prior to that, our home had been teeming with liveliness resulting from visiting Africans, most of whom were university students. They would hold lengthy political discussions and eat large quantities of food—especially rice—and drink beer.

When the fellow who had remained at my home that evening started making advances to me, I rudely dismissed him and sent him out of the apartment. Apparently, he had been sent by the others to "take care of my womanly needs," or it was a joke to see how desperate I was. Was that an African custom or something that he made up? I did not know, and it did not matter. The very thought of interacting with one of my husband's friends or countrymen turned my stomach. At that point, I knew I needed to tell Mama and Daddy Cook what was going on. I needed support and protection. They sent their son, Alfred, to stay with me for a while.

To occupy my mind, I kept busy. I let the babysitter keep my son as often as I could bear to be away from him, which was not long. I changed jobs. As time passed, I gained more control over my thoughts and dreams. I immersed myself in work, both on the job and at home. I cleaned places in my apartment that had never been cleaned and did not need cleaning. I read books, newspapers, and scientific journals. I began to dream. When I talked to people I knew, I never told them about my problems. Yet I always addressed theirs if asked. I did not let my anguish show on my face. A lifetime of needing to be strong in the face of adversity served me well in that regard.

After several months, my husband wrote to me, apologizing for the wrong that he had done and expressing his love for me. I was still angry. My wound was too deep, and I did not respond to his letter.

At night, I said a constant prayer: "Dear God, please deliver me from all evil, and protect me and my son. Help me find a way to support my son and myself. Forgive me for my sins." Yes, I had sinned. I had entertained very negative thoughts of my husband and my best friend. I had had evil thoughts that I did not try to control. I eventually divorced my husband and, later, even accepted another gentleman into my life. Of course, that relationship did not get off the ground either, and it ended quickly.

As I thought back over my marriage and the time leading up to it, I wondered if I had read all of the signals correctly. It is true that the person that I married had asked me to marry him. His parents gave him advice on the planned marriage, while Mama and Daddy Cook advised me to consider all of my options. Options! What options did I have? At the time, I was 23, lonely, and unmarried. The men that I knew, other than my husband, were not love interests of mine.

The man who had asked me to marry him was a handsome, pure-blooded African from the Grebo Tribe. He dressed neatly in pants tailored in England, and his shirts were made of the finest material. Yes, he was from a wealthy family in Liberia, West Africa. According to him, his father always wore a suit—even in the hot Liberian weather. His mother was a lady of class. She wore the finest of outfits and jewelry. She and I had communicated by letter after the marriage. In one of her letters to her son—my husband—she included her dress size, since she was requesting that he find a gown for her to wear to a special event. I bought a beautiful gown and sent it to her, but I never told her that her son did not pay for it. On another occasion, she sent me an African dress, which was very much appreciated. I never met my husband's mother or father since they were in Africa, and I was in America.

Our son was less than one year old when his father and I were divorced. Because my ex-husband was an unemployed foreign student at the time, it would have been absurd for me to request alimony and/

or child support. Keeping my son was my decision. For that reason, with the divorce decree, I became a single parent, accepting total responsibility for both a small child and myself.

As I look back over the situation, it appears that I was better off than most divorced women. I had a good babysitter for my son and a reasonably good job teaching mathematics at a well-known historically Black educational institute, Tuskegee Institute in Alabama. I had hoped that my appointment in the Mathematics Department would last until a position was available in the Chemistry Department. I had earned a master's degree in analytical chemistry a few months prior to getting the position in the Mathematics Department, following my stint as a research technician. Obtaining an appointment in the Chemistry Department became more urgent when I learned that I would not be able to move upward in rank in the Mathematics Department because I did not have a primary degree in mathematics; my major degree was in chemistry with a mathematics minor.

As months drifted by, life seemed to become empty. I felt as if I were going in circles. Certainly my evenings were filled with the joyful noises of my son, but something was still missing. I yearned to leave the area to start over again, but I did not know where to start. For that reason I continued to teach mathematics. When I was on the job, I felt good. I worked diligently and slowly began feeling that I was making progress in taming my emotions and recovering from shock. I came to another momentous decision—that I would have to remake myself yet again. I needed to develop a strategy to do that. First, I reviewed my previous plans, which I had made prior to marriage. I even reviewed the goals that I had set prior to college. Fortunately, while I thought long and hard about the future strategy for my professional development, an attractive opportunity presented itself.

From Alabama to New England: Change of Scenery

A s a mathematics instructor at Tuskegee Institute, my office was in Huntington Hall on the campus. There I spent long days preparing lectures, holding discussions with students, grading examinations and quizzes, and completing other tasks. Fortunately, Mrs. Campbell continued to serve as babysitter for my son, and she loved taking care of him.

One afternoon while I sat in my office, I received a call from Dr. Richard Wasserstrom, dean of the College of Arts and Sciences. He asked if I would meet with a representative of Brown University who originally had an appointment with another faculty member. That faculty member was not available on campus at the designated time.

I agreed to meet with the representative, Dr. Eugene S. Pysh. The plan was to listen to his presentation and receive brochures for distribution to my students. When Dr. Pysh arrived in my office, he did the planned information transfer. With the completion of the information transfer, he asked me about my own educational plans. I told him that I was satisfied with the educational status that I had achieved already. He then asked about my family and other personal matters. Then he asked me to complete a preliminary form for application to the doctorate program in chemistry at Brown University. Although I was surprised by the request, I completed the form and handed it to him, while explaining that I was not interested in any additional graduate education. When he left my office, I thought that the matter was closed.

A few days later, Dr. Pysh asked me by telephone to complete a longer application form that he had left with me. He told me that the Chemistry Department faculty of Brown University wanted to see my completed application. When I arrived at home, I called Mama Cook and told her the details. When I finished telling her about this matter, she was in a hurry to get off the telephone. Shortly after she hung up, the telephone rang with Daddy Cook calling. He asked me why I was not planning to complete the application to attend Brown University. I was surprised at his tone and concern, but it was clear that he and Mama Cook wanted me to earn my doctorate degree. It was also clear that they were willing to assist me in earning the degree in whatever way they could.

Each of my statements to the Cooks of why I could not earn my doctorate was met with an offer of support. I told them that I had a furnished apartment, a good job, a babysitter, a Pontiac Firebird, and a good salary of $6,000 per year. I thought that I was living well. I was particularly impressed when they asked if they could keep my son while I was at Brown. When I told them that I did not have any money to pay them for keeping him, they asked me whether they had ever asked me for any money. Once again, I was touched—in fact, emotionally overwhelmed—by their concern and generosity. I completed the Brown University application and mailed it that night. In a short time, I received acceptance to the Chemistry Department at Brown University.

After being accepted, I was informed by Dr. Pysh that Frank Starkey would be my "big brother" on campus. He was a Black graduate student, majoring in chemistry. He was familiar with the university, particularly the Chemistry Department. Therefore, he was able to respond to my questions from a student's perspective. Mr. Starkey and I talked by telephone and corresponded by mail a number of times. After receiving an acceptance letter from Dr. J. H. Gibbs, Chemistry Department chair, I was ready to head for Brown University. My assistantship included a stipend and tuition. After arriving on campus, I held long discussions on academic matters and life with a number of chemistry faculty members and graduate students. Talking with them made my adjustment to the campus much more pleasant.

When I left Tuskegee in 1970, I drove to Suffolk, Virginia, with my son in the passenger seat. The sun became too hot on him as it shone through the car window, and he began to cry. I quickly adjusted him in the seat so that he was comfortable, and the remaining hours of driving and rest stops were pleasant. Although there were racial incidents reported in the news, I did not experience any problems during my trip from Alabama to Virginia. After arriving at Mama and Daddy Cook's home, I sighed with relief. It was a long drive, but I was on a mission: to leave my son in a comfortable place where he would receive excellent care while I studied for my doctorate degree.

While in Suffolk, I gave my car to my baby sister, Mary Lee, made sure that I had everything that I needed in the trunk I would take with me, kissed my son good bye, and bid Mama and Daddy Cook and their son, Alfred, good bye. Then I left by bus for the trip to Providence, Rhode Island. I felt great. I learned afterward that one of my sisters was not pleased with my decision to leave my son with Mama and Daddy Cook. She felt strongly that I should have left him in her care. Obviously, I did not agree with her.

When I arrived in Providence on September 1, 1970, it was snowing. I could not lift the heavy trunk containing my clothes and other items to put it into a cab at the bus station, and the cab driver was an elderly man who could not lift it either. Therefore, I left it at the bus station. I did not have a heavy coat to wear in the snow, since my purple one—made for me so many years ago—was in my trunk. A few days later, some of my fellow classmates helped me transport the trunk to my new living quarters, which was an apartment shared with another graduate student. I unpacked and began preparations for my academic work.

Meanwhile the snow continued to fall. I felt sure that all classes at Brown University would be canceled due to that snow, but they were not. I made my way to the Chemistry Building, where I met with faculty members and several student chemistry majors. Details were worked out on classes and examinations that had to be taken. My fellowship was processed. In time, I passed all of my qualifying examinations and proceeded to interview eight faculty members, one of whom I chose to serve as my major professor. This was an extremely time-consuming process.

I had numerous things to consider even after I enrolled at Brown, and adjusting to the cold weather was one of them. I also continued to deal with my feelings for my ex-husband. I still questioned whether I was better off with or without him. I had to stop worrying about my son and the fact that he would have only one parent as caregiver. I had to adjust to the Ivy League environment and to being a student again. All of these thoughts had to be placed on the "back burner of my mind" while I oriented myself to new beginnings and addressed the academic challenges to be encountered.

Living near the campus made things easier. The apartment was alive with student activity, largely because of my apartment mate, who was friends with lively students, some of whom would later make a national name for themselves—such as André Leon Talley, who would become American editor-at-large for *Vogue* magazine and a famous fashion promoter. In a short time, however, it became clear that my roommate and I had very different academic and social lifestyles. I needed quiet and a stable routine to study chemistry and other scientific subjects while trying to control my emotions.

To accommodate my needs, I decided to move. Although on-campus housing was limited, I was able to rent a bedroom in a dormitory suite for graduate students. There were three or four students already in that suite, each of whom had a separate bedroom. We shared a bathroom with a shower, three or four sinks with faucets, and a couple of toilet stalls. A kitchen accommodated all of the suites on our floor. Everything looked new, convenient, and comfortable.

I interviewed eight faculty members in chemistry and the biological sciences before choosing my major professor, Dr. John N. Fain, who was in the Division of Medical Sciences. When I joined his research team, my fellowship funding from the Chemistry Department was replaced with financial support from Dr. Fain's research grant. This was necessary since I had changed from the Chemistry Department to the Division of Medical Sciences. After a few months of financial support from his grant, I applied for and received a national fellowship award from the Southern Fellowship Fund. This award was indeed a blessing. It included a stipend, paid tuition and supplies, and funding for a few trips to scientific conferences. Dr. Samuel M. Nabrit[23], the first African American to graduate from Brown University with a doctorate degree, was director of the fellowship fund at an office in Atlanta, Georgia. I was grateful for the support. In reading and hearing about Dr. Nabrit, it was clear that he was a role model who had achieved success.

The receipt of this national fellowship relieved me of my financial burdens, and I was able to immerse myself totally in my academic pursuits. I often started my day on campus before 7 a.m. and did not go home until 9 or 10 p.m. In addition to conducting research, I spent hours in the library reading about current developments in biochemistry, my major in the Division of Medical Sciences. All of these efforts paid off. A paper reporting my research results was published in the *Journal of Biological Chemistry*, an important scientific journal for my chosen field.

In science, submissions to such a journal are highly competitive, yet getting published is extremely important for establishing one's credentials and getting future positions. This was one of the first major steps in launching my career. Dr. Fain was pleased with my academic progress and research results.

Dr. Fain's research team consisted of about 20 researchers, most of whom were conducting research on fat cells. There were two African Americans, R. H. Pointer and Yvonne Clement, besides me in the research team. Another student, Naomi Das, was conducting research on isolated rat liver cells, and Dr. Fain suggested that I join her to form a two-member team focused on liver cell research. I immediately introduced myself, and we joined forces. We reported our research results every two weeks to Dr. Fain. Periodically, we presented our results to the team that was conducting fat cell research. We worked hard to meet our research schedule. It was amazing to me how easy it was to conduct successful experiments that generated useful data.

---

[23] Kimetris N. Baltrip, "Samuel Nabrit, 98, Scientist and a Pioneer in Education," *The New York Times*, January 6, 2004.

Shortly after, Naomi completed her research and began a hospital internship, consistent with her plan to become a medical doctor. After her departure, I assumed responsibility for the remainder of the liver cell research project.

One of the doctors in the fat cell group asked if he could assist with a particular component of the liver cell research, involving research on the production of a particular compound, cyclic adenosine monophosphate (cyclic AMP), referred to as a second messenger. It triggers physiological changes in cells that involve the transmission of signals for biological processes. Those results were added to several manuscripts I was already preparing for submission to a journal. I agreed to list the doctor as a collaborator and co-author on the article because of his contribution of original data, and Dr. Fain approved.

With the inclusion of the cyclic AMP data, the manuscripts were accepted for publication in the *Journal of Biological Chemistry* and *Metabolism*.[24]

By the end of my second year at Brown University, I had completed most of the requirements for a PhD in biochemistry. Even though I was doing quite well as a graduate student, I often thought of my siblings. Audrey Mae had moved to New York City. When I learned from my other siblings that she was living on the streets after being evicted from her home, I went to the city and found her, after a long, complicated search. I brought her to Providence, and we

---

[24]   M. E. M. Johnson (currently M. E. M. Tolbert), N. M. Das, F. R. Butcher, and J. N. Fain, "The Regulation of Gluconeogenesis in Isolated Rat Liver Cells by Glucagon, Insulin, Dibutyryl Cyclic Adenosine Monophosphate, and Fatty Acids," *Journal of Biological Chemistry*, 247:3229-3235, 1972; M. E. M. Tolbert, F. R. Butcher, and J. N. Fain, "Lack of Correlation between Catecholamine Effects on Cyclic Adenosine 3',5'-Monophosphate and Gluconeogenesis in Isolated Rat Liver Cells," *Journal of Biological Chemistry*, 248:5686-5692, 1973; M. E. M. Tolbert and J. N. Fain, "Studies on the Regulation of Gluconeogenesis in Isolated Rat Liver Cells by Epinephrine and Glucagon", *Journal of Biological Chemistry*, 249:1162-1166, 1974; J. N. Fain, M. E. M. Tolbert, R. H. Pointer, F. R. Butcher, and A. Arnold, "Cyclic Nucleotides and Gluconeogenesis by Rat Liver Cells," *Metabolism*, XXIV: 395-407, 1975.

lived in the suite that I had on campus. She had not been there long when I was called to the office of the director of Campus Housing.

The director told me that I could not have a non-student living in my room. Thankfully, the director helped us find an apartment off campus where the two of us could live. Because I spent long hours in the laboratory, I began searching for an activity to occupy Audrey Mae's time. I found an organization that offered a reading course for her. Although I took her to the facility where the classes were held and helped her register, she did not attend any of the classes. I was surprised to learn this when I visited her instructor. It seemed that she decided not to attend the classes and failed to tell me. Instead, she spent the time drinking and having a good time with other people. Later, I found employment for her as a custodian at Brown University. After a few months, she sent for her son to join us in Providence.

Although my academic work was challenging, I was pleased with my progress. By multi-tasking, I was able to meet my academic schedule even while addressing the issues of my sister and nephew. Although I tried to get Audrey Mae on a track to improving her life, my efforts seemed futile. No one else was available to help. Whenever I called family members in Virginia, they would tell me their problems without asking about mine. They talked about people I didn't know, because I had lost touch with the Saratoga community and the Norfolk Road area. I listened patiently, and when the conversations ended, I felt just as lonely as I had been before the call.

In time, I stopped calling family members and tried forming relationships with people in the area where I lived. I remained in contact with Mama and Daddy Cook. When I called them, I would have the opportunity to talk to my son, who would not say one word. I knew that he was listening to me, but I wondered if he had forgotten me. I wondered if he even regarded me as his mother, or if he thought that Mama and Daddy Cook were his parents. That possibility did not cause me any major concerns, because I believed that we would get reacquainted as mother and son when we were reunited.

As I continued my studies at Brown University, I met a graduate student who was majoring in linguistics. He had been in the military service, where one of his responsibilities was the translation of conversations spoken in Slavic languages. Eventually, he learned to speak several Slavic languages fluently. When his military service ended, he enrolled at Brown University to study those languages more intensively.

I found him to be fascinating—an African American who could speak Slavic languages. Even though he was dating a White woman when we met, I continued to show interest in him, and he in me. He was well spoken and attentive. We could talk for hours without becoming bored. On occasion, we had study dates. One day he invited me to dinner at the lovely home of his landlords, where we had a very enjoyable evening.

After being in their presence for a while, it became clear that the hosts were more than just landlords. They had taken a personal interest in my new friend. They wanted him to succeed in life—and find a good wife. After dinner, he invited me to the upper level of the huge house for drinks. I did not tell him that I did not drink alcoholic beverages. After surviving a father who drank profusely and became violent when he drank, I had no desire to drink alcoholic beverages. When my friend handed me a glass of orange juice, I had no idea that it was spiked with vodka. Although it tasted odd, I continued to drink, thinking it was juice. After a couple of sips, I began feeling that I was losing control of my thoughts. He found my inability to "hold my liquor" humorous. Obviously, he had no idea that it was a first for me.

As our relationship developed, he and I spent a great deal of time together. He even escorted me to social events at the home of my major professor, Dr. Fain, and his wife, Ann. At other times, I cooked special meals for him in the kitchen of the dormitory where I lived. When I moved off campus and into an apartment with my oldest sister, we continued to date. Before I had sufficient furniture for my apartment, he and I would sit on the floor and talk for hours. Of course, he and I studied together to ensure that we did not fall behind in our academic work.

When he asked me to marry him, I was overjoyed. Until then, I thought I would never remarry. We were concerned that neither of us had completed our graduate degree work, and that I had a son whom he had never met. He knew that my son lived with Mama and Daddy Cook in Suffolk while I completed my doctoral studies. Nevertheless, we decided to move forward with our desire to get married and live together.

In 1972, he and I married in the chapel on the Brown University campus. On the day of the wedding, I had to attend a seminar with both of Dr. Fain's research teams. The seminar seemed to continue forever. I had not told my major professor and other faculty members about my wedding. After the seminar, I had to rush home to dress and hurry to the chapel. As I ran to my apartment, another student noticed that I was in a rush and gave me a ride in his car.

I dressed in a short white dress and attached the lace head cover that I had made earlier in the week. I wore off-white stockings and shoes. I sprayed on some perfume and headed for the chapel. When I arrived—just in time—I found that my husband-to-be was a little tense, assuming that I might have changed my mind about marrying him. Also, it was important that I arrive in time because another wedding was to be held in the chapel immediately after ours.

A few of our friends[25] were in the chapel to witness the wedding. Dr. Fain and other members of his research group also surprised us by attending the wedding. In a short amount of time, the marriage ceremony was completed; we were married. We went back to my apartment to prepare for our future as husband and wife. Within a few weeks, we found a new apartment and moved into it, leaving the other one for Audrey Mae and her son. Our next few months alone were great. He continued with his studies, and I with mine.

---

[25]   Including Tophas Anderson, Lucy Hicks, Calbert Laing, R. H. Pointer, and other Brown University graduate students

On one occasion, Mama and Daddy Cook visited us and brought my son, Lawson, with them. Before leaving town, they brought Lawson to my laboratory and introduced him to Dr. Fain and members of the research group. It was interesting to see Lawson's reaction as Dr. Fain talked to him while holding him on his lap. He had never been held by a stranger, and he was curious to know who the person was who was holding him. He looked at him attentively and seemed relieved when Mama Cook took him back in her arms.

As time passed, my second husband and I decided to have my son join us in Providence. However, having a three-year-old boy sharing our lives was not what my husband expected. We disagreed on how to rear him. I was not pleased with his punishment style and reasons for punishment.

As my husband and I came to terms in reference to Lawson, he decided to adopt him. We obtained the birth father's permission, and the adoption was completed in a timely manner. I was pleased to have a family, with all of us having the same last name. Unfortunately, though, all was not well. My spouse began finding fault with many of my actions and daily activities. It was as if I could not please him.

I did not know what to do. After all the effort I had put into changing my life and my prospects for career and family, I did not want to face the possibility that my second marriage could be a failure like the first.

In time, my husband reached the point of finalizing his dissertation. He no longer needed to be on campus in order to do that; therefore, he accepted a faculty position at a university in Pennsylvania. Since my laboratory work had not been completed, I could not join him on a permanent basis. Therefore, I visited him whenever I could, and he came home to visit Lawson and me whenever he could.

During one of my visits with my husband, the president of the university and his wife invited us to dinner. The atmosphere was wonderfully relaxing, and the host and hostess were most gracious. As the dinner talk unfolded, the president asked me if I wanted to join the faculty. I told him that I had not completed my graduate work but that I would like to know about the available positions.

Not knowing my major, the president offered me the position of instructor of reading. I smiled graciously and advised him of my major, which was biochemistry. He was surprised and delighted. He immediately gave me the names of administrators and faculty members with whom I should speak in the Science Department.

Although I spoke with some of the individuals he identified, I chose not to accept a position there, since I already had one at Tuskegee Institute. I had worked at Tuskegee prior to enrolling at Brown University and had taken a leave of absence to earn my doctorate. In addition, I was using a Southern Fellowship Fund award that required me to return to the South and teach for at least five years after receiving my doctorate.

A long-distance relationship became more and more difficult to maintain. My husband was doing well in his new position; but his home and job were in Pennsylvania, which was hours of driving from my home in Rhode Island. Some weekends and holidays, he came to Rhode Island, and other times, I would visit him at his apartment, in a large, old white house across from the university campus.

On trips to visit him, I took Lawson, who was only about three years old. On one occasion, I traveled Route 1 for as long as that road would take us. I traveled that route because someone had told me that it was shorter than the more commonly used roads between Rhode Island and Pennsylvania, and that it would take me directly to the university. In fact, it went right past my husband's apartment. However, the route was unnerving since it was a truck route, and I was driving a small Pinto wagon. When I arrived at my destination, I promised myself never to take that route again. I was really tired from driving and comforting our son. After having something to eat, we all went to bed—my son on the sofa and my husband and me in the bedroom.

The next morning I was awakened by the sound of honking vehicle horns. As I turned over in the bed, I realized that my husband was not there. After looking at the clock, I realized that I had overslept and that he had gone to work. I went to the living room and found that our son was missing from the sofa. Panic struck. I ran to the window in the bedroom, pushed back the dirty gray lacy curtains and moved the sash upward in order to look out the window. Because the house was located on a hill next to the street (Route 1) that curved in that area, I could only see a part of the street and the vehicles on it. The vehicles were at a standstill.

My son was on the opposite side of the street where there was a high embankment. He had a long stick in his hand and was moving slowly in preparation for crossing the street back toward the house. I ran out of the apartment and onto the porch. I ran toward the edge of the porch that was in line with the street. I was prevented from running to the street by the screen that was around the entire porch. I turned in panic and noticed that the door to the screened-in porch was in the back of the porch. I pushed it open, ran around the house and into the street screaming as I ran. I was screaming, "Don't cross the street, Lawson!" "Stay where you are!" Unfortunately, he did not hear me or did not understand. He continued to move slowly across the street. As I reached the street, a car missed hitting me as I ran off the hill and down onto the street. I did not see it coming because of the curve in the road. I could not reach Lawson before a vehicle struck him. I picked him up and cuddled him, screaming my distress.

The middle-age White man and his two sons, who had been in the vehicle that hit Lawson, came to my side and asked what they could do to help. They apologized profusely and offered to take us to the hospital, since it would take a long time for an ambulance to arrive. A slightly yellowish liquid slowly drained from my son's ear. Others who were on the road gathered to watch. I felt helpless as I agreed to let the man drive us to the emergency room of the nearest hospital.

The man and his sons stayed with us at the hospital until the police arrived to record the accident. The policeman advised that the vehicle that hit Lawson was not at fault since he should not have been on that street anyway. I thanked the man for his assistance. He apologized yet again, as did his sons and said that they could not avoid hitting my son since they did not see him due to the curve in the road and his location in the street. No charges were lodged against them for this accident. My husband finally arrived at the hospital, visibly upset. We huddled together as doctors examined Lawson.

It was decided that the care that he needed could not be provided by that hospital, so we were all transported by ambulance to another hospital. The ambulance ride seemed to take forever. When we arrived at the second hospital, I was emotionally drained. My husband and I stayed at the hospital for a week. I slept in a chair near Lawson's bedside most of the time. On other occasions, I slept on a large chair in a nearby waiting room. Finally, Lawson was released from the hospital.

Because of the excitement of the incident, I completely forgot to call anyone at Brown University, especially my major professor, to tell them about the accident and let them know that I would be with my son until he recovered. I realized this slip in memory was a major blunder. When I returned to Brown University, a member of the fat cell research group cautioned me that my major professor was upset with me for not showing up in the laboratory for more than a week. I went directly to Dr. Fain's office and explained what had happened, and he calmed down. He asked me why I had not called, and he accepted my explanation for my thoughtlessness. I was grateful for his concern for me and my family.

Once my absence was accepted and forgiven, I resumed working on my research and other academic work. My remaining years at Brown were hectic ones. In response to a suggestion from Dr. Fain, I signed up for and completed several graduate courses. I also taught science and mathematics courses to future nurses and welders enrolled in night classes at the Opportunities Industrialization Center in Providence. In due time, my research was completed, and I presented my research results at several national and international conferences held in the United States. When I completed all of the requirements for my doctorate degree in biochemistry, I was appointed to the temporary position of assistant professor at Brown, and in that position, taught in the Transitional Program during the summer of 1973.

I did not receive my actual degree until 1974. By that time, I had returned to my faculty position at Tuskegee Institute with an official Brown University letter, which indicated that I had all of the rights and privileges afforded by a doctorate degree in biochemistry. When the graduation ceremony was held at Brown University in 1974, I did not attend.

While enrolled at Brown University, I had a lot on my mind. For one, my family was frequently in my thoughts, though most of my family members seemed to be settling down after years of turmoil. Audrey Mae and her son were doing well; they had moved out of the apartment and into a house in Providence with her boyfriend. My second oldest sister, Lee Vania, also moved to Providence, and she purchased a house. Lee Vania's husband had died from wounds inflicted while in the military several years earlier, and she never remarried. She served as caregiver for a few neighborhood children to supplement her income. Later, she adopted a baby girl and found joy in being a mother.

My thoughts frequently turned to my brother, Benjamin. He had enlisted in the U.S. Army and went to war in Vietnam in December 1967. He and I had kept in touch while he served in the Army, and afterward, he got married and settled in New York.

It was time to focus on my own relationship with my husband and child.

Part Three

Four Decades of Service

Return to Tuskegee: Teaching and Research

With the completion of my doctoral requirements and my summer teaching duties in 1973 at Brown University, I returned to Tuskegee Institute, where I was appointed to a faculty position in the Department of Chemistry. I taught chemistry and chemistry laboratory courses to chemistry, biochemistry, animal science, and veterinary medicine majors. I also taught science to nursing students and a general science course to non-science majors.

My husband, having completed his work in Pennsylvania, accepted an administrative position as associate director of the Freshman Studies Program at Tuskegee. Our son lived with us in Tuskegee for a while, but then my husband and I left on another grand adventure and parted with him again.

The summer after we moved back to Tuskegee, instead of returning to Brown University to attend my graduation ceremony, my husband and I got in our car, and I drove cross-country from Alabama to California. We left Lawson with Mama and Daddy Cook again. We would be crossing the tremendously hot Mojave Desert, and, upon our arrival at our destination, I would be busy with another valuable research opportunity. I had been accepted into a summer program for university faculty members at Lawrence Livermore National Laboratory in Livermore, California, the second government-owned energy-research laboratory at which I was privileged to work.

En route, we passed through many of the country's beautiful natural areas—from prairies and rolling hills to the stark contrasts of desert and mountains. Because of my commitments, however, we did not allow much time for stopping along the way, other than just to rest for the night. I wanted to take advantage of every minute available for learning and contributing to one of the preeminent scientific institutions in the United States. I felt like I had really come up in the world!

While I conducted research, my husband used the time to complete his dissertation. By the time I arrived at our rented apartment in Livermore each weekday, it was too late to go anywhere. Therefore, we entertained ourselves at home. On weekends, we toured places near the laboratory and the city of Livermore. As we looked into the distance, we could see the smog over San Francisco. However, because both of us were very busy, we did not venture far from the city in which we lived.

At the end of summer, we returned to our house and our son. Back at Tuskegee, after teaching and conducting research for another two years, I was recognized by the university as an outstanding teacher.[26] I was very surprised by the recognition and the award. However, I must admit that it made me feel special and that my work on the campus was worthwhile and appreciated. Although I was married and had a child to rear, I was proud to be able to keep up with my tasks and keep pace with my peers, who were primarily males.

After I had been on the faculty for a while longer, the mother of a high-school student, Reginald Murcherson, asked me to serve as her son's mentor. I accepted the challenge of guiding him in getting started with both his scientific education and his first research project. After school, on a regular schedule, he came to my office or to the laboratory that was a part of my teaching space to use the equipment for working on his own project.

As hard as I tried, I could not seem to make as much of a success out of my martial relationship as I could out of my advancing career. Every time I thought things were settling down and improving at home, life—or at least love—hurled another missile at me.

Initially, my husband and I rented housing owned by the university. Our usual mode of operation was to be on campus most of the day. Our son was in the kindergarten on the Tuskegee Institute

---

[26] "Dr. Tolbert Picked Top Teacher," *Suffolk News Herald*, May 19, 1976, page 10.

campus. At times, I went home at lunchtime to eat and relax. While at home one day, the telephone rang.

When I answered the telephone, the caller asked to speak with my husband. I told the caller that he was at work and that I could take the message and give it to him upon his return home. The person on the other end of the line asked for my relationship to the person for whom the call was intended. Puzzled, I told the caller my name and that I am the wife of the person for whom the call was intended. There was a pause. Then the caller said that my husband did not mention in his application that he had a wife. Imagine my shock when I learned that my husband had applied for a position at another university without telling me! When he came home that night, I gave him the message and waited for an explanation. It was obvious that he had not intended for me to learn about the application until he had a chance to tell me.

I was hurt. I had worked hard to establish a marriage based on trust and honesty, and it did not seem to be succeeding. In the end, he did not receive the job offer; therefore, he continued in his campus-wide administrative position at Tuskegee.

In contrast, my office mate in the Chemistry Department, Dr. Subramanya Krishnamurthy, and I were enjoying a very good professional relationship. This was somewhat surprising, considering that we were cramped into a small space filled with a continuous influx of students seeking tutorials, explanations about chemistry and biochemistry, or personal advice. Even though both of us were extremely busy, we found time to talk and get to know each other. Eventually, we began writing a book. In 1983, a few years after I returned to Tuskegee again in a different capacity, he and I published our 96-page book titled Stereochemical Insights into Biochemistry.

Returning to Tuskegee, the same area where I had previously lived and worked, posed a new round of marital problems for me. I was well known, and my new husband was initially unknown. He resented being referred to as "Margaret's Husband." Seemingly, he felt that he had lost his identity. Additionally, he was not as outgoing as I was, and he made friends quite slowly. We did not have friends in common.

After being in the city for a while, my knee baby sister, Eleanor, asked for assistance with moving to Tuskegee with her children. I helped her by allowing them to live in our home. With my husband's encouragement, I helped her find a home of her own. I also encouraged her to enroll in Tuskegee Institute to earn a bachelor's degree, and she did, earning her degree in social work in 1978. Before she finished her degree work, my baby sister, Mary Lee, also contacted me to ask for assistance in moving to Tuskegee with her family. My knee baby sister—Eleanor—and I helped her to rent an apartment, and I co-signed for her to purchase a car. All of this was done in response to her request. Unfortunately, I was later stuck with completing the payments on the car since Mary Lee and her husband failed to keep up the payments. As a result of my encouragement, however, at last Mary Lee enrolled at Tuskegee, initially in biology and later in nursing. She never completed her degree requirements.

While it made me feel good to be able to assist my siblings, my husband seemed to resent my close relationship with them and their families. At times he seemed happy to be with me, but he expressed displeasure at not being able to obtain a position in his field of linguistics. My position on campus seemed acceptable to him, but he expressed concerned about a particular incident that occurred. When a high-ranking official of the university asked him if an administrative position could be offered to me, he became angry. His sentiment was that he was the administrator in the family and that having two in the family would be too many. Personally, I didn't understand why the official would ask my husband such a question at all! Perhaps he thought that he was showing respect to my husband, or I had encountered a case of male chauvinism. Nonetheless, because of my husband's opposition, I turned down an offer for the position of associate provost.

I have often wondered why, even though he was in the university's administration himself, he did not want me to also have a position in that area. Perhaps it felt to him as if we would be competing, or that a female's role should be a lesser status one than those of males. Even more important, I wondered why he was not pleased that a major university appreciated my expertise and experience enough to consider offering me a major promotion. Where was the pride that spouses should have in each other?

It seemed that as soon as one problem was solved, others began to surface. Before we had completely adjusted to being a family of three, we became a family of five. My knee baby sister, Eleanor, had been hospitalized, and she needed someone to keep her two school-aged children until she completely recovered. The presence of additional children in the household seemed to irritate my husband, although he initially agreed to allow them to live with us temporarily. I concluded that he could not tolerate children for long periods. This was paradoxical, since he had adopted my son and was from a large Chicago family himself.

After a few weeks, my sister recovered and picked up her children; our family returned to its normal size of three. We began to move ahead with more ambitious housing plans. In the late 1970s, my husband and I bought a large house in the Bulls subdivision of Tuskegee. I really enjoyed living in that house, and my husband seemed to become more relaxed. At last, he had lots of space in which to do whatever he wanted to do. To both of us, I think it also represented a symbol of our success.

Following the move into our new home, I continued to keep in touch with my siblings. Slowly, additional marital problems began to surface. It seemed as if I could not do anything right. To relax, I would go window shopping at the mall in Montgomery or walk around in downtown Tuskegee. One night when all seemed peaceful, I received a call from Lee Vania, who lived in New York City. She was terribly upset as she told me about our brother Benjamin's condition. Benjamin worked at a regular job during the day and drove a limousine and taxi at night and on weekends in New York City. For those reasons, he did not have sufficient time to sleep, and according to Lee Vania, Benjamin did not have anyone to help him with his problems. Benjamin worked diligently to pay his family's bills, including a high mortgage. He also had what Lee Vania viewed as mental issues that were evident when he could not find his way home, even though he was on the next street from where he lived. Lee Vania asked if I could facilitate his admittance into the Veterans Administration (VA) Hospital in Tuskegee. I told her that I could indeed do that, and we developed a plan of action to transport Benjamin to Tuskegee and get him admitted to the Tuskegee VA Hospital.

Although Benjamin had served our country well years earlier, in Vietnam, his warrior spirit was not at peace. After his recovery at the Veterans' Hospital, he divorced his first wife and later married a lady from Tuskegee. Being a warrior at heart with love of America, he decided to serve our country again. When troops were needed in Saudi Arabia for Operation Desert Shield, he returned to combat, serving this time in the Middle East. He knew that the stakes were high. Weapons of mass destruction could have been deployed by either side. There was a lingering threat of chemical warfare. Yet, as he has told his story, his platoon moved steadily east toward the front lines of battle while continuously checking the enemy's defenses and boundaries. He was part of a mighty force of all-Black soldiers that showed much power and force on behalf of America.

Standing proud, my brother and his fellow soldiers would have resonated with Langston Hughes' words, "I, too, sing America. I am the darker brother. ..."[27] They knew that the prestige of the United States rode on their shoulders as they carried out their responsibilities, through the discharge of 88,000 tons of bombs, temperatures of more than 120 degrees, and hot desert sands, not to mention unfamiliar bugs and sand pests. I am sure their thoughts included anguish about whether they would ever see their families again.

Now, let's return to the time following Benjamin's service in Vietnam. Knowing Benjamin's background and his health problems

---

[27] Onwuchekwa Jemie, "Or Does It Explode?" a chapter in <u>Langston Hughes: Critical Perspectives Past and Present</u>, Henry Louis Gates, Jr., and K. A. Appiah, eds., Amistad, New York, NY, 1993, page 138.

following his return from combat in Vietnam, I was anxious to be part of the family's attempt to get treatment for him. Besides, he is my brother, and he had served our country well!

The conversation with Lee Vania, and our planning to help Benjamin, transpired in a single phone call late one night. As I settled back into bed that night, my husband and I had a major argument. He expressed his displeasure at my efforts to assist my brother with his emergency. His actions and tone left me shocked and scared. Rather than stay around to find out what he planned next, I jumped out of bed, ran to the bathroom, and locked the door. There I stayed for the rest of the night. I was relieved that our son was spending a few days with Mama and Daddy Cook in Suffolk at the time.

In the morning, after my husband left home, I dressed and went to work as usual, even though I was extremely upset. Was I now in a situation like that of my Mama? Heaven knows I did not want to endure the kind of treatment she received from my Dad, and I never imagined that I would be facing that type of predicament.

This situation demanded much thought, but I had no time for it now; I had a task to accomplish. I needed to speak with a doctor at the VA Hospital to secure Benjamin's admittance. After getting that done, I went to Montgomery to meet Benjamin, his wife, and Lee Vania at the airport. When I returned home, my husband was sitting there smiling, as if nothing had happened. If anything, this made me feel even more uneasy—I needed stability in my home life, not unpredictability.

Benjamin was admitted to the locked ward of the Tuskegee VA Hospital, where he was confined for months. I visited him almost daily. It gave me peace of mind to know that he was improving. At first, Lee Vania and Benjamin's wife stayed with Eleanor and Mary Lee, who were living in the same apartment complex by then. Shortly after Benjamin's hospitalization, his wife returned to New York—which surprised me. Although I had lived away from my husband several times for career reasons, in times of distress I thought I would always want us to stay near each other. Such was not the thinking of Benjamin's wife.

Although my brother was improving, my marriage was not. Since my husband and I earned approximately the same salary, the issue arose of which of us should pay for what. At one point, the agreement had been "spend as you please." However, I was learning that he and I had different financial-management styles. He seemed to disregard the high interest rates charged when bills are not paid in full. Eventually, he ordered me to give him my full paycheck so that he could pay all of the bills.

Evidently, he did not trust me to handle the finances, even though all of the bills for which I was responsible had been paid on time and in full each month. Or perhaps the issue was something else; perhaps, for example, he thought I was spending too much, or that I supported my sisters and brother too freely. Admittedly, I went window shopping, but I seldom bought anything. Shopping relaxed me. Although I complied with his order, I became angrier with the passing of each month that I gave my paycheck to him. I became concerned that he was merely trying to subordinate me, perhaps even testing whether I would break under the stress.

In 1977, a plan appeared on the horizon for a potential exit from Tuskegee. Perhaps, I thought, this could facilitate a break from the disturbing pattern developing at home.

Moving Around

My husband and I had been working diligently, and our son was a joy to have around. School and piano lessons kept him busy. As time passed, however, it became clear that my husband still wanted to find a position in the field in which he had earned his doctorate degree. Although I supported him in his efforts to find what he wanted, no such position existed on the Tuskegee Institute campus, and the same was true of nearby cities.

In order to satisfy his yearning for a position in linguistics, I figured that we needed to move elsewhere. He seemed to be engrossed in his work, spending long hours in his office at night. When he came home, he did not have much to say. The nature of my position on campus required that I also spend long days giving lectures and teaching laboratory techniques to students. Nevertheless, I recognized the urgency of finding employment elsewhere.

In 1977, I was invited by Dr. Charles A. Walker, dean of the School of Pharmacy at Florida A&M University, to teach pharmaceutical organic chemistry. After my husband agreed to my acceptance of the offer, I started preparing for relocation to Tallahassee, Florida. I finalized my research and teaching tasks at Tuskegee, packed, and prepared for my son and me to move to Tallahassee. My hope was that my acceptance of this new position would open opportunities for my husband in the same city, given that he was not satisfied with his position at Tuskegee Institute.

On the day of the move, a rented moving van was parked in front of the attractive split-level house in Tuskegee that my husband and I had financed with a bank mortgage. I stood quietly at the window and watched the activity. The house sat elegantly back from the street, accented by a well-kept lawn of zoysia grass that lay like a plush carpet in the yard. The only noise was from the four men grunting while lifting large pieces of heavy wooden furniture onto the van—furniture that my husband and I had accumulated through years of shopping up and down the East Coast. I loved that beautiful house and was saddened by the prospect of moving out.

Boxes of dishes, books, toys, papers and other household items were loaded onto the truck. Finally, the house plants were carefully pushed into small spaces between the furniture and boxes. It began to rain before the loading was completed, and everyone was tired. Curious neighbors peeped out of their windows, but only one came to say good-bye. At last the house was empty except for four rooms—kitchen, bedroom, office, and family room—to be used by my husband. He was planning to join us in Tallahassee as soon as he could find a position there. He travelled to Tallahassee with our son and me to help us move into a rented house, where the two of us would live while I worked at Florida A&M University. With his returned to Tuskegee, we would see each other on weekends and holidays.

Why did I choose to be a "weekend wife" over insisting that we move only if we could be together? The reasons are numerous and personal. My marriage was a union of two strong-willed, career-oriented people. I had a doctorate in biochemistry and a productive career in the sciences. My husband had a doctorate degree in linguistics and career goals of his own. Getting jobs in a region that both of us liked seemed close to impossible. I thought that if I accepted a position away from Tuskegee, he would find one too and follow me. To me, this seemed logical, since he was not having as much success in finding a job as I was. Since receiving my doctorate, I had received a number of very good job offers in my field.

Previously, I had refused job offers because my husband did not receive offers in the same geographical areas. After several lengthy discussions, it became increasingly clear to me that he would not have done the same for me: he would accept a position without considering my feelings or my chances of getting a job in the same vicinity. The relationship was one-sided. Perhaps he even felt threatened by a wife having a more successful career than his own. But none of that was ever stated, and I did not realize it for some years.

These emerging issues deserved much thought. My move to Tallahassee to become an associate professor included an increase in rank and salary with far better fringe benefits. I saw many more advantages than disadvantages associated with my acceptance of the offer. Yet I had a feeling of apprehension: I was taking on challenges in both job and marriage. I felt like I was assuming a big risk becoming a "weekend wife" again, as I had done when I was a student at Brown University and my husband worked at a university in Pennsylvania.

As I moved cautiously through each day, I looked back over previous days, checking the progress of my adjustment. The feeling of isolation that had been prevalent when I first moved into my new rented home disappeared, as did a period of sleepless nights. In addition to having more time for myself, I had more time to spend with my son and my young niece, Jacquelyn (Mary Lee's daughter), who had come to live with us shortly after my move to Tallahassee.

Although I prepared meals almost daily, my husband's requirement of having meals prepared every day at a given hour was gone, and I could take my time. My Saturdays were no longer consumed by washing, ironing, and performing other chores at the convenience of others. I performed these tasks when I saw fit to do so. No longer was I concerned about the fact that my husband spent long hours in his campus office or at home while not paying me any attention.

Once I moved to Tallahassee, my husband and I spent at least two weekends per month together. I must admit that his weekend visits were a bit disruptive. As soon as he arrived in the house, he began asserting his authority. In time, he curbed this behavior, and I noticed that he started paying more attention to me. We returned to entertaining each other and going out to dinner often. At last, I was beginning to feel special again—the way I had felt when we first married. Maybe this change was partially due to changes I had made within myself.

Certainly, I had done something unorthodox, putting my career ahead of my husband and becoming a "weekend wife," by choice, for a second time, but my intentions were good—to find employment where my husband had a better chance of finding what he desired in a position. At the same time, I had become self-sufficient, had stopped allowing myself to be battered verbally and physically, and was no longer allowing anyone to take me for granted. In my view, I had significantly advanced my self-development.

Furthermore, I was not spending all of my time at home, as many wives do. Even though I was caring for two children, I was making significant contributions to the scientific community by teaching, conducting research, training future scientists, publishing scientific articles, and actively participating in meetings. Perhaps it would have been impossible to carry out such ambitious career goals within the traditional boundaries of marriage, but I tried, and was ultimately unsuccessful. Marriage is an extremely personal relationship that can be approached in various ways. The approach I ultimately took—taking care of myself and my career, unintentionally at the expense of my marriage—ultimately failed. However, my previous situation—which pitted my career against my marriage—did not work for me either, by preventing me from being myself and growing as a person. For a marriage to be successful, I believe that each person must be allowed to grow without one becoming subservient to the other.

At this point, a major adjustment had been made in my life as well as in my thinking. I acknowledged my role as an African-American woman, a wife, and a mother. However, there was much more to me than that. I had worked hard and smart and made worthwhile accomplishments. There was no compelling reason to give that up.

In Tallahassee, I continued to live in the rented house. The thought still lingered that living in Tallahassee afforded plenty of opportunities for my husband to advance his career once he joined me. That thought kept me going. I enrolled our son in school and an after-school piano class. My husband remained in Tuskegee, and as far as I knew, continued seeking positions in Tallahassee.

Within a few months of teaching and conducting liver cell research in the School of Pharmacy, the dean of that school promoted me to associate dean. With that promotion, I was consumed with paperwork, while time for other responsibilities was minimal. I managed to continue supervising my students' research and to serve as mentor to a number of students, most of whom were minorities. Eventually, I purchased a house into which I moved with my son and niece. By this stage of my life, I was well aware of the prospect for making money by buying and selling real estate, as the economy boomed and real estate prices seemed to appreciate without end. So from then on, even when I held temporary positions in a new place, I looked for opportunities to purchase a home to sell later, thereby supplementing my income.

Weekend and holiday visits with my husband in Tallahassee and Tuskegee continued to be pleasant. After several months, he finally accepted an appointment at Florida A&M University. Shortly after moving to Tallahassee, however, he informed me that he wanted a no-fault divorce. I reluctantly agreed. If he did not want to be with me, what could I do about it? Although he remarried shortly thereafter, I remained single. I could not, and still cannot, figure out what I did that warranted a divorce. I can only speculate that perhaps my successful career was seen by him as competition for my attention or not in keeping with his more traditional views of marriage.

At any rate, I had been keeping my own company, and taking care of my son as a single mother, for so long, that the physical transition was not difficult, despite the emotional tangle.

During the summer of 1977, I made yet another physical and career move, at least temporarily. I went to Texas to conduct research at the University of Texas Medical School in Houston. One of my former Brown University classmates facilitated my getting a summer research appointment in the Department of Neurobiology and Anatomy and the Department of Pharmacology. The temporary change in scenery enabled me to think through my life issues, while expanding the scope of my knowledge and experience to additional scientific fields.

Admittedly, I was having a difficult time dealing with my failure to keep my marriage together. I felt as if I had been a failure as a wife. For the first time since becoming an adult, I felt an urge to get away from family responsibilities for a while. But a number of people besides my son were relying on me. My baby sister, Mary Lee, had already sent her daughter to live with my son and me. Although I certainly did not need the additional responsibility, I agreed to keep her daughter, even during the move from the rented house into the one that I bought in Tallahassee. This additional burden did not help me adjust to my surroundings or to my new status as a divorcee. The differences between my sister and me in the area of child discipline were too great for her daughter to be able to adjust easily to my home and household rules.

Upon my return to Tallahassee after the summer of research in Texas, the accumulation of emotional burdens became too much for me to bear. I was spending so many nights crying that it was taking a drastic toll on my physical health. I was experiencing enormous pain while sleeping and arising from bed each morning. In hindsight, I am amazed that I was able to keep up with my son's and niece's school routines.

I recognized that a more drastic change was needed to get my life back on track. I sent my sister's daughter back to her and asked Mama and Daddy Cook to keep my son for a year. I had found yet another opportunity that would allow me to change my surroundings. This time, I would literally "get away from it all." My plan was to conduct research in Europe—at the International Institute of Cellular and Molecular Pathology (ICP) in Brussels, Belgium. My former major professor, Dr. Fain of Brown University, helped me find a host at the institute, and I also found a sponsor to fund the trip: the U.S. National Institute of General Medical Sciences.

I packed up everything in the house and put everything there on hold. I rented the house in Tallahassee, to the same realtor who had originally rented me a house there. In fact, he later bought the house from me. Next, I drove my growing son to the Cook's house in Suffolk, Virginia, and got on my first intercontinental flight. I headed for Europe and a drastically different way of life.

In Brussels, I conducted research on liver cells as part of an international research team. I kept myself occupied in the evenings and weekends by going on walking tours of the city. It didn't take me long to discover that the chocolate candy available in Brussels was delicious. That alone was a boon to my scrambled emotional state. I loved the Grand Place, the central market section of Brussels with its beautiful flowers and shops and eateries, and I attended ballet performances at the opera house, which took me back in my mind to my high-school days, when I was a member of the modern dance club.

In addition to working and playing tourist in Brussels, I traveled to Switzerland, England, France, and other places. My co-workers at ICP invited me to their homes to discuss culture and research, and they took me on tours of the city. To my surprise, I observed White-on-White racism, among the French and the Flemish, in Brussels.

At one point, an African-American woman who was also an ICP visiting scientist and I enrolled in a course to study conversational French. Although we could already speak some French, having studied it in school, we wanted to speak it like Belgians. The course was fun, and we learned much more about the local culture.

After several months in Brussels, I returned to the United States, but instead of returning to Florida, I went back to Brown University. As I noted earlier, I moved around a lot! After my experience overseas, I realized I wanted to return to active research and generate publishable research data—a very important part of moving up within the competitive scientific community.

I obtained an appointment in the research laboratory of Dr. Elizabeth LeDuc at Brown University and completed a project in collaboration with Dr. Fain's research group. Dr. Fain had been my major professor; and his continued support would prove to be useful several times as my career advanced. My sponsor at Brown remained the National Institute of General Medical Sciences, which funded my visit to Brussels. My research results were again published in scientific journals.[28]

---

[28]   M. E. M. Tolbert, A. C. White, K. Aspry, J. Cutts, and J. N. Fain, "Stimulation by Vasopressin and Alpha Catecholamines of Phosphatidylinositol Formation in Isolated Rat Liver Parenchymal Cells," *Journal of Biological Chemistry*, 255: 1938-1944, 1980; B. B. Hoffman, M. E. M. Tolbert, T. Michel, D. M. Kilpatrick, R. J. Lefkowitz, H. Gilman, and J. N. Fain, "Agonist versus Antagonist Binding to Alpha-Adrenergic Receptors," *Proceedings of the National Academy of Sciences of the United States of America*, 77, No. 8: 4569-4573, 1980.

The Carver Research Foundation

As it turned out, a return to Tallahassee, Florida, was not to remain on my agenda. I sold the house there because I found another opportunity elsewhere. As I was completing my latest research project at Brown University, I was contacted by Dr. Andrew P. Torrence, who was then provost of Tuskegee Institute, on behalf of the Tuskegee Institute president, Dr. Luther H. Foster. Dr. Torrence advised me of a position on my old campus—director of the Carver Research Foundation (CRF) of Tuskegee Institute.

This was a position that excited me. The research foundation was established in 1940 by Dr. George Washington Carver, and I knew I would be proud to follow in his footsteps. After considering the challenge, I submitted my application for the position. Within a few weeks, I received an invitation for an interview. I learned that there were numerous applicants, and I was the only female.

When I was appointed to the position of CRF director in September 1979, I became the first female to serve in that capacity. These were very exciting times for me, as well as for the foundation. With my appointment, I was following in the footsteps of several successful scientists: Dr. George Washington Carver, Mr. Austin Curtis, Dr. Russell Brown, Dr. Clarence T. Mason, and Dr. James H. M. Henderson.

Bottom left to right, then top right to left, each with period(s) of service:
Me (Dr. Margaret E. M. Tolbert, 1979-1988 including a
sabbatical leave period in 1987-1988), Dr. J. H. M. Henderson (1968-
1975), Dr. Clarence T. Mason (1953-1954 and 1958-1968), Dr. Russell
W. Brown (1944-1953, 1954-1958, and 1976-1979), Mr. Austin W.
Curtis (1943-1944), and Dr. George Washington Carver (founder and
former director, 1940-1943). Dr. B. D. Mayberry who served as Interim
Director while I was on sabbatical is not shown in this sketch.

Here I am with Mr. Austin Curtis, the second director
of the Carver Research Foundation.

When it was first established in 1940, CRF had a central focus: continuing Dr. Carver's scientific endeavors in agriculture and industry, and developing young scientists. While I was director, the foundation's scope expanded to include four divisions: natural science research directed by Dr. Linda Phaire Washington, behavioral science research directed by Dr. Paul Wall, Agricultural Experiment Station directed by Dr. Walter Hill, and international and domestic outreach directed initially by Dr. Theodore Pinnock and later by Dr. T. T. Williams. The contributions of researchers at CRF over the years are noteworthy. In addition to Dr. Carver's initial research, for example, Dr. Russell W. Brown and Dr. James H. M. Henderson, both of whom are former CRF directors, led research on HeLa cells—a very popular line of cells used in research throughout the country for decades. They developed a method for the mass production and live preservation of cells so that they could withstand the process of being mailed to research centers throughout the United States, primarily for use in vaccine evaluation procedures.[29]

---

[29]   R. W. Brown and J. H. M. Henderson, "The Mass Production and Distribution of HeLa Cells at Tuskegee Institute, 1953-55," *Journal of the History of Medicine and Allied Sciences,* Vol. 38, No. 4, October 1983, pages 415-431.

I was pleased to oversee a second period of tremendous expansion at CRF. As director of CRF from 1979 to 1988,[30] I oversaw ongoing research and the development of new research throughout the Tuskegee Institute campus. This included managing budgets, negotiating grants and contracts, managing a group of research scientists, and supervising quality control and safety programs (e.g., radiation safety, biohazards safety, laboratory animal care, human research review, patents and copyrights, and varietal release procedures) for the entire campus. Another role in this position was providing advice to the university president and members of the CRF Board of Trustees on research policies, budgets, and research and development programs. A selection of photographs of CRF activities is shown below and on the next page.

I am discussing agricultural research and development with Dr. George Cooper.

I am meeting with my graduate students at the Carver Research Foundation.

I am performing an experiment in my laboratory at the Carver Research Foundation.

I am listening to a graduate student explain the research he conducts, using an electron microscope.

---

[30]   My tenure as CRF director did not end in 1987; that was the year that I went on sabbatical leave to the Standard Oil Company of Ohio, which later merged with BP and became BP America, Inc. In 1988, I resigned from the position of CRF director to accept a permanent position at BP America, Inc.

Dr. Boyle of ORAU and I are discussing the involvement of Tuskegee Institute with ORAU. I represented Tuskegee Institute on the ORAU Council.

I am discussing Carver Research Foundation research programs with guests.

Dr. P. K. Biswas and I are inspecting the biomass gas generator.

As if all those responsibilities were not enough to handle, my position as director was concurrent with that of full professor of chemistry, an appointment I received in 1980. Even though I had a wealth of duties in those two positions, I also conducted my own research, served as research advisor and mentor for a small group of graduate and undergraduate students, and published scientific papers and articles.[31]

---

[31] Publications during this time included: Margaret E. M. Tolbert, Johnson A. Kamalu, and Garnette D. Draper, "Effects of Cadmium, Zinc, Copper and Maganese on Hepatic Parenchymal Cell Gluconeogenesis," *Journal of Environmental Science and Health*, B16, No. 5, 1981, pages 575-585; M. C. Datta, J. Josephs, M. E. M. Tolbert, J. Anderson, and H. Dowla, "Acetylsalicylic Acid Antagonizes the Bleeding-Induced Changes in Hemoglobin Proportions in Normal Adult Rats," *Biochemical and Biophysical Research Communications*, 137, No. 1, 1986, pages 69-75; Sheila Bhattacharya, P. K. Biswas, and M. E. M. Tolbert, "Comparison of the Effectiveness of Various Pretreatment Methods on the Enzymatic Hydrolysis of Sweet Potato (*Ipomoea batatas* L.) Biomass," *Biological Wastes*, 19, 1987, pages 215-226; and S. Bhattacharya, J. F. Eatman,

After I had begun serving my dual role as director of the Carver Research Foundation and professor of chemistry, my previous office mate, Dr. Krishnamurty, and I published our book on stereochemistry as previously noted. In the following year, I wrote additional articles and reports, and initiated an ambitious project to edit a book—Focus: Energy Issues for the Eighties, published in 1984—for which I invited several authors to contribute. Those authors were from a variety of institutions: the Alabama Department of Energy, U.S. National Science Foundation, U.S. Agency for International Development Asia Bureau, U.S. Department of Energy (DOE), Howard University, University of Alabama, University of Health Sciences in Missouri, WED Enterprises of California, Active Solar Systems/Aircraftsman Solar of Alabama, Oak Ridge National Laboratory, and the Institute for Energy Analysis.

The diversity of interactions that were stimulated by this collaborative publication was new to the Carver Research Foundation, and served as a launching point for obtaining funding for the work of the foundation. During my tenure as the foundation's director, I received grants from the Mary McCants Stewart Foundation, Upjohn Company, National Aeronautics and Space Administration (NASA), U.S. Department of Agriculture (USDA), U.S. Department of Energy, Alabama Department of Energy,[32] U.S. Nuclear Regulatory Commission, and National Institutes of Health, as well as other agencies.

This was another turning point for me: learning the value of networking and making connections. I found it easy to do, and the rewards far surpassed the amount of effort it took. This insight would serve me well for the rest of my career.

I was fully employed as CRF director, professor, researcher, and mother during my first year back at Tuskegee. In addition, I

P. K. Biswas, and M. E. M. Tolbert, "CO2 Enrichment and Its Relationship to Bioconversion of Cellulosic Biomass of Sweet Potato (*Ipomoea batatas L.*) into Fermentable Sugars," *Biomass*, 15, 1988, pages 259-268.

[32] Joe McFadden, "One Small Step," *The Montgomery Advertiser*, March 29, 1982, page 4.

was called that year to again take up the mantle of responsibility for extended family members. My brother, who had spent several years recuperating in the Tuskegee VA Hospital, needed a place to stay until he could get "on his feet." I invited him to stay in my home with me and my son. I was glad I was able to help my brother once again.

Within a year, Benjamin got married for the second time, and he and his wife moved into their own house in Tuskegee. Within a few years, he seemed to me to have everything that a man could want: a wife, several children, and a stepchild. However, his military service—including combat in Vietnam and the Middle East and continued service in the Reserves—continued to weigh heavily on his mind, even after treatment at the VA hospital.

I did not know it at the time he came to live with me in Tuskegee, but my brother had suffered for years from what is referred to today as post-traumatic stress disorder. Also, he had developed cancer in one of his kidneys, and the other one failed shortly thereafter. For this reason, dialysis is required three times each week. His suffering has been mitigated somewhat by the support of his wife and his pride in his children, all of whom enrolled in college. At this point, several have earned undergraduate and graduate degrees while others are making progress toward that goal. These are accomplishments of which Benjamin and his wife are very proud, and so are other members of the family, including me. His oldest son, who died in 2013, earned a doctorate degree in materials science and mechanical engineering at Tuskegee University in 2010. With the receipt of that degree, he became the second person in my family to earn a doctorate degree. I am the first. Benjamin's second son, David B. Mayo, earned a doctorate degree in aerospace engineering in 2014 from the University of Maryland at College Park. As a result, he is the third person in my family to earn a doctorate degree. More doctoral degree recipients are anticipated.

During the first years of my tenure as CRF director, assisting my brother was just one of my many concerns. Perhaps I was at risk myself for becoming overwhelmed by everything that was going in in my career and family. Or, perhaps it was my jam-packed workload that kept me sane. Either way, I initiated a lot of new projects at CRF.

Throughout this period, my staff and I aimed for continuing the research tradition at CRF even while we also worked to enhance its visibility. We launched a publicity campaign, distributing information to the public and potential supporters through brochures and newspaper articles, and establishing an Annual Carver Lectureship. The first speaker was Dr. Thomas Ellis Malone, deputy director of the National Institutes of Health.[33]

The complexity of CRF required the use of all of the talents and skills I had developed in my personal and professional capacities, and I loved every minute of the work. Each day was a new adventure. I met people from places that I had never seen. They came from domestic locations as well as foreign countries to talk about research, Dr. Carver, Tuskegee Institute, contracts, grants, and life. We held many, many discussions about science and research.

When Dr. Richard E. Lyng, who was then the U.S. Secretary of Agriculture, visited the campus to give a speech and participate in the ceremony on the wreath laying on Dr. Carver's grave, I had a leadership role in the ceremony. When the Honorable Howell Heflin, U.S. Senator, visited the campus, I had a leadership role in activities surrounding his visit and the program in which he participated. Additionally, I served as hostess for a campus visit by the director of a NASA research center, and I did the same for other dignitaries from federal agencies and private sector companies. This was an exciting time in my career.

---

[33] "Carver Lectureship Features Dr. Malone," *The Tuskegee News*, May 22, 1980, page 13.

USDA Secretary Lyng (left)
TU President Payton, Me (Dr.
Tolbert), and other officials
participating in the wreath laying
ceremony at Dr. Carver's grave site
on the Tuskegee Institute campus

USDA Secretary Lyng and
Tuskegee Institute Officials
Participating in a Luncheon

One visitor who was important to establishing a long-term partnership with Tuskegee was Dr. William "Bill" Wiley, director of the Pacific Northwest National Laboratory (PNNL) in Richland, Washington. PNNL, a government-owned energy-research facility, was operated by Battelle. Dr. Wiley and I, after much discussion and negotiation, developed a memorandum of understanding (MOU) between PNNL and the Carver Research Foundation[34] to conduct research that would benefit both parties. The MOU enabled the awarding of several contracts to CRF for research work. One example was research on the removal and prevention of mold development on Walla Walla sweet onions.

I visited PNNL on several occasions between 1984 and the end of my time as CRF director. During one visit, I had the honor of delivering a speech and responding to questions[35] from PNNL personnel. I also discussed with personnel at PNNL how we might

---

[34]   This document was signed on April 3, 1986, by Dr. William Wiley, Dr. Benjamin F. Payton, Dr. J. E. Bostic, Jr., who was then the chairman of the CRF Board of Trustees, and me.

[35]   Scott Fisk, Editor, *The Greenie* (a publication of Battelle's Pacific Northwest Division, PNNL), Vol. 21, Issue 44, November 9, 1984, page 4.

work together to enhance the quality of scientific training and research at Historically Black Colleges and Universities, such as Tuskegee, through a proposed foundation.

On other occasions, I visited officials elsewhere to publicize CRF's research capabilities—meeting with, for example, the executive director of DOE's Office of Minority Economic Impact and officials at Oak Ridge National Laboratory in Oak Ridge, Tennessee.

As a result of the many connections I established, research partnerships with Tuskegee grew. The U.S. Department of Energy funded a project in which an alcohol production plant was constructed and legally operated on the Tuskegee Institute campus.[36] This was a project that was in operation before alcohol was widely used as an alternative energy source. Other agricultural projects were sponsored by the U.S. Department of Agriculture (USDA). For one of the USDA major projects, I was responsible for overseeing the renovation of several buildings on the agriculture side of the campus. The results were appreciated by faculty, administrators, and students, especially those in agriculture. However, there were a few who openly expressed concern about a woman having that type of responsibility, control of funds, and, perhaps, power. As always, I held my temper and focused on working with those who appreciated my contributions.

CRF trustees were very supportive of my productivity, and some even introduced me to potential collaborators. One CRF trustee, who was also an official at NASA, invited me to meet NASA scientists and engineers in Washington, DC, and to observe satellite launches in Florida. In response to an invitation from me, a team of NASA scientists visited CRF and discussed possibilities for partnering on research. One result of the discussions was a successful experiment at CRF's Agricultural Experiment Station in growing sweet potatoes in soil-less culture, funded by NASA. My leadership in developing the initial collaboration was applauded.

---

[36] "Objective – Energy Efficiency," *The Tuskegee News*, March 4, 1982, page 2; and David Oakes, "Moonshine with a Twist," *The Montgomery Advertiser*, February 27, 1982.

I also developed good relationships with the Tuskegee Institute trustees. At one point I was invited to accept the award for the posthumous induction of the late Dr. George Washington Carver into the Alabama Business Hall of Fame. For that occasion, I was accompanied by Mr. and Mrs. A. G. Gaston. Mr. Gaston was then a member of the Tuskegee Institute Board of Trustees and a prominent banker in Birmingham, Alabama. Also among those who accompanied me to the induction ceremony were several representatives of Tuskegee Institute and the community, including Dr. Carver's former secretary.

In the above photograph made in 1980, I am in the center, holding the plaque awarded in honor of Dr. Carver on the occasion of his posthumous induction into the Alabama Business Hall of Fame. Among the others shown (from left to right) are Dr. Julian Thomas, Mrs. Jessie Abbott—Dr. Carver's former secretary, Mrs. Virginia C. Hawkins, Mrs. Carolyn Ford, Ms. Noel Mitchell, Mrs. Minnie Gaston, Mrs. Hattie West Kelly, Mr. A. G. Gaston, and Dr. Elva Howell.

Here I am sitting beside Mr. A. G. Gaston, a Tuskegee University trustee and Birmingham businessman at the Alabama Business Hall of Fame banquet.

Over the years, funding to Tuskegee Institute increased, and eventually some of it was designated for a redesign of the CRF Building and for increasing its endowment.[37] The Alabama Department of Energy funded the preparation of architectural plans for a new wing that was added onto the CRF Building, and I oversaw the planning and construction. Funding for construction was obtained from various sources. The new wing included a large office for me and adjacent offices for my secretary and a special assistant. It also included a conference room, kitchen, and more laboratories and offices for researchers. Also, a small number of solar panels were installed on the roof to supplement the electrical usage needed in the building.

Another important milestone took place in 1983. CRF had been serving as host to a number of dignitaries in foreign affairs, including an Ambassador who was a guest-in-residence for several months. With the increase in international activities over the years, the international component of the CRF Division of International and Domestic Outreach was moved from the CRF organizational structure. With that move, the Tuskegee Office of International Affairs was established. Dr. Eugene Adams was appointed in 1983 to become the first associate provost for International Affairs, reporting directly to the university president. With that change, a similar-level position was established for me: the title of associate provost for research and development[38] was added to that of CRF director in my portfolio of responsibilities. This structure—moving one of my functions into the higher level of university administration, outside of CRF—acknowledged the benefits the university enjoyed because of CRF's activities and contributions to society.

The increase in Tuskegee's foreign connections allowed me to expand my career at CRF to another dimension: international networking and collaboration. I once led a team of scientists to

---

[37] The CRF endowment had increased by 30% by the end of Dr. Tolbert's tenure as director.

[38] "Tolbert, Adams Reassigned at TI," *The Tuskegee News*, August 18, 1983, page 2.

Liberia, West Africa, to review programs of the Teachers Training Institute there. Tuskegee Institute had a leadership role in establishing that training institute in 1963, and its implementation was led by a team of Tuskegee faculty members under the leadership of Dr. Adele McQueen, under a contract funded by the U.S. Agency for International Development.

Of course, Liberia held a special attraction for me, having been married to a Liberian. I was especially curious to get to know more about that country's culture and the relationships between men and women there.

I experienced some initial confusion getting into the country, because my last name from my second marriage, Tolbert, happened to be the same as that of the late president of that country, the Honorable William R. Tolbert, Jr. President Tolbert was assassinated in a military coup d'etat led by Master Sergeant Samuel Doe, and the officials who detained me served under Doe's command. I was rescued by the U.S. Agency for International Development director in Liberia and her staff, just in time, as military officials at the airport were preparing to put me in prison. They were of the mistaken opinion that I was the daughter of the late president and had returned to Liberia for revenge.

After that close call, I proceeded with my team to the Teachers Training Institute in Monrovia and also to Cuttington University and a health clinic in Suacoco. Cuttington University has the distinction of being the oldest four-year private, co-educational, degree-granting institution in Sub-Saharan Africa. The president of Cuttington University, Dr. Stephen M. Yekeson, was a graduate of Tuskegee Institute. For that reason, the time spent with him, his family, university staff, and faculty was special. Shortly after returning to Tuskegee, I was saddened to learn that the president of Cuttington University was killed during the fighting that followed the coup d'etat after our departure.

In Monrovia, we also met with the U.S. Ambassador, the Minister of Education, and the Minister of Science. Overall, the tour in Liberia, and later ones in Senegal and Sudan, prompted return visits to CRF by officials of those countries and opened the door to potential collaborations.[39]

At another time while serving as CRF director, I was invited to participate in a women's conference in Libya. I accepted the invitation and prepared presentations on diabetes and on rural development. I also planned for discussions on encouraging scientific careers for women of that country.

The trip was exciting from beginning to end. For safety, we stayed two team members per room, and our rooms were located on the same hotel floor. Our two male drivers, who also served as interpreters, accompanied us everywhere we went.

Prior to the conference, the American team of women, which included me, submitted a list of activities in which each of us wanted to participate while in Libya. The list included a proposed visit with political leader Colonel Muammar Qaddafi. Of course, we thought that a visit with him would not become a reality. Surprisingly, all of our wishes were granted, although some of them resulted in some interesting occasions. For example, on a trip to "the beach," we were taken only to a mountaintop that overlooked the sea, where some sparingly clad White women were sunbathing and enjoying the water. When our hostess was asked why we were not permitted to go down the mountainside to enjoy the water, she responded that Libyan women did not disrobe in public.

As a matter of fact, most of the Libyan women covered their entire bodies, leaving only the left eye visible, in public. In closed quarters, where they did not wear the covering, we learned that they wear beautiful clothing underneath. Some Libyan women wore what appeared to be regular Western-style clothing, although they wore long sleeves and blouses closed to the neckline. Young girls who dressed liberally on the college campus would switch to traditional Libyan attire when around older relatives.

One evening the team members were guests at the beautiful home of the Libyan Women's Leader. The special features of the evening

---

[39] "African Leader Visits Tuskegee," *The Tuskegee News*, October 8, 1981, page 1.

included the appearance of a bride-to-be, dancing, interesting conversations about the Libyan culture, and a tour of our host's home. Although most of the interior of the house was decorated in French furniture and a number of elaborate chandeliers, there was a room that was called the Libyan room. There I spent time with the host as she talked about the features of the room and her role as the Libyan Women's Leader.

Here I am making a presentation to participants
in the women's educational conference in Libya.
Of course, an interpreter was used.

Here I am in the home of the hostess of the women's educational conference in which a team of American women, including me, participated in Libya.

One day at our hotel, we heard the call to prayer broadcast on all televisions, radios, and outside. Immediately, all of the men removed their shoes and went into a room off the lobby area to pray. The experience kindled a desire in me to see the origin of the multiple calls to prayer each day.

The next day the team was taken on a tour that included a mosque, a mall, and a rural development center. In order to enter the ornate mosque, each female team member had to cover her head with a scarf. At the time of our visit, two elderly men were sitting on the floor rotating rocks in their hands and praying. There were no chairs in sight. In a small room was modern electronic equipment used for the calls to prayer. What I saw was an "eye opener." This was my first, and only, visit to an Islamic mosque.

When the team toured one of the traditional shopping malls, I noticed that most of the women stood back while purchases were made by men. At the rural development center, the female director told us about the initial difficulty in getting women to attend classes at the center; the husbands would not allow their wives to go. To convince them to allow the women to participate in activities such as learning how to cook and preserve food, tend beehives for honey production, sew, care for children, and do household chores, the men were invited to the center and shown the equipment and services available.

Before they agreed to allow their wives to participate in the programs, however, the men demanded that each woman would be given the item of equipment that she learned to use while in training at the center. For example, if a woman learned sewing, a sewing machine was given to her for use at home. Since funding was not a problem, the director agreed, and the program began. This was, indeed, a lesson on a different culture.

We were not informed in advance when each of our activities would take place. One day, we learned that it was time for the meeting with Colonel Qaddafi. As we approached the gray building where his office was located, I noticed that military tanks were recessed into the outer walls. A red carpet marked the stairway entrance. We were seated in a beautifully decorated lounge to wait for our meeting with the Colonel. Then we were ushered down the hallway, where he stood at his office door to receive us and shake our hands. His office had large windows, black leather seating, a number of large bookcases holding lots of books, a prayer rug hung on a bronze stand, and a huge desk equipped with several recessed monitors.

Colonel Qaddafi sat at his desk and began to talk. He told the group that his problem was not with the American people but with the American government. He was poised, generous with his time, and articulate. He promptly answered each question that we asked in English. When I had seen him on TV prior to visiting Libya, he spoke in Arabic, which was translated by an interpreter. When asked about his language skills, he pointed out that when foreign people are in America, they are expected to speak English; yet when Americans visit foreign countries, they fail to speak the language of those countries. I had to agree that this was true. In general, however, I reminded myself that this man was a terrorist and that I needed to be aware of his propensity for propaganda. Since I was in the country for educational purposes, with a focus on women's activities, it was not difficult to keep things in perspective.

While in Libya, we also visited an oil refinery in the desert, a university, and a medical clinic. At the clinic, I noticed that a large number of people were being treated for diabetes and other health problems. The medical staff members were from many countries, and one of their goals was to encourage Libyans to move into health-care fields after earning medical degrees. Oil money was plentiful, and it was used to sponsor foreign teams of doctors and nurses to staff the clinics and help train Libyans in medical fields.

The original intent was that the visit to Libya would last for 14 days. A few days before we were scheduled to depart, however, the leader of the team received a telephone call at an early morning hour. She was advised urgently that the drivers were coming to transport everyone to the airport and that we should rush to depart. We packed and departed immediately; in fact, when we arrived at the airport, we were told to run to the screening area and to the waiting airplane. There were a large number of Libyans standing outside the airport, but no one said anything. The quiet was disturbing. We cleared the screening area and boarded the airplane. As soon as the last team member boarded the airplane, the doors were closed, and the airplane immediately took off.

No one said anything about why we had to flee three days early until we arrived at the New York City airport and heard the reason on television. The TV reporter announced that the Libyan Embassy in Washington, DC, was ordered closed by the U.S. Government and that the Libyans who served in that embassy had been expelled from the United States. Had we remained in Libya, undoubtedly our lives would have been in danger. I was relieved to be on American soil after the close call. I returned to Tuskegee with a wealth of cultural information and many stories to share.

I also led a team of Tuskegee Institute scientists and administrators to Senegal, Kenya, and Sudan. Discussions in those countries primarily centered on health issues, policies regarding educational institutions, education programs, and potential collaborations of the Tuskegee Institute with educational institutions of those countries. At each place, we also found time to do some sightseeing and absorb the local culture.

In Sudan, I was holding a discussion with my team in the hotel lobby when I noticed a gentleman sitting nearby, paying close attention. He was dressed like a rich sheik. He said to one of my male teammates that he found me to be very intelligent, and he asked my male teammates if he could make me one of his wives! My teammate explained that I was an educated woman and would not be interested. I did not say a word—but returned to my room immediately. My team members teased me for days about that incident.

Governing Boards
Add a New Dimension

In 1981 when Dr. Benjamin F. Payton was newly appointed as president of Tuskegee Institute, I went out of my way to keep him informed about the work of the Carver Research Foundation. In return, several requests came my way to serve on committees and councils, both on and off campus. In the early 1980s, Alabama Governor George C. Wallace appointed me to serve as a member of the state's Energy Advisory Council.[40] It seems to me that this visibility, heightened by my research activities on campus, played a role in my receipt of other appointments. Also, it was unusual in those days to have a female serving in a high-level university position.

Two special invitations came my way during my tenure as CRF director to serve on boards outside of the university: the Board of Trustees of the University of Alabama System followed by the Board of Governors of the Birmingham Branch of the Federal Reserve Bank.[41] In addition, I was informed by letter that I had been appointed by the interim president at the University of Oklahoma to the position of adjunct professor of pharmacy—a surprise. That role, which did not require leaving my position at Tuskegee, included interactions with faculty in the university's Health Science Center, service on the dissertation committee for PhD students (especially that of one of my former master's degree students, Abraham Weaver), and the possibility of occasional lectures.[42]

I was invited in person to serve on the University of Alabama System's Board of Trustees by its chairman, Winton Malcolm "Red" Blount, Jr. Although the president and provost of Tuskegee gave me a tepid response to the idea of my taking on obligations outside

---

[40] "Tolbert to Serve on Energy Council," *Tuskegee Gram*, Vol. XXII, No. 4, July 28, 1983, page 3.

[41] "Dr. Tolbert Is Appointed," *The Tuskegee News*, June 6, 1985.

[42] "Jischke Named Professor," *The Tuskegee News*, March 28, 1985, page B-1.

Tuskegee University, I accepted the invitation. I did not understand why the president was not pleased that someone on the university staff was invited to serve on such a prestigious board.

Dr. Russell Brown—a former CRF director—stated that my appointment was a great step forward and real recognition for Tuskegee Institute and CRF. I was interviewed by a writer for the local newspaper and took that opportunity to describe the appointment as "a challenge I see ahead of me." I also said, "The one way I think we can reach out of poverty and economic hardships is through education. With this position, hopefully I can make a contribution to higher education in the [whole] state."[43]

While attending the first meeting of the board, I learned that numerous matters required the attention of members and that an effort was being made to racially diversify its membership for the first time in its history. Three African Americans (including me) were among the seven people invited to serve on the board.[44] All of the appointments had to be approved by the Alabama legislature before they became official.

The board held social events in conjunction with its meetings, which enabled everyone to become acquainted. One of them was a grand affair held in the garden of Mr. and Mrs. Blount's home in Montgomery, complete with a live band, delicious food, interesting people, and conversation. It was an opportunity for persons under consideration for board membership to meet key officials. This was where the movers and shakers could be found who had roles in the administration and future of campuses of the University of Alabama System, which included campuses in Birmingham, Huntsville, and Tuscaloosa. When board members visited each campus, the accommodations were excellent, and the people were most cordial.

---

[43] J. J. Johnson, "UA Trustee Says Education Way Out of Economic Hardships," *The Tuskegee News*, Vol. 117, No. 34, November 18, 1982, page 1.

[44] Sidney Bedingfield, "7 New UA Trustees, Including 3 Blacks, Attend 1st Meeting," *Birmingham Post-Herald*, February 4, 1983, page C1; Jack Wheat, "UA Board Expands, Adds Women and Blacks," *The Tuscaloosa News*, January 30, 1983, page 10B; and Sonny Brasfield, "UA Trustees 'Change with Times," *The Journal Advertiser*, 1983.

On one occasion, the group had the opportunity to attend a University of Alabama football game. There was much excitement about Bear Bryant (Paul William "Bear" Bryant), the football coach for 25 years. He was extremely popular, having won 323 games, including six national championships and 13 conference championships. The board group sat in the bleachers in 28-degree Alabama weather (believe me, it was that cold in Alabama) just to see him come onto the football field on the shoulders of his players. There were cheers beyond belief. Of course, I cheered too, although I am not a sports enthusiast.

Holding dialogue with legislators was important to gaining final approval for board membership. Consequently, I met with one legislator in the capital building in Montgomery. After that meeting, however, I became concerned about how to fit in more of such meetings as well as the future responsibilities the board position entailed. I concluded that I needed to withdraw my candidacy and focus on my responsibilities at Tuskegee.

Later, when the list of approved members was made public, I learned that five of the seven nominees were not approved by the legislature. This caused a controversy that was aired in the news.[45]

I am deeply grateful to Mr. Blount for inviting me to serve on the University Of Alabama System Board of Trustees and introducing me to a number of key figures in Alabama. I appreciate having had the opportunity to serve in that prestigious position for a short period, which gave me a platform for raising awareness of the issues that minorities encounter while attending majority institutions.

Even though my life seemed fully occupied, I continued to add additional activities—a recurring pattern in my life and career! Shortly after my brief membership on the University of Alabama System Board of Trustees, I was invited to serve as a member of the Board of Governors of the Birmingham Branch of the Federal

---

[45]   Noted in an editorial in *The Birmingham News*, July 3, 1983; also see Michele MacDonald and Jean Lufkin Bouler, "Baxley Singled Out in UA Trustee Furor," *The Birmingham News*, July 3, 1983.

Reserve Bank of Atlanta.[46] This was a major milestone for me, and important to my position at CRF, which required me to be business savvy and to interact with business and industry. Later, I became chair of that board.[47] In addition to representing the Branch at meetings in Atlanta, Georgia, and Washington, DC, I held board meetings locally and made regular reports on economic conditions in Macon County, as well as neighboring counties. Another noteworthy contribution that I made to that board was organizing tours for board members of counties being discussed at closed meetings. The board members visited Tuskegee Institute once while I was chair.

When I later left Tuskegee, Alabama, to accept an appointment in private industry in another state, I resigned from the board since I would not be able to perform my duties while out of state. In recognition of my contributions, I was presented an award, a plaque; a copy of the wording follows.

FEDERAL RESERVE BANK OF ATLANTA
THIS CERTIFICATE
is awarded to
Margaret E. M. Tolbert
in recognition of her distinguished service
to the Federal Reserve System as a
Director of the Birmingham Branch
April 29, 1985 – June 30, 1987
and in sincere appreciation of her excellent
contribution to the Bank and to the
economic progress of the Sixth Federal Reserve District

(This certificate was sealed and attested by the chairman, president, and senior vice president of the Birmingham Branch of the Federal Reserve Bank of Atlanta.)

---

[46] *The Tuskegee News*, June 6, 1985; and "Ms. Tolbert Named to Reserve Branch," *The Alabama Journal and Advertiser*, June 2, 1985, page 1 (Business in Brief section).

[47] "Reserve Board to Meet," *The Alabama Journal and Advertiser*, May 4, 1987.

Throughout my tenure as CRF director, I devoted my energies primarily to addressing programs and activities throughout Tuskegee Institute. As mentioned, however, I also participated in organizations in the community. A part of my life during this period was devoted to my religious life. I have always believed, as Maya Angelou wrote, "… in a power larger than myself and other than myself which allows me to venture into the unknown and even the unknowable."[48] In 1982, I converted to Catholicism, and my son and I began attending St. Joseph's Church in Tuskegee. My close relationship with God has continued throughout my life, in good and bad times.

During this period, my son—Lawson—also benefited from my position at Tuskegee. In 1984, I developed and implemented the Hi-Tech Program to provide hands-on experience in high-technology areas predominantly for minority students, ages 13 to 16. The program was held after school and on weekends. My son was a participant in the program, which was designed to encourage students to choose careers in science and engineering. At Tuskegee, they participated in courses and laboratory sessions in science, technology, engineering, physics, and computer techniques. To relate the classroom instruction to the real world, the students toured high-technology firms in Alabama, Georgia, and Florida. There was always a high demand for enrollment.

Another activity in which my son participated was a student project in the Tuskegee School of Veterinary Medicine. There, he worked after school under the supervision of an epidemiologist who had a sizeable research team. My effort in encouraging such participation was to stimulate my son's interest in education, with a focus on the sciences.

Throughout this period, I needed to balance the time I devoted to my son, my position at CRF, and my own research interests. I managed a small research team and a couple of technical specialists

---

[48] Maya Angelou, Wouldn't Take Nothing for My Journey Now, Bantam Books/published by arrangement with Random House, Inc., New York, 1994, page 34.

and conducted a limited amount of research. For example, the radiation specialist, Dr. P. A. Loretan, and I joined forces and wrote a user's manual on the disposal of radioactive waste.[49] Most of my efforts were in planning and implementing programs that directly benefited CRF, however.

I feel certain that the contributions made by CRF staff during my time there in the 1980s were valuable to the nationwide research community. Our work helped identify problems and solutions that would ensure that the university stayed in the mainstream of research, diversified its research and development portfolio, obtained grants and contracts for new research projects, and fostered collaborations among scientists and engineers, most of whom were previously isolated in their narrow research areas.

To carry out the latter goal, I worked hard to establish partnerships and launch projects with major research facilities. As a result, Tuskegee Institute received more contracts than ever to perform research. These included the memorandum of understanding signed between CRF and PNNL, the NASA work, the USDA projects, and partnerships with the private sector. During several summers in the 1980s, my research team of graduate students and I traveled to the U.S. Army Research Institute of Environmental Medicine in Natick,[50] Massachusetts, to conduct research. The experience served to broaden their scopes in research and job opportunities.

At the same time, I was participating in activities of scientific and professional societies, including the American Chemical Society, Sigma Xi, American Association for the Advancement of Science, and the American Association of University Women. I attended seminars and held discussions about issues pertinent to women in

---

[49]   M. E. M. Tolbert and P. A. Loretan, "User's Manual for Applicants Proposing On-site Burial of Self-Generated Radioactive Waste," Tuskegee Institute Press, 1986.

[50]   D. Wilbert D. Bowers, Jr. who was the Chief of the Experimental Pathology Branch of the Cold Research Division at the Army Research Institute of Environmental Medicine in Natick, Massachusetts, was the supporter for my research at that facility in the late 1980s.

university positions with a number of community leaders, including the Mayor of Tuskegee.

Here I am (right) with Mrs. Claudine Penson, Dr. Dora Johnson, and Mrs. Beluah Johnson (left to right)—members of the Tuskegee Chapter of the American Association of University Women (AAUW) for which I served as chairwoman—observing Tuskegee's Mayor Johnny Ford (center) as he declared March 25, 1975, as AAUW Legislative Day in Tuskegee.

Although each day my life was full of meaningful activities, I found time to hold company with a handsome gentleman who was a faculty member. His educational background was similar to mine. Although we had a lot to talk about relative to education, he was a very private person. My questions about his family, former marriage, and friends almost always went unanswered, and I never told him how frustrating that was. I knew that he was concerned about my safety, since I lived alone after my son enrolled in the boarding school in Covington, Louisiana. He even parked his light blue car on my lawn for a long time, giving the impression that more than one person lived in my home.

I was disappointed that the relationship did not develop into a long-term one. Admittedly, I was preoccupied with my son and my job, while also serving on external boards and committees. I had served in a lot of capacities for a long time, and sometimes that got in the way of my personal life.

As the years went by, I noted that getting dates was never an issue for me; however, finding a man with whom to spend the rest of my life was. Perhaps I did not spend enough time developing relationships that might have led to another marriage. I devoted much more of my time to taking care of my son and planning how to progress in my career.

Perhaps it was time for a change. After years on the job at Tuskegee, I began making plans to take a sabbatical.

Just prior to my departure from CRF for a sabbatical, my staff presented to me several gifts, one of which was a beautiful rocking chair made of brown wood. Now that I have the time to do so, I love to sit in that chair and rock while thinking of my early years, my family, the people that I have known, and the diversity of my career path. It crosses my mind now and then that my work was very productive, and my contributions much broader than described here.

I also pursued a few personal projects on the side. One of them was research into Dr. George Washington Carver's life. I met on several occasions with his former secretary—Mrs. Jessie Abbott—and with Mrs. Hattie West Kelly, a graduate of Tuskegee and former dean of women. Both knew Dr. Carver well. With the first-hand information obtained during meetings with these two ladies, I completed a slide-tape program on Dr. Carver titled "A Life That Stood Out."[51] Funding for the slide-tape program on Dr. Carver was obtained from the Alabama Department of the Humanities. Additionally, I completed a booklet on Dr. Carver's assistant, Austin

---

[51]   David Oakes, "Foundation Tells Carver Story Through New Slide Program," *The Montgomery Advertiser*, February 8, 1982, page 16; "Slide Project Ready," *The Tuskegee News*, Vol. 116, No. 37, December 3, 1981, pages 7-8; and Virginia Smith, "Tuskegee Prof Produces Acclaimed Slide Show," *Ledger-Enquirer East Alabama*, February 4, 1982, page 4.

W. Curtis,[52] who was also the second director of the Carver Research Foundation.

During one of the meetings, Dr. Carver's former secretary gave me a small milk jar over which Dr. Carver had crocheted a beautiful cover. I later donated it to the National Park Service for display in the Carver Museum on the Tuskegee campus.

[52] M. E. M. Tolbert, <u>Austin Wingate Curtis, Jr.</u> (assistant to Dr. George Washington Carver, 1935-1943, director of the George Washington Carver Foundation, 1943-1944), Tuskegee Institute Press, 1984.

Working in the Private Sector

I was participating in a conference of the White House Initiative on Historically Black Colleges and Universities when I met Dr. Jeanette Griselli of the Standard Oil Company of Ohio. During an informal discussion, I asked her to host a few Tuskegee faculty members at her company for the summer. Back at my campus, I found no one willing to accept a summer appointment in Ohio because of the high cost of living there. A temporary appointment would require continuing to pay their mortgage or rent in the Tuskegee area while also paying for housing in Ohio.

Dr. Griselli then asked if I would be interested personally in taking a sabbatical leave from my positions at Tuskegee to spend a year at the Standard Oil Company of Ohio. I accepted and moved to a suburb of Cleveland—Warrensville Heights—to work at the Standard Oil research laboratory there.

While I was preparing for my sabbatical, Lawson earned his high-school diploma from St. Paul's Catholic School, the boarding school he attended in Covington, Louisiana, and he accompanied me to Ohio. Shortly after we were settled into an apartment, he accepted a job as a busboy at a nearby restaurant. During the day, I worked at the research laboratory of the Standard Oil Company. At night, Lawson used my car for transportation to and from work.

One day, I woke up early and did not find Lawson sleeping in his room. Even after I was ready for work, he still had not come home nor had he called. Even though the suburbs of Cleveland, Ohio, where we lived did not seem like a particularly dangerous area, I began to worry. After several abortive attempts to reach anyone by telephone at the restaurant where he worked, I called the police, who put out a call for officers to watch for Lawson and my car.

Just before 9 a.m. I received a call from my son, who said he was using a pay telephone near a highway toll booth. I was shocked to hear that he had been abducted and had escaped! He was safe, but he did not have any money to pay the toll to return home. The police department was notified, and a policeman was on the scene by the time Lawson returned to the toll booth.

After a couple of hours he arrived home, with a terrifying story. He had gone into an area of Cleveland where there were many people and cars on the street. He drove down a dead-end street and, when he pulled into an alley to turn around, a man stuck a gun through the car window and poked it into his face, ordering him to move over so that he, the gunman, could drive.

The gunman picked up another man carrying a package and ordered Lawson to get into the trunk of the car and keep quiet, which he did—fearing for his life. The two men drove a long distance before stopping in an isolated area of tall grass. Both men left the car to talk to another man, whose headlights shone onto the back of my car. Lawson was able to open the trunk slightly so as not to attract attention. However, he could not hear what was said. Lawson said that he was afraid to get out of the trunk and run because he did not know where he was and did not know his way home.

After the package and other items were exchanged, the second car left the scene, and the two men in my car opened the trunk. They told my son that they would release him if he did not tell the police about the incident. They took his wallet with all of his money. Of course, he promised not to tell.

The men disappeared into the night, and Lawson drove off. He was very fortunate that he was not physically harmed, though the incident took a severe mental toll on him. After searching for a while, Lawson found a way home, and that was when he encountered the toll booth. I was relieved to have my son safely home. After he finished telling me about his ordeal, he fell soundly asleep, and I went to work at the laboratory.

At work that day, I was fully occupied and did not tell anyone about the incident, although it was heavy on my mind. In addition to my regular duties, one of my responsibilities at Standard Oil was to serve as mentor for a small group of high-school students, who came to the laboratory after school to learn laboratory techniques and efficient computers operations. I couldn't help worrying about their personal safety as well as their future careers.

My year at the Standard Oil Company of Ohio passed rapidly. One of my roles as senior planner and senior budgets and control analyst involved analyzing and providing insights on engineering projects and corresponding budgets. In those capacities, I often contrasted work at a private-sector company with work at Historically Black Colleges and Universities (HBCUs).

Hugh differences! When budgets were discussed at HBCUs, the dollar amount was usually in the thousands. Rarely were there any individual projects at the million-dollar level. When officials at the company spoke of budgets in the private sector, the dollar amounts were frequently in the multi-millions or billions. Seemingly, lack of money was never an issue. Decisions were made rapidly, and they were based on sound data.

Furthermore, discussions by company officials about the "minority" had nothing to do with race; they were about the number of shares held by the company. During my time at the company, it was taken over by British Petroleum Company (BP). This was accomplished by first gaining control of a large block of minority shares. The company's name was changed to BP America, and a number of British managers and scientists moved in, replacing Americans in high-level positions.

Since I was at the research center on a one-year sabbatical, I was not particularly concerned about the changes taking place. However, as the personnel changes took place at BP America, I was eventually called to the office of the vice president to discuss my status. I assumed I would return to Tuskegee as planned. To my great surprise, I was offered a permanent position, along with several amenities for remaining at the Research Center.

After speaking with my son, and with the president of Tuskegee Institute, from which I was on sabbatical leave, I accepted the offer within a few days. The company facilitated the sale of my Tuskegee house, funded my move to Ohio, and, within the limits of the law, helped me fund the purchase of a house in Twinsburg, Ohio.

Shortly after the paperwork was completed, I moved out of my apartment and into my new home in Twinsburg, a predominantly White community with new houses near a golf course. The transition went well. Twinsburg was quiet and a short drive to the research center where I worked.

Prior to moving into my new home, I accompanied Lawson to Howard University in Washington, DC, and assisted him in settling into the dormitory on campus. Although he had selected another university as his first choice, he was not accepted there. At Howard University, he initially chose to study computer-based information systems and later changed his major to finance. I sighed with relief at his successful enrollment.

With his entry into a university, I felt that he would be safe and happy, and upon graduating from the university, he would have made great progress in his preparation for a productive and successful life. I wanted him to have a better life than I was having, despite making what I thought had been wise choices.

Lawson, like everyone else, however, was born with the power of choice. After less than two years at Howard University, he chose not to complete the requirements for a bachelor's degree. Needless to say, I was disappointed.

At BP America, people were generally cordial. I continued with my budget and planning responsibilities and joined various committees at the company. One of the committees was responsible for making decisions on funding educational institutions. While on that committee, I negotiated and gave strong support for a proposal submitted by the School of Engineering at Tuskegee University (Note: Tuskegee Institute was renamed Tuskegee University in 1985). This led to a sizable monetary award to the university. It made me feel good that I was able to help Tuskegee in that way.

On another occasion, I served as a "loaned executive," representing BP America at other organizations. As a result, I met a large number of executives who were employees of companies in Cleveland. Interactions with these individuals helped to expand my management expertise and broaden my network of professionals.

Living alone in my new home in Twinsburg was not without its problems. On several occasions in the early hours of the morning, my telephone would ring. When I answered, the caller would not say anything. Additionally, my home alarm system would sound at times, indicating a home intrusion. The local police department was unable to determine the origin of the calls, and the alarm system company could not find the problem with my security system. Thankfully, a police officer was assigned to park on the street near my home for security at night. Still, from time to time, I stayed in a hotel overnight just to quiet my nerves and get some sleep.

Although I worked diligently at the BP America Research Center, I found time to socialize. I joined the Cleveland-Tuskegee Alumni Club and continued my membership in the American Chemical Society, the American Association for the Advancement of Science, and Sigma Xi. Prior to moving to Twinsburg, I completed a principles-of-accounting course at Dyke College in Cleveland. During the same period, my son also completed a finance course there.

One day while getting a facial makeover at a cosmetic counter in a department store in downtown Cleveland, the attendant asked if I wanted to be a model for a Fashion Fair luncheon and show. I said "yes"—what a novel opportunity! Why not? I modeled products of the Fashion Fair makeup line. During the program I met John H. Johnson, founder of the Johnson Publishing Company. He was one of the most significant African-American businessmen and publishers in the United States, for whom a postal stamp was later issued in his honor. I was very excited to be on the same program at which Mr. Johnson was the guest speaker.

Despite the hectic job and outside activities, I was lonely in Ohio. After about three years of employment at the BP Research Center in Warrensville Heights, Ohio, I decided that I needed to be closer to my family.

Promoting Diversity in Research at the National Science Foundation

O ne day as I was reading a prominent journal, *Science*, I saw an advertisement for a temporary position at the National Science Foundation (NSF). I applied and received the appointment in 1990. I immediately contacted my son, who was still a student at Howard University, and asked him to assist me in finding an apartment to rent while I searched for a house to buy in Virginia. He was successful in identifying a small apartment in The Pennsylvania Building located on the corner of Indiana and 6th streets in Washington, DC.

After making arrangements by telephone, I asked my son to pick up the key to the apartment for me. When I arrived, I found that he had already moved his things into the apartment. That was unexpected. However, we stayed there together until I bought a condominium on South Pickett Street in Alexandria, Virginia. The Washington, DC, area was experiencing a huge boon in real estate prices, and I had arrived just in time to benefit from it.

On most days, I had conversations with my good friend and professional advisor, Dr. Charles A. Walker. When he and I reconnected, I had begun work at NSF and he was starting employment at a major library in Bethesda, Maryland. He had previously served as chancellor of the University of Arkansas at Pine Bluff. I had worked for him when he served as dean of the School of Pharmacy at Florida A&M University. He was the one who hired me to serve on that faculty, and he was the one who promoted me to the position of Associate Dean of the School of Pharmacy.

When Dr. Walker moved to the area, we continued our professional interactions, meeting with presidents and faculty members of colleges and universities in the Washington, DC, metropolitan area. We informed them about federal opportunities and encouraged them to advise their students of potential careers in science and engineering. Before we could fully implement our program by including a larger number of institutions, Dr. Walker became ill. He was hospitalized and died, leaving behind three adult children. During his hospitalization period, I spent a great deal of my after-work time at his side. His death really saddened me, and I did not continue the program that we initiated.

At NSF, I managed the Research Improvement in Minority Institutions Program—something I was well qualified for, given my experience at Tuskegee.

As part of my temporary appointment, I was assigned to work with the Federal Coordinating Council for Science, Engineering, and Technology. Dr. William McHenry and I wrote a booklet titled Resource Guide to Selected Undergraduate Programs of 10 Federal Agencies, 1993-1994, to assist colleges and universities in finding federal grant funds. The booklet was published in 1994 under the auspices of the council's Committee on Education and Training.

Since I was seeking a permanent appointment, I constantly reviewed NSF job announcements. However, I was unsuccessful in finding a permanent NSF position, and my position ended after three years, in 1993.

Following the end of my NSF appointment, I turned my attention to family-oriented tasks and a temporary appointment at the Howard Hughes Medical Institute in Chevy Chase, Maryland, through the TeleSec Agency. More details on this position are provided later.

Unfortunately, my dear long-time supporter, Daddy Cook, had been murdered a few years earlier. Mama Cook's health had gone downhill ever since, and one of my priorities was to move Mama Cook into my home. I used most of my time to prepare her house and household furnishings for sale, and I took over management of her rental properties. I worked tirelessly on these tasks.

During the same year (1993), my oldest sister, Audrey Mae, died in Providence, Rhode Island. For more than a half century, she had alternated between living in joy and other times in frustration. Much of the time, she hid behind mind-dulling corn liquor—just like our Dad had done. Maybe it made her forget her hard upbringing. Perhaps it was due to the fact that she was pushed into marriage at age 15, that she had a husband who did not appreciate her, and that she had difficulty taking care of her son. She never learned to read and write. Dipping snuff was another of her pleasures, or should it be called a vice? I believe that her drinking while taking medication to control seizures finally caught up with her. At 4:32 p.m. on August 16, 1993, she passed away. Some thought that she had a seizure while asleep and never woke up. Her death certificate cited several conditions.[53]

The window of her bedroom in the house on Vineyard Street in Providence, Rhode Island, was kept open for several days by her best friend, Dave, who had lived with her since the early 70s. Dave sat by the window and mourned her death while my second oldest sister, Lee Vania, me, and several other relatives raided the house for the nice things—clothes and jewelry—that Audrey Mae had accumulated. We felt certain that our sister wanted us to have her possessions, celebrating her death not in sadness, but with joy, by holding something of Audrey Mae's in our hands.

Of course, our perceptions were shaped by the amount of violence and death we had experienced in our lives. As a result, we did not normally display our sadness openly. As a matter of fact, we had a beautiful, lively wake and funeral for Audrey Mae at the Bell Funeral Home in Providence. Audrey Mae's husband, from whom she had been separated for years, adorned the casket with flowers. I didn't know who had notified him of her death. Audrey's boyfriend knew that she was married to someone, but that did not matter to him. He loved her and had endured her drunken ways—even her cursing and leaving home for long periods without letting him know where she was.

At the funeral service, everyone was somber until a lady that nobody knew came into the room. She made it clear that she and Audrey were drinking buddies. She said, "I came to pay my respects to my friend." She stood before the casket and stared at Audrey's

---

[53]   Cause of death was listed as arteriosclerotic heart disease; other conditions listed were hypertension and seizures.

corpse. After a long silence she said, "I have to go; I need a drink." Then she left as quickly as she came. I thought, "That is a fitting tribute to my sister. A drink is what she always wanted whenever she felt sad."

My sister, Eleanor, wrote a poem about Audrey Mae on the occasion of her funeral. It follows:

Audrey Mae[54]

Hi, do yu know me? I do. I know me.
I'm Audrey Mae … And Yea, I know me.
I'm short, fat, big eyed,
With short kinky hair and bow legs.
But look at me.
I'm cute as can be.

Have yu ate? I know ye not hungry.
Try this cornbread, collard greens, and chit'lins.
I fried some chicken too.
And there's a pot of homemade spaghetti in the frig'.
You don't have to be hungry.
Just sit a while, and eat with me.

Dave, I love you. You too Roy Lee.
Lee Vania, I got to go see Elma, Margaret, and Mary Lee.
This bus trip is too long; might as well go see Benjamin
And the rest of my relatives too.

Are you my friend? Are you really my friend?
Yea, Johnny Walker, J&B, you and Cutty Sark were there
When no one else understood me.

---

[54] Poem by Eleanor Olivia Mayo Minns, 1993; permission granted June 6, 2014, to include it in this book.

Why do you ponder, or weep just for me?
I'm happy, really happy. Can't you see?

I've lived my life to the fullest.
Junnie, can't you see.
No need to bellow;
All my pain is now beyond me.
Life dealt me an awful task,
And I lived it freely.

I loved, let love, and I did some deeds.
Now most of all, can't you see,
I'm free.

I admired the beauty of a piece of Audrey Mae's jewelry, turning it over and over in my hand. It was the only thing I took from her house, while my siblings cleaned out the rest. It was a gold broach, as wide as four fingers placed side-by-side. An oval topaz stone was mounted in the center, on top of a locket. A mesh design encircling the locket portrayed ten flowers, each with leaves and blooms. It was indeed beautiful. Even today, I sometimes wear that broach to provide a ritzy look to my business suits, and each time it makes me think affectionately of my sister.

Onward and Upward:
The Argonne Experience

A s my time at NSF was ending, I was not sitting idle waiting for anyone to help me. I was networking inside and outside of NSF. At a conference held in Washington, DC, my conversation with a NASA manager about my predicament was overheard by Dr. Barbara Filner, an official of the Howard Hughes Medical Institute (HHMI). During a conference break, Dr. Filner asked me if she heard correctly that I was looking for employment. She needed someone to work on a temporary basis on an international program that she was managing.

When we spoke on the telephone, I provided information on my background and job interest, and she advised of an agency where temporary appointments were available. I applied to that agency and was successful in getting a temporary appointment to a position at HHMI. The responsibility of this position was to review proposals received from research scientists in Eastern Bloc countries and recommend which ones to fund. Apparently, HHMI was expecting about 200 proposals, but more than 2,000 were received. A few additional individuals also served as proposal reviewers along with me. We worked as a team, reviewing and ranking proposals each weekday for several weeks. We worked well together, and I was overjoyed to have the position. Dr. Filner served as my strong supporter throughout the months that I was employed in this temporary position.

We identified 400 proposals to recommend to HHMI officials for further consideration. Officials of HHMI took over at that point, and those 400 proposals were further reviewed by teams of HHMI awardees in the United States. It was a complex process, but I was confident that the best scientists received awards.

While I worked at HHMI, several of my job applications were under review. On weekends, I continued sorting the enormous amount of furniture and household items in Mama Cook's home in Suffolk. I contracted with an antique shop in Suffolk for the sale of most of the items, partly at an in-house sale, and partly at the shop. Most of the resulting funds were used to support Mama Cook once I transported her to my condominium in Alexandria, Virginia, where I lived at the time. The remaining funds were given to her heirs.

It was clear that Mama Cook was in the early stage of Alzheimer's disease and no longer capable of caring for herself. Additionally, she had cancer, which was in remission at the time. I could not work in Chevy Chase, Maryland, and take care of her in Suffolk, Virginia—almost four hours away. Her niece, Ann, and I had joint power of attorney for her, but Ann and Alfred (Mama Cook's son) also lived too far away to assist with her care.

Once in Alexandria, I enrolled Mama Cook in an adult daycare center so that I could work during the day. She was not in any condition to be left alone in my condominium while I was away. However, while enrolled in the daycare center, she did a number of things that I attribute to her being in the early stage of Alzheimer's disease: she was uncooperative with the attendants and twice walked away from the center. Clearly, the daycare center was not equipped to handle a person with Mama Cook's needs either. That put me in a bind. It was clear that her son Alfred would not be able to take care of her. Therefore, I had to act fast to find a way to accommodate Mama Cook's needs while I continued my temporary jobs at NSF and then at HHMI.

While I was accomplishing all of these tasks, I received an invitation to interview for the permanent position of director of the Division of Educational Programs at Argonne National Laboratory.

In anticipation of possibly moving to Illinois, I began searching frantically for a place for Mama Cook. Luckily, her son found a facility that could accommodate her condition. Quickly, I completed the application and got her into that facility, which was located a long distance from Washington, DC. She did not do well there, and a few years later, I moved her into the Sunrise Assisted Living Facility in Springfield, Virginia. This was a new facility with a well-qualified staff that was able to accommodate her needs. I felt confident that she would receive excellent care. She liked the Sunrise facility, and she adjusted rapidly.

By the time I started the job at ANL in 1994, I knew Mama Cook was in competent hands, and I could focus completely on my new responsibilities.

At some time during the course of my career, working hard and smart, and excelling in every position, had become an obsession with me. I believe it was at least partially an emotional ploy; I would be so busy I would have no time to ponder the hard times and heartaches I had endured. Somewhere along the way, I made a conscious decision to devote myself wholeheartedly to my jobs and perform superbly at all of them.

In some ways I had it easier than most people; despite my qualms about whether I may have been at fault for the breakup of my marriages, those insecurities did not carry over into the academic and professional aspects of my life. I was relaxed at job interviews, confident that my merits would shine through. I was able to speak about my skills and experience and answer questions easily, free of nervous tension or fear of embarrassment.

The same applied to starting new appointments; unlike many people, I do not recall ever feeling unsure of my ability to carry out the responsibilities of a job or even to change them if I saw fit.

In fact, in at least this realm of my life, I was feeling downright competitive—willing to fight for a job against other candidates, to take on a challenge and overcome obstacles, and to excel even when the odds were unfavorable. You might say I was finding my professional voice. Was it a reaction to failed marriages and family relationships? Yes, probably. Was I overworking myself as a result? Yes, probably. Did it feel good to finally be recognized for my accomplishments? Yes, absolutely.

By the time my appointment at ANL ended, I had led or overseen the development and implementation, or refinement, of numerous programs and projects at both universities and government-owned laboratories. I had held administrative, managerial, research, research management, teaching, mentoring, and strategic planning positions. I had built networks of connections that numbered in the hundreds, for myself, among universities and organizations, and between government and private entities.

First, though, I had to get the position at ANL. After several preliminary telephone conversations with ANL officials, I went to Illinois for an interview. There were several applicants who made the interview list for the division director position. I was prepared to compete; in the end, though, I seemed to have obtained the position quite easily.

As part of the competition, I was required to present a seminar and respond to questions. I also interacted with both staff and interviewees at a social gathering. While on a tour of the laboratory, Alice Essling, the chemist who had served as my research advisor during my earlier ANL internship in the summer of 1966, invited me to stop by her laboratory.

I was pleasantly surprised that Ms. Essling remembered me and still had the notebook in which I had recorded research data while I was an intern. We had a nice chat, and she introduced me to other chemists. Shortly after returning home, I received a letter of appointment to the position of director of the Division of Educational Programs (DEP) at ANL.[55]

I was responsible for developing educational programs, recruiting students and faculty for program participation, placing them in research laboratories that matched their interests and skills, assessing programs, and participating in DOE and ANL programs, both onsite and at headquarters.

I was also responsible for the DEP budget, training and hiring of staff, development of proposals for funding, interacting with the U.S. Department of Energy headquarters officials, and leading the provision of services that would enable universities to make use of

---

[55] "Grad Named to Post at Argonne Laboratory," *Tuskegee Gram*, Vol. 32, No. 43, April 15, 1994, page 2.

ANL research resources (e.g. equipment, expertise in science and education).

One of the first things I noticed was that only a limited number of minorities applied for participation in DEP programs. Even fewer were successful in obtaining on-site internships. To address this problem, I recruited a highly qualified, senior African-American scientist, Dr. Linda Phaire Washington. Together we organized teams of staff members and charged them with identifying problems associated with the low representation of women and individuals from minority groups in DEP programs, as well as other ways to strengthen the DEP portfolio of programs.

My staff and I established several programs for increasing the number of minorities in research and expanding the science and engineering opportunities to community colleges, technical institutes, and small undergraduate institutions.[56] Some of the women who worked at ANL established the annual Science Careers in Search of Women Conference. And I served on the advisory committee of the Second Annual Technical Women's Symposium, which focused on similar goals. Outside of my regular responsibilities, I also participated in activities, such as Science Careers in Search of Women, specifically designed to encourage girls to choose science, technology, engineering, and mathematics (STEM) careers.[57]

As a result of my efforts and those of my staff, the participation in ANL student and faculty research programs by women and minorities increased from ten to 40 percent in various programs. Our programs and initiatives still serve as models for other organizations.

---

[56]   The Student Interdisciplinary Research Training Program was established to increase the number of minorities in ANL research programs. The Science and Technology Technical Associates Program provided opportunities for developing skills in science and engineering for faculty members and students from community colleges, technical institutes, and small undergraduate educational institutions.

[57]   Janita Poe, "Role Models Opening Doors of Lab to Girls," *Chicago Tribune*, MetroDuPage Section, April 18, 1994, page 1.

I also oversaw initiatives for university student participants in telecommunications and high-performance computing, to take advantage of the growing opportunities to use high-tech channels to share, access, and process scientific data.[58] Other training programs for university students and faculty members were very popular.

Dr. Linda Phaire Washington, DEP senior program leader, guiding a student in an experiment that required the use of a microscope

Dr. Emmanuel Brako giving a lecture to students on proper laboratory techniques

Dr. Germàn R. Nùñez interacting with students as they show him how much they have learned from his lectures and guidance in research

---

[58]   In the Telecommunications Program, developed by Dr. Samuel Bowen, DEP senior program leader, more than 2,000 Illinois teachers were trained in the use of computers, with special emphasis on internet aspect of the program. Another program (the Tuskegee University program), which was funded by the National Science Foundation, enabled the establishment of the high-performance computing infrastructure to link Tuskegee University with ANL's Division of Educational Programs, Mathematics Division, and Computer Science Division as well as with programs at Oak Ridge National Laboratory.

An instructor giving students guidance on how to handle laboratory data in calculating their research results

A senior-level student assisting a research participant in computer techniques

Argonne National Laboratory, Summer 1996
Faculty Research Participation (RFP) Program

In this photograph are participants and instructors in the RFP, a program of DEP/ANL. I am third from the left on the front row.

Photographs: Courtesy of Argonne National Laboratory

The pace of the job was relentless. Or was it just the pace that I had adopted for myself? Whenever new programs were in progress, they seemed to take on a life of their own. Before one program was completed, another one was being planned.

With the expansion in the DEP portfolio, a strong evaluation program was needed. Therefore, a few members of my staff, led by Dr. Louise Monegain, took on the challenge of developing criteria and processes for assessing program results. I also reorganized DEP for more effective operation, including streamlining the process for applying for DEP programs. A strategic plan was put in place, and I developed scenarios for reducing budgets in science education programs and leveraging funds. For the latter endeavor, the manager of the DEP Washington, DC, office (Dr. R. D'Annucci) was of tremendous assistance in developing and strengthening ties with federal agencies and managing a couple of programs. At the DEP location on the ANL site, other staff members (e.g., Dr. H. Myron, Dr. F. Vivio, Dr. L. P. Washington, Dr. D. Ettinger, Ms. L. Ousley, Ms. J. Botcher, and others) participated in a variety of program development, strengthening, and reporting activities and in implementing education programs.

At the same time, there was no end to the need for routine reports, proposals for field work, and proposals for work-for-others projects by DEP staff. When staff members work as hard as mine did, it is imperative that actions be taken to maintain their morale at a high level. This was critical during a period when the prevailing atmosphere was becoming negative due to reduced funding and reductions in programs and staff.

I was determined that DEP would not become isolated or under-funded. In that regard, I employed the skills I had gained in networking and creating connections among diverse organizations to pursue cost-sharing opportunities. I worked with such agencies as the National Institutes of Health, National Science Foundation, U.S. Agency for International Development, U.S. Department of State, and the Howard Hughes Medical Institute to identify ways to interact and leverage funding. I also worked with universities, and oversaw joint development of an environmental science internship with Northwestern University.

In the face of a potential threat to eliminate science education programs at DOE facilities, I joined forces with other education directors to develop strategies for offsetting the potential threat. As I continued my aggressive work in science education, I found myself serving as chair of the DOE Science Education Directors Council, and as a member of the steering committee from November 1994 to March 1996.

It was a time of change at DOE, and I was determined to make sure that science education was adequately funded. I even worked with others to brief Congressional staff members of the potential impact of budget cuts on science education.

With the wealth of information that I had gained in my two years in this job, I shared some of it in an article published in the *Journal of College Science Teaching*.[59]

Because DOE's and Argonne's energy and nuclear portfolios were of global importance, my work as DEP director frequently branched out into the international arena. I participated in meetings at the International Atomic Energy Agency (IAEA) in Vienna, Austria. In turn, member states of that agency enhanced and strengthened efforts to identify and sponsor scientists, engineers, and technical managers employed at nuclear facilities to DEP for training in radiation safety. My key trainer, Dr. Jan van Erp, was an exceptional instructor of these adult foreign students. The international training program was popular, and it received many compliments from foreign guests. In order to reach this point, I held discussions on program development and implementation strategies with individuals from numerous organizations and institutions.

---

[59] M. E. M. Tolbert, "Strengthening the Nation's Educational Systems through Programs at Argonne National Laboratory," *Journal of College Science Teaching*, 26, No.: 18-25, 1996.

Me holding dialogue with
Dr. Walter E. Massey,
former ANL director

With Dr. Ali El-Saiedi of the IAEA,
I am discussing the importance
of IAEA in its relationship
with ANL, especially DEP.

I am discussing women in science
and engineering ideas with
conference participants at ANL.

With Dr. Schulzcraft of the
IAEA, I am discussing DEP/ANL
education and special training
programs and IAEA involvement.

Whether in my office or in other locations, I continue holding dialogue
on educational and research programs and topics on women and
minorities in science and engineering with interested individuals.

This was an interesting meeting with First Lady of Ghana— Her Excellency Nana Konadu Agyeman Rawlings (second from the left, also in the insert in the upper right corner of this photograph), a representative of the Government of Ghana (far left), an official of the U.S. Department of State (far right), and me (second from the right) in Accra, Ghana, in 1995.

Here I am in South Africa with Dr. Martha Krebs of the U.S. Department of Energy and two additional officials to visit universities and hold discussions with university officials on potential university-government linkages.

Here I am giving a speech at Freund Lodge on the Argonne National Laboratory site in Argonne, Illinois.

At one point, I provided technical advice and support to DOE headquarters on a program to link South African universities with ANL. My involvement included a fact-finding trip to South Africa with DOE officials, including Dr. Martha Krebs, head of the Office of Energy Research. My travel to South Africa was planned in combination with another initiative on the African continent. In 1995, I led a multi-agency team that conducted a workshop in Ghana, formerly the Gold Coast, which required spending several weeks in that country.[60]

Participants in the National Cancer Program Workshop held in Ghana

Prof. F. K. Nkrumah who directs the Noguchi Memorial Institute for Medical Research, Prof. F. K. A. Allotey who directs the Ghana Atomic Energy Commission, Dr. A. L. Goldson who directs the Radiotherapy Department at Howard University, and another Ghanaian official

---

[60] Team members included Dr. Linda Phaire Washington, an immunologist and senior program leader from DEP/ANL; Dr. Louise J. Monegain, an evaluator from DEP/ANL; Dr. Carrie P. Hunter, a medical oncologist and special assistant to the director of the National Institutes of Health's Office of Research on Women's Health; Dr. A. Olufemi Williams, a pathologist, cancer expert, and senior scientist from the National Cancer Institute of the National Institutes of Health; and Dr. Alfred L. Goldson, professor and chairman of the Department of Radiation Therapy at Howard University.

Ms. J. Briggs, Chargé d'Affaire, U.S. Embassy in Ghana giving a speech at the National Cancer Workshop

Me, Prof. Allotey, and others on a panel at the workshop

The Ashanti King—His Excellency Otumfuo Opoku Ware II—being greeted by Drs. Washington, Williams, Goldson, Monegain, and Hunter of the U.S. team

The son of the Ashanti King with four of the U.S. team members

Me, Dr. Mary Grant, and other dignitaries in Accra, Ghana

The workshop in Accra, Ghana, was titled "National Cancer Program for Ghana," and was sponsored by the U.S. Department of State. Our host agency was the Ghana Atomic Energy Commission for which Prof. F. K. A. Allotey served as director. My team had extensive interactions with high-ranking officials, including Ghana's President Rawlings and his wife. They were beautiful people who welcomed us and treated us with the utmost respect and cordiality. The team also met with the Ashanti King and his son, as well as officials from the U.S. Agency for International Development Mission in Ghana, the Ghana Ministry of Health and Ministry of Science and Technology, and Ghanaian medical institutions. [61]

The workshop resulted in discussions and exchange of information on radiotherapy and cancer and the refinement of Ghana's National Cancer Program. The workshop had the concurrence of the IAEA, which was one of the agencies that supported the construction of a radiotherapy facility in Ghana.

One important result of the workshop was a joint manpower development project. While the workshop was taking place, the IAEA-supported radiotherapy facility was under construction in Accra. As part of the manpower development project that I directed, a Ghanaian doctor, Dr. Verna Vanderpuye, received post-graduate specialty enrichment at host universities in the United States. She returned to Accra to work in a leadership position at the radiotherapy facility and to serve as an international consultant in the cancer field. Additionally, our work in Ghana enriched the dissemination of cancer information throughout the country, raising awareness of cancer problems and treatment.

Before leaving Ghana, my team took advantage of the opportunity to visit the Elmina Castle, which was initially a site for trading gold

---

[61]   Including Dr. Owusu, dean of the University of Ghana Medical School; Dr. F. K. Nkrumah, director of the Noguchie Memorial Medical Research Institute; and officials of the Korle Bu Teaching Hospital.

and ivory. It later became the principal export site for the slave trade.[62] Visiting that castle was an emotional event.

Various Photographs of Elmina Castle and Nearby Scenes

After completing my international duties in Ghana and South Africa, I returned to ANL and resumed my primary responsibilities in education and training. I continued to address issues pertinent to DEP, including the ongoing effort to strengthen programs and

---

[62] Tony Hyland, <u>The Castles of Elmina: a Brief history and Guide</u>, Series No. 3, Ghana Museums & Monuments Board, page 12, 1971

identify ways to increase the diversity of participants. Throughout my tenure at ANL, I had strong support from a large number of laboratory officials including the laboratory director (Dr. A. Schriesheim), associate laboratory directors (e.g., Dr. F. Fradin and Dr. H. Drucker), division directors (e.g., Dr. M. Thurnauer), as well as others.

Even though I was very busy, I participated in local activities. I served as a judge for science fairs at schools in Chicago and oversaw selected Science Bowl activities at ANL and at DOE headquarters. Not all of my endeavors were academic. For example, when a high-school student from Cabrini Green, a public housing section on the Near North Side of Chicago, needed assistance, a few of my co-workers and I assisted her in working through her personal problems. In addition, I participated in a modern dance class at a center in Chicago and toured museums, tourist sites, and neighborhoods. The latter tours were taken with the intent of identifying areas in which ANL might help provide improvements.

While serving as DEP director, I lived in Chicago. In the beginning, I lived in a rented apartment. In the end, after a long search, I purchased a condominium in the Gold Coast section of the city. Since this condominium was one block from Michigan Avenue, I could walk to shopping areas. The drive to and from ANL was not bad, even when it was snowing, since roads in that area were cleared of snow as a priority. The snow and the wind velocity in Chicago were legendary, and it was not like any other place where I had lived.

While I was living in Chicago, my son Lawson had gotten married and had children. He and his family continued living in my condominium on South Pickett Street in Alexandria, Virginia, purchased while I was working at NSF. My two grandsons stayed with me in Chicago for a summer, while they were very young. While I was at work at ANL, they participated in programs at the Chesterbrook Academy nearby. Often we had supper in the community near ANL before returning to Chicago. To keep them occupied during the drive between Argonne and Chicago, they listened to tapes on "Hooked on Phonics," a learn-to-read program.

Naturally, I wanted to encourage them to study science. We also toured Chicago, visiting such sites as the museums, Navy Pier, McCormack Place, malls, and city viewing towers. It was an exciting time for the three of us.

At another time, Alfred, the son of Daddy and Mama Cook, with whom I was always close, stayed with me for several months before moving to a new home in California, where he currently resides. Also at different times during my stay in Chicago, I was visited for short periods by my son Lawson; nephew James "Ezysarel" Washington Mayo; Benjamin Mayo, Jr., and Ifayet Mayo—my nephew and niece-in-law, respectively; and my sister Lee Vania Mayo Williams.

Nuclear Chemistry at New Brunswick Laboratory

A lthough being the director of ANL educational programs was interesting and full of satisfying responsibilities, I yearned to have a role in which I would be more directly involved in science. When I learned that the position of director of the New Brunswick Laboratory (NBL) was available, I applied and was successful in receiving the appointment in 1996.

NBL is a government-owned and government-operated facility, unlike ANL and PNNL, which are government owned and contractor operated. In this new position, I did not need to move from my condominium in the Gold Coast section of Chicago because NBL is on the same site as ANL. I had only to move my office from one building to another.

With this change, I became a federal employee—a move that would offer significant fringe benefits well into my retirement years. My reporting changed to officials of the U.S. Department of Energy. As NBL director, I reported to senior-level officials of three DOE offices: the Office of Security, the Office of Safeguards and Security, and the Chicago Operations Office.[63] An additional change was that I had to obtain a security clearance, via a federal investigation of my background.

NBL is a nuclear analytical chemistry laboratory that is part of an effort to ensure worldwide nuclear safety. In this role, NBL serves as the U.S. Government's official laboratory for measuring nuclear materials, setting standards for calibrating measurement instruments

---

[63]   During my NBL tenure, Joseph S. Mahaley was director of the Office of Security at DOE headquarters in Washington, DC; Owen B. Johnson was director of the Office of Safeguards and Security in DOE headquarters in Germantown, Maryland; Marvin Gunn, Jr. was manager of the Chicago Operations Office in Argonne, Illinois, following Dr. Sam Martin's tenure in that position who succeeded that of Cherri Langenfeld.

at other facilities, evaluating nuclear safeguards, and certifying nuclear reference materials.[64]

In addition to its national role, the laboratory is internationally recognized for its expertise in these areas. It is a networking facility of the International Atomic Energy Agency. In this role, it provides technical expertise to the IAEA and other nonproliferation organizations. The goal of global nonproliferation efforts is to account for, safeguard, and reduce the spread of nuclear materials worldwide.

All of these activities needed to be enhanced and strengthened. When I took over the laboratory, its status with the IAEA was not at its best. By 1997, efforts to strengthen NBL were in full force. One of many actions I took was to sign an "Agreement in Principle" with the director of the Institute for Reference Materials and Measurements (IRMM) located in Geel, Belgium. That institute is responsible for ensuring common measurement standards throughout Europe. In the agreement, we agreed that our facilities would continuously work toward improving the quality of measurement worldwide and expand our existing cooperation in the certification of nuclear reference materials.

To oversee this formal agreement between the U.S. and European laboratories, I travelled a number of times to IRMM in Geel, Belgium, for face-to-face discussions with the IRMM director and other officials. As my laboratory increased its involvement with the IAEA, I also travelled to its headquarters in Vienna, Austria, for meetings. Although I never traveled to Russia, I had oversight for a team of NBL scientists who monitored the blend-down of uranium in that country. The need for blend-down is to return uranium,

---

[64] Reference materials are controls, or standards, employed to ensure accurate analytical measurements and for calibrating instruments used for such work. In the field of analytical chemistry, they are important for determining the composition and tracing the origin of chemical samples. Whereas NBL is the primary U.S. institution for certifying nuclear reference materials according to standard criteria, the National Institute of Standards and Technology (NIST), in the Department of Commerce, is the primary U.S. institution responsible for certifying non-nuclear reference materials.

after it has been used in nuclear-power reactors, to a state in which it cannot be used for nuclear weapons, prior to returning it to its country of origin.

We regularly hosted visitors from nuclear facilities in the United States and foreign countries, and participated in international conferences.

On the domestic front, NBL had close ties with the U.S. National Institute of Standards and Technology (NIST), formerly known as the National Bureau of Standards. In 1981, NBL assumed some of NIST's former responsibility for maintaining and distributing nuclear reference material.[65] NBL, as a government-owned and –operated facility with a history of producing special nuclear materials, had the best and most secure infrastructure in the country for handling and storing such materials.[66]

I oversaw interactions with NIST that included sharing information on certified reference materials (CRMs) and advising government officials on nuclear materials policies and programs.[67]

Although NBL was and still is small, its work became better known among national and international officials as a result of the activities I initiated or oversaw. I was pleasantly surprised to receive numerous congratulatory letters for the progress that my staff and I made. Among those who sent letters were U.S. Secretary of Energy Bill Richardson and Professor F. K. A. Allotey, director of the Ghana Atomic Energy Commission. Also, complimentary letters were received from The Honorable Spencer Abraham during his tenure as Secretary of the U.S. Department of Energy, Joseph S. Mahaley who was the director of the Office of Security of the U.S. Department of Energy, and a number of other officials.

---

[65] July 22, 2014, e-mail message forwarded to Dr. M. E. M. Tolbert by Dr. Willie May of NIST, who received the historical information from Dr. Dave Holbrook via Dr. Jason Boehm, both of whom are NIST officials.

[66] Ibid.

[67] Dr. Thomas Gills and Dr. Willie May of NIST were helpful in providing guidance and introducing me to scientists in this field.

Of all the positions I have held, the NBL one was the most crucial to national and international welfare, given its critical role in nuclear matters. As such, I used all of my management skills and business acumen to stay on top of developments and make sure no mistakes were made. Yes, this created pressure on me. But, just like my previous jobs, I enjoyed my work and was willing to devote myself to it.

On the administrative side, I supervised scientists, engineers, and support staff, and managed research and development activities. I oversaw the development and implementation of business plans and the publication of information about NBL.[68] As I had done at other facilities, I identified stakeholders and potential partners, and instituted scientific collaborations on the local, national, and international scales.

Some of the challenges at NBL were evident; however, I was just as concerned about those that may not have been obvious. Therefore, during my time there, the laboratory conducted two sweeping self-evaluations, to identify any actions needed to bring its work up to date and to ensure its continued safety, efficiency, and effectiveness.

First, I oversaw an in-depth assessment of the certified reference materials produced by NBL. As a result, eight additional materials were developed and issued, or re-certified and re-issued. These are listed in an appendix of this book, along with definitions and explanations.

Second, we completed an overall self-assessment, examining the laboratory's strengths and weaknesses in all areas—strategic

---

[68] M. Irene Spaletto, Maureen Clapper, and Margaret E. M. Tolbert, "Second NBL Measurement Evaluation Program Meeting: A Summary," *Journal of Nuclear Materials Management*, Vol. XXVI, No. 1, Fall 1997; *Progress Report*, New Brunswick Laboratory, Oct. 1995 through Sep. 1996, NBL-341, 1997; *Progress Report*, New Brunswick Laboratory, Oct. 1996 through Sep. 1997, NBL-343, 1998; *Progress Report*, New Brunswick Laboratory, Oct. 1997 through Sep. 1998, NBL-351, 1999; *Progress Report*, New Brunswick Laboratory, Oct. 1998 through Sep. 1999, NBL-358, 2000; *Progress Report*, New Brunswick Laboratory, Oct. 1999 through Sep. 2000, NBL-368, 2001.

planning, customer focus, human resources, business operations, and management of processes. Identified weaknesses needed to be addressed immediately, and I did as much as I could with the available resources. By this time in my career, I was quite experienced in doing a lot with a little.

I authorized a restructuring of the laboratory, and strengthened teamwork and collaboration among the newly organized divisions and teams. To support the scientists and cut operating costs, I hired post-doctoral and pre-doctoral fellows to assist with laboratory projects headed by senior staff members.

Drawing on the leadership capabilities of key staff members, a tracking and reporting system for laboratory-wide documents was refined to increase accountability and documentation. Together, my staff and I found new program sponsors and ways to leverage funding received from those sponsors to cover improvements completed throughout the laboratory.

All of these activities were successfully carried out with a small staff and an inadequate budget.

I devoted a fair amount of effort to human resources issues, especially diversity. When I began serving as NBL director, the laboratory staff was ten percent minorities. Although diversity issues were being addressed at DOE headquarters, minimal action had been taken to address similar concerns at facilities outside of Washington, DC, such as NBL.

Efforts to increase the percentage of minorities were hampered by the lack of available positions; therefore, whenever a position was vacated, I focused on identifying well-qualified female and minority candidates. I was successful in employing three well-qualified chemists from minority groups, resulting in better representation of the population as well as greater diversity of ideas.

I also determined that NBL (and other national laboratories) needed a larger pool of trained and qualified scientists overall, to draw from as positions became available. To meet this national challenge, I introduced a proposal for an outreach program that would provide on-site training for students in chemical analysis of nuclear materials, computer science, statistics, and program management. I modeled the proposal on examples of successful programs that I had directed at ANL.

After the proposal was developed, funding was identified to implement and support it. The program was open to all students, especially those from Historically Black Colleges and Universities and Hispanic-Serving Institutions.

This new program experienced rapid success. In the first year, 2001, a graduate student from Howard University worked for a year at NBL, analyzing nuclear materials. During the summer of 2002, seven students from universities, especially HBCUs, worked at NBL under the mentorship and supervision of senior scientists. The program grew to include increasing numbers of undergraduate and graduate students as well as pre-doctoral and post-doctoral fellows.

These and other internship programs provided a needed service to the nation by developing the capabilities of young scientists, and placing more trained scientists in the pipeline for future jobs—all without a huge budget. These activities also heightened NBL visibility and staff morale.

During my time as director, there was an increase in the proportion of minorities on the NBL staff to approximately 20 percent, achieving our diversity goals. I was recognized by DOE for addressing diversity issues and was appointed to serve as the Diversity Champion for the Chicago Operations Office. In this role, I assisted other parts of DOE in achieving similar successes.

Meanwhile, the technical side of the job needed equal attention. In the year 2000, the Department of Energy began implementing an Integrated Safety Management System—which combined the agency's environment, safety, and health programs into an integrated whole.

Although NBL had a long-standing safety system, overseeing the implementation of this new, broader system at NBL required thorough knowledge of how all the processes of the laboratory fit together. I worked closely with senior staff to ensure that safety was addressed at all levels and in all types of work (e.g., operations, maintenance, and chemical analyses). In the process, we considered all potential hazards (e.g., chemical, occupational, environmental, nuclear, electrical, and transportation) to workers, the public, and the environment.

All aspects of staff safety training were updated, and more than 150 baseline documents were reviewed to ensure compliance with applicable guidelines. I arranged for special training for NBL Environment, Safety and Health Team members responsible for implementing and verifying the efficacy of the new system. Meanwhile, I continued my interactions with DOE site managers and other officials, gaining valuable information and insights on how they addressed management matters. Also, I shared with them my approaches to various issues.

As a federal employee and director of a federal laboratory, I gained a much greater appreciation for the role of the agencies in Washington, DC, in nurturing the nation's scientific community. When an opportunity presented itself, I took a three-month temporary assignment at DOE headquarters in Germantown, Maryland, a suburb of Washington, DC. My title was acting associate director of the Office of Laboratory Operations and Environment, Safety, and Health. The position was located in DOE's Office of Science. Essentially, this office oversaw the operation of all of DOE's government-owned laboratories and their research.

In addition to broadening my scope of experience (and opening my eyes to how a large bureaucracy operates), the location of my assignment enabled me to interact more often with my son and grandsons, who were living in Alexandria, Virginia, which is approximately an hour's drive from Germantown, Maryland. My son and I had a lot of quality time together, during which we talked about his life and path forward. My grandsons spent a few fun weekends with me, touring Washington, DC, discovering the seafood at Joe's Crab Shack, and getting to know the area.

At the end of the assignment at headquarters, I returned to my work at NBL in the outskirts of Chicago. As usual—the common theme throughout my career—I initiated several new programs and projects.

A project that had particular significance to me was the book drive. Through discussions with school officials in the local area and in Chicago, I learned that a large number of books in some school libraries were woefully outdated. I knew that an effort for the donation of books to local schools would fit within the Secretary of Energy's Adopt-a-School Initiative to provide 2,000 books to schools throughout the nation by the year 2000.

I was excited about addressing real needs under the umbrella of this national initiative. I served as champion of the book drive and invited volunteers to assist me. We selected several schools and asked each one to submit a list of needed books, and found an innovative (and legal) way for staff members of DOE's Chicago Operations Office—including NBL—to contribute books to the project, by purchasing books directly from vendors then having volunteers distribute the books to schools.

School officials expressed a great deal of gratitude for the donated books. The Secretary of Energy expressed his appreciation by presenting me with the DOE PRIDE Award.

Another memorable occurrence that followed my return from Maryland was an increase in NBL funding from DOE headquarters. With some of those funds, I approved the recruitment and hiring of two new staff members as well as the installation of a computer-based system useful for updating documents on regulations and standards, tracking the movement of nuclear materials, tracking staff assignments and training, and monitoring action items.

With the use of this new Laboratory Information Management System, the movement of nuclear material was tracked from the day it was received at NBL until it was sent to another facility—a big improvement in accountability.

Furthermore, DOE's Office of Security recommended the acquisition of a new facility to replace the aging building that housed NBL, and the office director committed to providing some of the funding. Those funds were to be augmented by funds obtained from work-for-others projects—work the laboratory performed for "paying" customers, such as other federal agencies.

Things were looking great for NBL. Under my management and with the increase in funding, NBL began operating more efficiently and effectively.

Our biggest improvements were the increase in the efficiency of preparing and selling certified nuclear reference materials.[69] These materials are used to calibrate instruments that are in turn used to measure the amounts of nuclear materials in samples. The improvements were critical to address complaints from domestic and foreign customers about the amount of time it took to receive the materials they ordered. My goals were 1) to satisfy customers without sacrificing quality, 2) to operate NBL like an efficiently managed business, and 3) to keep staff members motivated. With the staff's help, we met these goals and got the laboratory on track.

In 1997, we mapped the processes involved in our Reference Materials Program, which is focused on CRM sales and services. We identified problem areas, such as the needs for more certified shipping containers, freight forwarders, a tracking mechanism, and dedicated staff members to handle the receipt and processing of orders and shipments. Ultimately, we reorganized the staff of the program and redefined their tasks for more efficient operation. Two freight forwarders were identified to assist with shipments to foreign countries. NBL was then in a better position to sell CRMs globally. The international involvement of NBL was strengthened, and its position as a network laboratory of the IAEA gained respect.

The changes initially required a great deal of direct supervision to keep the program on target. Strategic planning, flexibility, and continual learning were part of the job. These were critical in dealing with foreign customers with different cultures, languages, and management styles; with DOE headquarters; and with changing rules and regulations for the transportation and receipt of nuclear material.

---

[69]   See footnote 64 for more information.

As a result of NBL's greater efficiency, sales in 1998 increased by 82 percent over 1997. In FY 2000 the sale of certified nuclear reference materials reached an all-time high of more than a half million dollars. In addition, the time required to process and ship orders to foreign customers decreased from eight or more months in 1997 to two or two and a half months in 2001. At last, special orders could be shipped on the same day or within a matter of days.

Customer reactions were positive in regard to the timeliness of product deliveries and satisfaction with NBL services. The new operating style of NBL was praised in sessions held at the IAEA in Vienna and at the European IRMM.

While participating in scientific meetings in the United States, I learned that most individuals did not know the purpose of nuclear safeguards laboratories such as NBL. I decided that the scientific image of NBL had to be improved further. Also, we needed to establish and nurture partnerships with other nuclear safeguards laboratories, which would increase nuclear security throughout the world.

After discussing my vision with others in the field, a plan was developed for holding a full-day session to discuss topics of mutual interest to scientists and managers at nuclear safeguards analytical laboratories throughout the world. I proposed that the Institute for Nuclear Materials Management (INMM) provide the forum, a plan that was received with enthusiasm. I solicited an international panel of experts to address the chosen topic, "The Role of Analytical Laboratories in Safeguarding Nuclear Material."

Officials participated from nuclear laboratories in seven countries—the United States, Japan, Belgium, France, Austria, Germany, and the Russian Federation. I chaired the panel discussion, held during the 39th Annual INMM Meeting in Naples, Florida, in July 1998 in addition to being its primary organizer and implementer. As a result of its success, I was invited to organize similar sessions for future annual INMM meetings. Feedback was quite positive from participating countries, and partnerships continued to grow as ideas and lessons learned were exchanged.

The full-day sessions of the annual INMM meetings are still being held, with participation by representatives of several foreign laboratories. Collaborative endeavors have been developed as a result. Additionally, partnerships between NBL and other safeguards laboratories were strengthened. As a direct result of the sessions at INMM, four papers for which I served as author or co-author were published between 1999 and 2001, one in the conference proceedings and three in the *Journal of Nuclear Materials Management*.[70]

Within DOE, I shared my insights and information on NBL with other managers by participating in DOE Site Managers' Meetings, serving on various committees, and participating in programs.

While serving as director of NBL, I received several awards. Among them was the Women of Color in Government and Defense Technology Award for managerial leadership in government. On the occasion of the program where the award was presented to me, Joseph S. Mahaley and Owen B. Johnson—the director of the office of Security and director of the Office of Safeguards and Security respectively—were in attendance to support me. In participating in the program, which was a grand affair, Mr. Mahaley applauded my productivity and success during the speech that he gave at the award ceremony.

---

[70]   K. Mayer, M. E. M. Tolbert, R. Wellum, S. Deron, R. E. Perrin, and B. Mitterrand, "Preparing for the Future Today," *Journal of Nuclear Materials Management*, Spring 1999, ages 4 and 18; R. Wellum, J. Tushingham, and M. E. M. Tolbert, "International Safeguards V – International Certified and SI Traceable: The Ultimate Aim for Reference Materials II – Panel Discussion," Fall 1999, *Journal of Nuclear Materials Management*, Vol. XXVIII (No. 1), pages 27-28; M. E. M. Tolbert, "Organization and Implementation of the Full-Day Session on Reference Materials, in Session H: International Safeguards IV – International Certified and SI Traceable: The Ultimate Aim for Reference Materials I," INMM 40th Annual Meeting on CD ROM, July 1999; and D. Donohue, M. E. M. Tolbert, and P. De Bievrè, "Deliberations on Safeguards Measurement Uncertainty," *Journal of Nuclear Materials Management*, Vol. XXIX (No. 2), Winter 2001, pages 27-30.

Here I am with Joseph S. Mahaley who was then the director of the Office of Security/U.S. Department of Energy, on the occasion of my receipt of the Women of Color in Government and Defense Technology Award for Managerial Leadership in Government

My success in heightening and strengthening NBL's credibility within the nuclear community and in the day-to-day management of NBL was recognized at the highest levels within the U.S. Department of Energy. During my tenure as NBL director, as well as director of DEP, I had the honor of meeting and working with three secretaries of energy: The Honorable Hazel O'Leary, The Honorable Bill Richardson, and The Honorable Federico F. Peña.

Here I am in the photograph with The Honorable Federico Fabian Peña (top center)—8th U.S. Secretary of Energy, and Ms. Cherri Langenfeld who was then the manager of the Chicago Operations/DOE.

Here I am with The Honorable Hazel R. O'Leary (left of me in photograph)—7th U.S. Secretary of Energy.

Here I am with The Honorable William Blaine "Bill" Richardson (right)—9th U.S. Secretary of Energy. Dr. Martha Krebs (on the far left) of DOE, Mr. Marvin E. Gunn, Jr. (second from the left)—DOE's Chicago Operations Manager, and the Mayor (third from the left) of Washington, DC, are also shown in the photograph.

Return to the National Science Foundation

I was extremely busy both at work and at home while serving as director of NBL. I took time to assist my son, Lawson, now divorced, who lived in my condominium in Alexandria, Virginia, with his sons. I also continued to take care of Mama Cook, who lived in an assisted-living home in northern Virginia. I wanted to be closer to both. So I began making plans for my departure from NBL and Chicago.

I received confirmation of an appointment to the position of senior advisor at the National Science Foundation in Arlington, Virginia, a permanent position in the Senior Executive Service (SES)—the highest management rank of the federal government. I put my Chicago condominium on the market and identified a moving company to pack up and store my things.

The transition from Illinois to Virginia took place late in 2002. The drive to Virginia was made easy by my nephew, James Washington Mayo, who accompanied me on the trip. It was a tense in the Washington, DC, metropolitan area, as a sniper was on the loose, shooting people at random. The area was locked down and wary. This made house hunting difficult. I stayed for a while in a hotel in Alexandria, Virginia. I could not wait to get settled in a house with a yard for flowers and shrubbery and a place for my grandsons to play.

When I found and purchased a house in a very good neighborhood, my son and two grandsons moved in along with me, so that I could sell my Alexandria condominium. The market was good for selling and buying homes, and the process went quickly.

On September 22, 2002, I officially began my tenure as senior advisor in NSF's Office of Integrative Activities (OIA). OIA reported directly to the NSF director and performed activities that required coordination across multiple offices within the agency. Initially, my primary responsibility was to promote efforts to increase the participation of underrepresented minority groups, women, and persons with disabilities in science and engineering research and education.

To accomplish the objectives of my position, I served as NSF's executive liaison to the congressionally mandated, national Committee on Equal Opportunities in Science and Engineering (CEOSE). CEOSE focuses on policies and programs to encourage participation by women, underrepresented minorities, and persons with disabilities in science, technology, engineering, and mathematics (STEM).

Eventually, my accomplishments would include a leadership role in the publication of four CEOSE biennial reports to Congress plus a special congressionally mandated report.[71],[72] Before my work began in full, I had to be sworn in as a member of the SES. This was taken care of expeditiously by the Federal Executive Institute of the U.S. Office of Personnel Management (OPM). Judge R. J. Leon served as the official for the swearing-in ceremony.

Me and The Honorable R. J. Leon at my SES
swearing-in ceremony in 2002

---

[71] Science and Engineering Equal Opportunities Act, 42 U.S.C. § 1885(c) Committee on Equal Opportunities in Science and Engineering.

[72] Each "CEOSE Biennial Report to Congress" for 2003-2004, 2005-2006, 2007-2008, and 2009-2010, plus "The 1994-2003 Decennial Report to Congress" were prepared under the guidance of Dr. Margaret E. M. Tolbert who was then CEOSE Executive Liaison.

After being sworn in as a senior executive, I began functioning fully in my NSF position. I enjoyed interacting with members of CEOSE. Managing this committee was both challenging and rewarding. Holding dialogue with officials at NSF and other federal agencies was stimulating. I enjoyed holding discussions with them on topics of mutual interest. CEOSE members and I had similar concerns about issues pertinent to gender and racial diversity and the low representation in STEM fields of women, underrepresented minorities, and persons with disabilities.

I was fortunate to have Dr. Nathaniel Pitts, the director of OIA, as my supervisor as well as mentor. He was knowledgeable about NSF policies and programs, and he shared information freely as he guided me along the path of success at NSF. He respected the capabilities of all of his staff members and always took the time to provide guidance when needed. In particular, he listened to and respected my ideas and allowed me to fully employ my skills and capabilities in managing the committee.

Also, he realized quickly that I was a self-starter and a diligent worker.

As I was getting started with my original assignment, Dr. Pitts assigned me a second major responsibility: managing the nationwide competition for the multi-million-dollar Science and Technology Centers (STC) Program. This is a program that was established in 1987, and my assignment was to take charge of the competition for which preparations had to begin in 2003. The centers are national showcases, addressing select, high-level national needs with innovative research and development strongly tied to relevant education for future scientists and engineers.

The centers are a source of great pride for NSF, consisting of dozens of scientific hubs across the nation in which professionals from multiple disciplines work together on specific areas of research. The centers are always selected for federal funding via a competitive review of proposals. The proposals are submitted by teams of researchers who have novel ideas about how to solve particular problems, and are reviewed by peers who conduct similar types of research.

I was responsible for developing and implementing the procedure to be used for the competition. With two major concurrent assignments, I felt that I had been thrown into the "briar patch." But by this time in my life and career, I was immune to thorns. Multi-tasking was something I was good at, and it was good for me. And, in both endeavors, I received outstanding support from NSF staff members and contractors.[73]

In organizing the competition for new STCs, I included in the criteria the requirement that each center's staff would have training in strategic planning and program implementation. Also, I ensured that each center would strive for diversity in its staffs and that education would be part of its program, whether the center's research focus was in science, technology, engineering, or mathematics or a combination of these.

Although the workload was heavy and the assignments were tough, I prevailed. In recognition, Dr. Pitts, my first and my longest serving supervisor at NSF, wrote the following about my performance:

Dr. Margaret Tolbert and the Office of Integrative Activities, National Science Foundation

"Dr. Margaret E. M. Tolbert was working in the Education and Human Resources Directorate at the National Science Foundation (NSF) as a rotating program manager when I first became knowledgeable of her talents. At the time, she was directing the Research Improvement in Minority Institutions Program. (This would have been about 1990-1993). I actually got to know her credentials through an internal review panel. I had been assigned to help evaluate the credentials/applications of candidates for a division director position in the Education and Human Resources Resources Directorate, and Dr. Tolbert was one

---

[73]   Dr. Walter V. Collier, president of C&A Technologies, Inc., and his staff members served as a consultant group for the six STCs, NSF staff involved with the six STCs, and CEOSE; and later Ms. Corinda Davis, president of Beyond The Bottom Line, Inc., and her staff provided consulting service for CEOSE.

of the candidates. I thought, on paper, she was the best candidate, but I was out-voted. Later, she came to talk with me before leaving the NSF on her way to a new position at Argonne National Lab. While at Argonne, she and I had a few lunches when she came to Washington, DC, on business. It was during one of those lunches that I realized that she really wanted to be in Washington because of family, basically her two grandsons. So, knowing her abilities and special interests, I started paying attention to positions opening up at NSF that might fit her talents.

"One day Joe Bordogna, then deputy director of NSF, came into my office with a special request. He wanted me, or my office, to take over the oversight and staff support of CEOSE, the Committee on Equal Opportunities in Science and Engineering. This is a Congressionally-mandated committee that reports annually to Congress. CEOSE is composed primarily of high-level university and college faculty members recommended by the NSF director. Its main function is to make recommendations to the NSF and Congress about ways to improve the involvement of women, underrepresented minorities, and persons with disabilities in science and engineering research and education at NSF. There are other such committees in many other U.S. Government departments. NSF, however, always had a leadership role in these types of activities (i.e., educating Americans in science and engineering) across the government. I decided that Dr. Tolbert, with her background, would be perfect to oversee CEOSE. So, she was recruited and selected to be a senior advisor to the Office of Integrative Activities (OIA). Her initial, main function was to become the 'lead' in the oversight of CEOSE. Dr. Tolbert was hired by the NSF, brought into the Senior Executive Service, and started this position in September 2002.

"Her management of CEOSE required her to be the Executive Secretary and the NSF Executive Liaison to the committee. And, while on paper she reported to the director of OIA, in practice she reported to the Office of the Director of NSF for this particular function. Within the Office of the Director, she normally held discussions with the deputy director of NSF. But often the NSF director needed to be involved in her discussions. Dr. Tolbert, being a senior scientist and manager, had no trouble, in principle, holding discussions with the only two political appointees in the NSF (the NSF director and deputy). She was confident, assertive, impeccably dressed, and had no organizational or other issues with people who may have considered themselves senior to her. Her documentation was always extremely thorough, and that always satisfies scientists and engineers. However, a major issue that arose was the fact that this CEOSE management function had originally resided with the Office of the General Counsel, and there were principals remaining within that organization that still wanted to be involved in the decision-making regarding the management of CEOSE. Therefore, Dr. Tolbert had to deal with that element for some time.

"Early in her tenure as Executive Liaison to CEOSE, she and I had discussions on things that 'might' be done with CEOSE, but we cautioned each other that the Foundation leadership may not be ready to accept 'radical' changes or directives coming from CEOSE. So, initially I tried to get her into contact with some political forces outside the NSF that could provide her with political cover, should she need it in the future.

"Dr. Kathie Olsen was the associate director for science, in the Office of Science and Technology Policy of the White House. She was willing to entertain the CEOSE issues, particularly those dealing with women, and she held one of the FIRST meetings of representatives of most federal government departments that have committees similar to CEOSE. There were about 15 to 20 committees represented in this meeting, discussing their functions and processes inside their agencies. The meeting took place in the White House conference center. It was quite successful from the White House perspective.

"Dr. Tolbert had a major role in the planning and implementation of the meeting with representatives of multiple federal agencies. She followed up that meeting with Congressional staffers coming to the CEOSE meetings and holding discussions with the CEOSE membership. She, along with other members of CEOSE, was able to invite other high-ranking officials and university administrators to their meetings in order to pursue their agenda.

"After the first few meetings, the chair of CEOSE came to visit with me and to tell me what an excellent addition Dr. Tolbert had been, and that her style was exactly what CEOSE needed in order to become more functional and have more impact. The CEOSE members, all senior scientists and accomplished faculty in their own right from all over the country, also had only complimentary things to say about Dr. Tolbert's management style.

"Dr. Tolbert always had the chair and co-chair of CEOSE meet with the NSF director and/or deputy director in order for them to explain the CEOSE Annual Report to Congress. This meeting was always preceded by the NSF director or deputy attending one of the CEOSE working meetings for negotiation purposes. The committee membership was always pleased and satisfied by these interactions and could see that Dr. Tolbert was making a difference in their deliberations and effectiveness.

"After Dr. Tolbert had managed CEOSE for at least a year and had overseen the production of the CEOSE Annual Report to Congress, she and I were having follow-up discussions. At that time, OIA was missing a senior staff member to oversee the Science and Technology Centers:

Integrative Partnerships Program (STC) competition. When I mentioned this to Dr. Tolbert, she casually volunteered to run that competition. At that point, she seemed to have total control of the CEOSE management issues and was looking for more scientific issues in which to become involved. I thought about it for a bit, knowing that this was a major time commitment, and then accepted her initiative to be responsible for overseeing this next STC competition.

"The STC Program is a major cross-Foundation program inside the NSF. It is a multidisciplinary program, and all directorates are involved in the review, selection, and management of chosen STCs. Basically, these centers are chosen for their proposed: 1) cutting-edge research agenda; 2) agenda for the integration of research and education; 3) knowledge and/or technology transfer agenda; 4) agenda for educating Americans, especially women and underrepresented minorities; and finally 5) management plan. Each center received about $4-5 million per year for no more than 10 years, after successful annual reviews. Usually, about 260 preliminary proposals are submitted to this competition; and after Foundation-wide review, about 50 are selected to submit full proposals. After review of this set, about 12-16 are selected for additional review and site visits. From this final set, a Blue Ribbon Panel selects the new 'class' of STCs. Usually, about six new centers are selected after each competition, and the centers represent all areas of science from biology to physics to geology to engineering. An STC competition is held about every three years, but the NSF budget dictates the frequency. This is a very political competition within the NSF because each research directorate or division wants to get a center, hopefully in their most exciting, new research areas. Also, since the money for these centers is held in the Office of the Director (OIA, specifically) until the centers are selected, these funds are viewed as additional money for a research division or directorate. This raises the political stakes even higher.

"Although, as with most competitions of this magnitude, there are hiccups along the way, Dr. Tolbert managed this competition without any major issues. Of course, she had help from a very capable OIA staff, which had held these competitions in the past.

However, Dr. Tolbert did not complain even when the many political issues came to the fore during this competition.

"Still, there was one major political issue that upset everyone within the NSF community regarding this competition. After the Blue Ribbon Panel had made its selection of six new centers, the new NSF director, Dr. Arden Bement, decided that he only wanted to award three centers in that fiscal year and would consider awarding three new centers in the following fiscal year. He was looking for money for his new initiative, cyberinfrastructure, and he could get some from the funds kept in OIA, which was an Office of the Director. These specific funds were in OIA for the purpose of funding the new class of STCs.

Ultimately, two STCs were funded initially. So, Dr. Tolbert was stuck with the responsibility of dealing with the research community regarding this reduction of centers and funding. She handled this with style. And the next four STCs were funded early the following year. But now, Dr. Tolbert had to deal with managing six centers, established at very different times, within a program of ongoing, mature centers. The management of this situation was awkward at best. But once again, Dr. Tolbert handled it gracefully.

"Because this STC Program was a highly visible program, OIA reported separately to Congress on the achievements coming from this program. This program was also annually audited by the Office of the Inspector General. Therefore, annual evaluations were held with STCs reporting on various metrics. Those metrics most properly were determined by the original evaluation criteria upon which the centers were chosen. This made the evaluations straightforward with no surprises. Dr. Tolbert was responsible for ensuring the centers activated a strategic planning exercise and were knowledgeable about the ensuing annual evaluations. She hired and managed contractors when possible to support her activities.

"The combination of managing CEOSE and a class of STC centers allowed Dr. Tolbert a unique vantage point from which to view the NSF. She had the ability to observe and understand more fully how high-profile programs, like the STC Program, interact with the Foundation-wide policies, such as those recommended by CEOSE. And, on the specific issue of women and underrepresented minorities, she had a direct view regarding how these programs progressed, and she assessed their progress focused on inclusion of these groups in the research and education enterprise.

"The STCs Dr. Tolbert oversaw, managed, and legally established were the: 1) Center for Coastal Margin Observation and Prediction; 2) Center for Layered Polymeric Systems; 3) Center for Microbial Oceanography; 4) Center for Multi-scale Modeling of Atmospheric Processes; 5) Center for Remote Sensing of Ice Sheets; and 6) Team for Research in Ubiquitous Secure Technology. Each of these had multiple partners. Overseeing these centers required Dr. Tolbert to do a great deal of traveling across the country for an assortment of meetings, evaluations and reviews, and team-building sessions required by the STC Program. Dr. Tolbert was exceedingly efficient and very skilled at organizing documentation that would be useful for anyone inquiring about processes and actions as a result of center evaluations and reviews. This skill came in handy for the many and varied inquiries that resulted, because of the political nature of this program and because of the amount of money related to the STC Program and each STC.

Dr. Pitts' words are gratefully acknowledged and appreciated. His guidance and support throughout my NSF years were superior. With his guidance and support, I was able to accomplish a great deal.

As I began preparing for the STC competition that started in June 2003, personal responsibilities tugged on my time. While handling my personal responsibilities, I worked overtime at NSF to keep on schedule. There were guidelines that had to be written for various aspects of the program, for which the annual budget was estimated to be a minimum of $20 million. The management of the program had to be coordinated with NSF personnel. The paperwork was seemingly unlimited, and the calls endless: did I have a minute to spare? I did not.

I knew that I had to better organize my personal responsibilities to prevent overload. Mama Cook's health had continued to deteriorate. I moved her into my home for her comfort and convenience, and for economic reasons. I invited Mary Lee, my sister, to serve as her paid live-in caregiver. Mama Cook died on November 13, 2003. She had been a long-time resident of Suffolk, Virginia; a long-time survivor of Alzheimer's disease; and was thought to be among the longest living breast-cancer survivors. At the time of her death at age 88, her son, Alfred, lived in California, so I organized her funeral in Suffolk and burial next to her husband, Daddy Cook, at the Southview Cemetery in Franklin, Virginia. Rest in peace, Mama and Daddy Cook.

After Mama Cook's death, my sister stayed in my home for several years, along with Rod, her son, who still lives with me. Outside of my home, I took care not to reveal to anyone except persons very close to me how heavy a weight I was carrying as I addressed my family responsibilities. During my hours at work, I set aside thoughts of home.

At work, I was pleased to be part of an organization whose research endeavors were of national importance and would eventually benefit most Americans. I wanted to give it the full complement of my time and expertise.

As indicated by Dr. Pitts, each of the six STCs selected in the competition that I oversaw was led by a major U.S. research institution. Each had multiple partner institutions that worked toward common goals in research as well as STEM education. These six winning STCs and their current directors are listed below, with the lead and current partner institutions.[74]

 **Center for Coastal Margin Observation & Prediction**

Lead Institution: Oregon Health and Science University
CMOP Partner Institutions: Oregon Health and Science University / Oregon State University / University of Washington / Portland State University / Columbia River Inter-Tribal Fish Commission / National Oceanic and Atmospheric Administration / Saturday Academy / Translume, Inc. / United States Geological Survey / Wet Labs. Inc.

•

---

[74]   More information on these STCs is available on their websites, as well as that of the NSF Office of International and Integrative Activities at www.nsf. gov/od/iia/programs/stc. Logos are being used with the permission of the STC directors.

 **Center for Layered Polymeric Systems**

Website: www.clips.case.edu

Center Director: Dr. Eric Baer

Lead Institution: Case Western Reserve University

CLiPS Partner Institutions: Case Western Reserve University / Naval Research Laboratory / University of Southern Mississippi / University of Texas at Austin / Northwestern University / Kent State University / Cleveland Metropolitan School District / Fisk University; **CLiPS Affiliates:** Bowie State University / Central State University / Kentucky State University / Rose-Hulman Institute of Technology / Youngstown State University / West Virginia State University / Winston-Salem State University

•

 **Center for Microbial Oceanography**

Website: www.cmore.soest.hawaii.edu **Center Director:** Dr. David M. Karl

Lead Institution: University of Hawaii

C-MORE Partner Institutions: University of Hawaii at Manoa / Massachusetts Institute of Technology / Woods Hole Oceanographic Institution / Monterey Bay Aquarium Research Institute / University of California, Santa Cruz / Oregon State University / Columbia University

•

Center for Multi-Scale Modeling of Atmospheric Processes

Website: www.cmmap.colostate.edu
Center Director: Dr. David A. Randall
Lead Institution: Colorado State University
CMMAP Partner Institutions: Colorado State University / Colorado College / George Mason University / National Center for Atmospheric Research / Scripps Institute of Oceanography / Stony Brook University / University of Colorado / University of Utah / University of Washington / University of California at Berkeley / University of Corporation for Atmospheric Research / University California, San Diego

●

Center for Remote Sensing of Ice Sheets

Website: www.cresis.ku.edu
Center Director: Dr. S. Prasad Gogineni
Lead Institution: University of Kansas
CReSIS Partner Institutions: University of Kansas / Elizabeth City State University / Indiana University / Pennsylvania State University / University of Washington / Los Alamos National Laboratory / ADMI (Association of Computer/Information Sciences and Engineering Departments at Minority Institutions) / Centre for Ice and Climate, Niels Bohr Institute, University of Copenhagen / Centre for Polar Observations & Modeling (CPOM) / Indian Institute of Technology, Kanpur / NASA Goddard Space Flight Center / NASA Jet Propulsion Laboratory / The Kansas City Plant (NNSA and Honeywell FM&T) / University of Magallanes

●

 **Team for Research in Ubiquitous Secure Technology**

Website: www.trust.eecs.berkeley.edu
Center Director: Dr. S. Shankar Sastry
Lead Institution: University of California at Berkeley
TRUST Partner Institutions: University of California at Berkeley / Carnegie Mellon University / Cornell University / San José State University / Stanford University / Vanderbilt University; **TRUST Industrial Partners**: BT / Cisco Systems / DoCoMo USA Labs / EADS / ESCHER Research Institute / Hewlett Packard / IBM / Intel / Microsoft / Oak Ridge National Laboratory / Pirelli / Qualcomm / Selex Sistemi Integrati / Sun Microsystems / Symantec / Tata Consultancy Services / Telecom Italia / United Technologies

The review and selection process for these STCs was lengthy and detailed. After managing the review and selection processes, I assumed my role as the NSF's lead manager with oversight for these six STCs. In that role, I oversaw the centers, ensuring that goals and objectives were met, that strategic and implementation plans were used and continuously updated, and that management and staffing were handled in accordance with NSF guidelines. I joined with each NSF scientific/engineering expert in leading annual site visits at his/her assigned center. An NSF education expert was included as a member of each NSF team. Site visits were conducted by outside experts in the field(s) of research, management, and education at each STC. With oversight by me, the NSF and external experts worked together throughout my involvement with the STCs.

The teams conducting these site visits were diverse in race and ethnicity as well as in professional expertise. After reports on the site visits were prepared and reviewed, they were submitted to the NSF director to approve the continuation of funding or close the unsuccessful center(s).

Fortunately, all six centers are making noteworthy contributions to society, and they are addressing planned goals and objectives.

Details are available on the website of each center. Additionally, the NSF website contains details on the overall program, as well as these centers. In 2007, a publication titled "Profiles in Team Science" was released. It contains substantive information on these centers.[75] The six centers were continuing to operate and thrive when this book was written, and each center director continues to express appreciation for the support that I provided while employed at NSF.

Fortunately, my NSF responsibilities did not inhibit my involvement in scientific organizations. As always, I found a few hours here and there to participate in meetings, conferences, and seminars, sometimes serving as guest speaker or moderator of a conference session.[76] I was particularly pleased to speak at conferences

---

[75]   Deborah Illman, "Profiles in Team Science," University of Washington (NSF Grant #0609451), pages 48-71, 2007 Edition.

[76]   Dr. Margaret E. M. Tolbert served as invited speaker at the following (selected list): Alpha Chi National Honor Society Initiation Ceremony at Talladega College in Talladega, Alabama (2011); Women's Leadership Symposium hosted by NOBCChE in Atlanta, Georgia (2010); Colorado-AMP Meeting hosted by the Ute Indian Tribe (2009); program for graduate students and faculty members at the University of Alabama at Birmingham in Birmingham, Alabama (2008); the Quality Education for Minorities Network Workshop in Washington, DC (2008); Brookhaven National Laboratory – Historically Black Colleges and Universities Consortium (2008); Minority Graduate Student Program at the University of Alabama at Huntsville in Huntsville, Alabama (2007); Faculty Program at Brown University in Providence, RI (2007); Carver Convocation at Tuskegee University (2007); Conference at the Mississippi E-Center/Jackson State University in Jackson, Mississippi (2006); Honors Convocation at Alabama State University (2006); NSF Program at the University of Maryland in College Park (2006); NRCEN Conference at the University of Michigan in Ann Arbor, Michigan (2006); Programs at Tuskegee University in Tuskegee, Alabama (2006); Black History Month Program at Texas Tech University Health Sciences Center in Lubbock, Texas (2005); and Black History Month Program at the Albuquerque Operations Office/U.S. Department of Energy in Albuquerque, New Mexico (2001). Invited group moderator at the Purdue University conference titled "Women in Academia: Institutional Change to Enhance Success," which was held in West Lafayette, Indiana, on May 16-18, 2005, and in meetings with members of various organizations and national committees (e.g., AAAS,

and write about women—especially minority women—in STEM fields, as well as broadening the participation of minorities in those fields. With the limited amount of free time that I had, I wrote and published an article on the scientific contributions of a Chemical Heritage Foundation scholar.[77] My plan is to publish more articles on minority women in STEM.

Another important milestone for me was an invitation from the Chemical Heritage Foundation scholar who was the subject of the article I published in 2008. She requested to interview me for an oral history and content for a book to be published as part of the Chemical Heritage Foundation Oral History Program. I agreed to participate in the video-recorded interview on August 13, 2009.[78] The NSF media-relations staff facilitated our use of an NSF recording studio. During the interview, I spoke about all aspects of my work. In doing so, I incorporated the contents of a statement about my contributions in research. That statement had been provided in 2005 by Dr. John Fain, my former research professor from Brown University. His thoughts on that topic follow:[79]

ACS, NAS/COSPUP, NRCEN, INMM, and CEOSE). I organized and implemented the AAAS Workshop on "Broadening Participation in the Science and Engineering Workforce," held in Washington, DC (2005). Panelists consisted of the chair of the National Science Board, chair of CEOSE, and officials from NSF.

[77] Margaret E. M. Tolbert, "Jeannette Elizabeth Brown," African American National Biography, Vol. 1, Editors in Chief: Henry Louis Gates, Jr. and Evelyn Brooks Higginbotham, Oxford University Press, 2008, pages 617-619.

[78] Margaret E. M. Tolbert, interview by Jeannette E. Brown at the National Science Foundation, Arlington, Virginia, August 13, 2009 (Philadelphia: Chemical Heritage Foundation, Oral History Transcript #0648); first printing of Margaret E. M. Tolbert: Oral History by the Chemical Heritage Foundation, January 24, 2011.

[79] Email message dated February 9, 2005, from Dr. John N. Fain to Dr. Margaret E. M. Tolbert.

"The studies done by Margaret E. M. Tolbert for her doctoral dissertation under my supervision at Brown University were among the very first studies in signal transduction to point out that there are rapid effects of ligands [hormones] that did not involve RNA or protein synthesis and occur by some intracellular messenger other than cyclic AMP. At that time cyclic AMP had only recently been discovered and all rapid effects of hormones not involving gene transcription were attributed to this messenger.

"Later when Margaret came back for a sabbatical at Brown, she demonstrated that the so-called alpha effects of catecholamines involve phosphoinositide breakdown and an elevation of intracellular ionic calcium. Subsequent work has established that the breakdown of phosphatidyinositol 4,5-bisphosphate gives rise to diacylglycerol and inositol 1,4,5-trisphosphate and the latter open calcium channels to release bound intracellular stores of calcium. This pathway is now well accepted, and it is recognized that there are many intracellular messengers in addition to cyclic AMP."

--John N. Fain, PhD

In thinking over my career for the purposes of the interview, I thought that my time spent conducting research was worthwhile. The same is true of the time that I spent as a university administrator, faculty member, program manager, proposal reviewer, director of a nuclear analytical chemistry laboratory, and director of a major education division of a national laboratory. Additionally, it was an honor to be closely aligned with individuals who were passionate about alleviating injustices that result in the low representation of minorities, women, and persons with disabilities in STEM fields. In most positions that I have held, I addressed issues pertinent to that topic.

In 2011, as I was nearing my retirement date, I had an "earth-shaking" experience that, fittingly, reminded me of the importance of scientific research. On August 23, which was a beautiful day, I was eating lunch in a restaurant near NSF in Arlington, Virginia, when the building began to shake violently.

With much urgency, a waiter asked everyone to gather under an archway in the restaurant until the violent shaking stopped. Immediately thereafter, the buildings in the area, including NSF, were temporarily evacuated. When it was safe to enter the NSF building, employees were encouraged to get their personal items and go home. Needless to say, traffic moved slowly that day. We also experienced several aftershocks.

I had experienced one of the very few recorded earthquakes in that region—my first. Fortunately, there was no damage at my home or to the NSF building, except anxiety.

It was, perhaps, a fitting way to end my service to the nation, given the number of times that I had attempted to be a "mover and shaker" in order to accomplish my goals.

Upon my retirement from the NSF, several former and present chairs of CEOSE presented a plaque to me with the following inscription:

Honoring
Dr. Margaret E. M. Tolbert

In recognition of ten years of devoted and professional service and of your generous gift of pragmatic wisdom and guidance to the NSF Committee on Equal Opportunities in Science and Engineering (CEOSE), we former Chairs of the Committee give you our deepest appreciation, respect, and affection.

Wesley L. Harris	**Beverly Hartline**	**Richard E. Ladner**
Robert Lichter	**Theresa Maldonado**	**Samuel L. Myers, Jr.**
Indira Nair	**Willie Pearson**	**Muriel Poston**

A few months before retiring from NSF, I had been nominated for the position of Tuskegee University president. During preparation for the competition, I met with several individuals who had a wealth of information to share with me about the role of a university president.

As the competition unfolded, I was interviewed twice. The competition was complicated, and I was well along in completing the process of retiring from NSF. When the first competition for the position of Tuskegee University president stopped abruptly, I chose not to participate when it was begun again. Instead, I went on to enjoy my December 31, 2011 retirement, and I am most pleased with my decision.

Part Four

Living in the Here and Now

T he poet Langston Hughes wrote "Well...I'll tell you: Life for me ain't been no crystal stair."[80] I certainly could say that about my life.

Nevertheless, I have made the best of it.

For the first 19 years of my life, I lived in the rural section of Suffolk designated for Colored people. Over time, the name of my race changed from Negro to Colored American to Black to Afro-American. Now, my race is generally referred to as African American.

Since I was born in Suffolk, Virginia, I refer to myself as a Suffolkian—an African-American Suffolkian. Times have changed there. From its roots as a small agricultural community of 10,000, Suffolk has grown to a city of more than 80,000,[81] with more than 1,500 employers[82] and miles of lakefront development. It boasts of being urban, suburban, and rural simultaneously.

Likewise, I have grown and changed, and I have become an amalgamation of all my choices and experiences. My life now is very different—socially, physically, economically, and emotionally—from that of my early years while living in the city in which I was born.

Over the years I have bought, lived in, and sold nine different homes in five different states, usually making a good profit on the sales. During my employment history, my income increased from less than three dollars per week when I was a child to an annual six-figure salary before retirement.

I have traveled a great deal in the United States and in foreign countries, learning about other cultures, hearing other languages, and enjoying different food. According to Maya Angelou, "It is necessary, especially for Americans, to see other lands and experience other cultures."[83] Regardless of where I am, I feel blessed to be able to greet each day with joy.

---

[80] Onwuchekwa Jemie, "Or Does It Explode?" page 137.

[81] City Profile & Statistical Digest FY 2012-2013, City of Suffolk, Virginia.

[82] Virginia L. "Jinks" Babey, Editor, *Discover Suffolk 2009*.

[83] Maya Angelou, <u>Wouldn't Take Nothing for My Journey Now</u>, Bantam Books/published by arrangement with Random House, Inc., New York, 1994, page 11.

Whenever trouble came my way, I have landed on my feet with clarity of thought and gratefulness for survival. I made choices that served me well. I pray daily, giving thanks for life and family, and I attend St. Augustine Catholic Church in Washington, DC.

Some may think that I am resting on my laurels since my retirement at the end of 2011, but that is not totally true. I say to you: this Suffolkian has been through some rough times and some good times, and they did not end with my retirement.

Although I have enjoyed working in my various positions, traveling, and living in different areas, my current focus is on immediate family members. My plan is to continue assisting them in accomplishing more in their lives, especially in reference to completing formal education and gaining upward mobility—opportunities that came to mean so much to me over my lifetime.

My son is comfortable with the choices he has made. And, as with most grandmothers, my grandchildren mean the world to me. In 2013, my older grandson lost his leg in a car accident. He is doing well despite the injury, and he is continuing his high-school education. He will graduate from high school in 2015 and begin his college/university education. My second grandson is attending school and participating in sports. I have been blessed with the birth of a third grandchild, a girl, who is learning fast and growing as fast as a weed. Oh my goodness, I feel blessed!

Recently, I joined my siblings in establishing a program of monetary awards and recognition for the educational successes of descendants of Grandma Fannie and Granddaddy Benjamin Mayo. I serve as administrator of the program. On July 26, 2014, two of my nieces (Rachel M. Mayo Winston and Martha D. Mayo) and two of my nephews (David B. Mayo and Quentin R. Mayo) were recipients of awards through this program. David B. Mayo received his doctorate degree in aerospace science and engineering in 2014, thereby becoming the third member of my family to earn a doctorate degree. Hopefully, the other three that received Mayo Education Fund Awards will continue their formal education and receive doctorate degrees in their chosen fields of computer science/

computer engineering, nursing, and professional health sciences. Also, it is hoped that they will help to encourage other family members to earn formal education degrees.

Additionally, I am addressing items on my bucket list. Periodically, I sponsor Mayo family reunions, named the Mayo Family Pilgrimages. When time permits, I conduct research on the history of my family.

In addition to family activity, I have not lost touch with the academic community. I informally recruit individuals to attend colleges and universities, and I continue to serve as mentor for several graduate students. I keep in touch with some of my former classmates from Tuskegee University and Brown University, former members of CEOSE, former co-workers, my former Brown University research advisor, some of my former supervisors, and individuals for whom I serve or have served as mentor. Participating in these and other activities keeps me busy, and the interactions are refreshing.

Thanks to one of my former NSF co-workers, I am on the invitation lists for Congressional events, such as public forums or panel discussions held by Congresswoman Eddie Bernice Johnson and Congressman John Robert Lewis. The subjects discussed at these events are often ones that are meaningful to me, such as STEM education, racial equality, retirement security, and economic development.

All of these activities and so much more keep me extremely busy as I continue to climb the ladder of life and help others to rise. Keeping active in meaningful ways is important to me. Occasionally, luncheon meetings with former NSF co-workers, and visits and conversations with friends and former associates, from near and far, are very enjoyable. Regular interactions with my neighbors give me a sense of being a part of a thriving community.

Photographs of Me at Various Stages of My Life

As life continues for this Suffolkian, Margaret Ellen Mayo Tolbert, it is not entirely calm, or without obstacles; but overall, it is good.

It took me a long time to get to this point, and I firmly believe that it was not just fate, but choice, that led me to accomplish so much in the face of such overwhelming odds. I feel blessed to have been given the chance to travel this path and to have been part of a growing and changing family, a supportive circle of friends and associates, a number of important organizations, and several active communities.

In my view, that is the definition of success.

Appendix 1
My Family

As described throughout this book, I have five siblings. I would like for you to meet them.

Left to Right: Audrey Mae, Lee Vania, Me (Margaret), Benjamin, Eleanor, and Mary Lee in the late 1980s on the occasion of a family reunion held in Tuskegee, Alabama

Left to Right: Lee Vania, Me (Margaret), Benjamin, and Eleanor in 2013 in Courtland, Virginia

Mary Lee in 2013 in Washington, DC

My oldest sister, Audrey Mae Mayo Holley, was born in Suffolk, Virginia. We lovingly call her Augie Mae. She and her husband had one son, Roy Lee Holley. She lived in New York in the 1960s and migrated to Providence, Rhode Island, in 1971. She liked Providence so much that she remained there for 22 years.

At one point in her life, Audrey Mae had the misfortune of being hit by a car, but that did not change her zest for life. She was short and bow-legged, and she was known for her big bright eyes. Having never completed elementary school, she was able to handle employment in a major jewelry factory and a restaurant. She was employed briefly as a custodian at Brown University.

When she began spending a great deal of time at home, she became a day-care provider for several children in her community. She had a special friend, David "Dave" Lawrence, who lived with her until her death. In her later years, Audrey Mae suffered from arteriosclerotic heart disease, hypertension, and seizures. She died in her sleep in 1993, in Providence, Rhode Island, and she is buried in Oaklawn Cemetery in that city. Her son died in 2005.

My second sister, Elder Lee Vania Mayo Williams, was pleasantly known as Frenchie. She was quite a migratory person, a title she earned since she often moves from place to place. She was married to Andrew Lee "Bay" Williams, who died of a military-related wound in 1958. She has one daughter, Shaneen Williams Lipscomb, who gave her three grandchildren, and her adult grandchildren have given her great-grandchildren.

In her young adult years, Lee Vania worked as a caregiver for children in Providence, Rhode Island. She was licensed to preach the gospel in 1985, and she was ordained to "The Christian Ministry" in 1992. Lee Vania was an Elder in her church in Providence, Rhode Island where she lived just prior to moving to Virginia in 2015.

She resembles Shirley Caesar and her singing voice was reminiscent of Shirley's, prior to Lee Vania having an operation to remove an aneurism from the top of her head. During her singing period, she performed in churches in Virginia, Alabama, and several New England states. Previously, Lee Vania spent a great deal of her time in church and reading religious literature. As her health continues to decline, living alone is not an option for her; therefore, I serve as her caregiver in my home.

Jessie Benjamin Mayo, Sr., is known as Benjamin. He was educated in Suffolk, Virginia, and he worked for Kurtwizer Hardware Store in Suffolk on Saturdays during his high-school years. He also did odd jobs for Mama and Daddy Cook, and he spent a summer working at the Sally Walker's White Horse Lodge and Paradise Resort in Cuddybackville, New York. After graduating from high school, he worked full-time at the previously named hardware store.

During the time of the draft, Benjamin volunteered to enlist in the U.S. Army and served in the Vietnam War, Desert Storm, and Desert Shield, and in the Reserves. Before retiring from the Army, he received numerous medals, ribbons, and accolades for his contributions to our country.

After marrying Conchita Denise Johnson of Tuskegee, Benjamin worked in Opelika, Alabama, and later he owned a lawn-care business in Tuskegee, Alabama. He and Conchita have several children: Chiquita Nico (Nikki) Mayo-Murray, David Benjamin Mayo, Rachel Margaretta Mayo Winston, Clifton Jessie Mayo, Quentin Reuben Mayo, and Martha Denise Mayo. He is the only member of the family that named some of his children after our parents. Some of Benjamin and Conchita's children have earned or are earning college degrees in aerospace science engineering, nursing, physical education, and computer science.

Benjamin had one son from a previous marriage, Jessie Benjamin Mayo, Jr., who earned his doctorate degree in Materials Science and Mechanical Engineering at Tuskegee University in 2010. In 2013, my nephew Jessie died of kidney failure and heart disease. Additionally, Benjamin claims the daughter, Sheila Harrison Lyons, of his first wife as his own. Benjamin has several grandchildren and great grandchildren. Although Benjamin suffers from military-related health issues, he still finds time to interact with his family members.

Eleanor Olivia Mayo Minns, my knee baby sister, is affectionately known as Elma. She earned a bachelor's degree in social work at Tuskegee Institute in 1978. She completed several graduate-level courses in social work at Norfolk State University and numerous on-the-job training hours, thereby earning continuing education units (CEUs).

She is an active member of her church and has spent several years serving as a Juvenile and Domestic Relations Court Services Worker for the 5th District of the state of Virginia. After retiring from the state of Virginia, she worked as a behavioral specialist for the Western Tidewater Community Services Board.

Eleanor has five children: Birran S. Outlaw, William Calvin Jones, Jr., Pattrena C. Howell, Erin R. Minns, and Eric N. Minns. She has 13 grandchildren and seven great grandchildren. Eleanor is a community activist and makes excellent speeches on social issues. She loves to sew and interact with her children, grandchildren, and great grandchildren. Additionally, she manages her personal rental properties in Suffolk, Virginia. Although she is retired, she serves as a community resource, exercising her professional expertise.

Mary Lee Mayo Brown, my baby sister who is called "Murlee," was married years ago. She has four children: Jacquelyn Aurora Mayo Daniel, Jessie Clarence Brown, Mildred Margaret Brown Taylor, and Rodrick B. Brown. Mary Lee also has grandchildren and great grandchildren.

Mary Lee completed courses in biology and nursing at Tuskegee Institute. While completing those courses, she worked at the Carver Research Foundation on the Tuskegee Institute campus. After moving back to Suffolk, Virginia, Mary Lee worked at the Nansemond Credit Union and the Suffolk Shelter for the Homeless. While living in Springfield, Virginia, she worked at Walmart. For a short period, she served as a caregiver for senior citizens at the Sunrise Assisted Living facility in Springfield, Virginia. After that, she served as an in-home caregiver for the elderly in Springfield and Tuskegee. She loves to read and tell oral histories.

Over the years, using the tools of genealogy research, I have been able to locate some records about other members of my extended family.

Grandma Fannie was born in Newsome, Virginia, in 1887.[84] She was the daughter of Chestine and Margaret Hunt Johnson.

My Granddaddy, Benjamin Mayo, died on September 20, 1931, at age 65 in Southampton County, Virginia, long before I was born. On his death certificate, he is listed as a pauper.[85] However, he had been a farmer in his early years.[86] Although the Virginia Bureau of Vital Statistics does not have a record of Granddaddy's birth, my siblings and I calculated from the information on his death certificate that he was born in approximately 1866. Benjamin and Fannie had five children: John, Clifford (my Dad, also known as Clifton), Armeania, Maebell (known as Aunt C), and Margaret Ellen. Margaret Ellen had a son, Joe Louis Bullock.

Information on my Mama is scanty at best. In a search of the records in the Division of Vital Records of the Commonwealth of Virginia, her birth certificate was not found. However, according to her death certificate (#18016), she was born in 1921, and her parents were George Cherry and Erma Taylor. However, she was reared by another family in the Saratoga section of Suffolk, Virginia, where she met my Dad. I do not know if she had any sisters or brothers. Before being placed in the community hospital in Suffolk where she died in 1951, she lived with my siblings and me in Suffolk.

The last names of some of the other relatives in my family are Bullock, Daughtry, Hunt, Myrick, Palmer, and Rawlings.

---

[84] Certificate of Death #12966 for Fannie Mayo.
[85] Certificate of Death #22596 for Benjamin Mayo.
[86] According to Certificate of Birth #23640 for his son, Jessie Clifford Mayo.

Appendix 2
The Education of My Son

One of my major accomplishments was raising my son, Lawson, who continues to be an integral part of my life. His guidance, support, and education have always been high priorities for me. Fortunately, I have lived to see him become an adult, husband, and father.

Lawson when he was a baby

Lawson and me

Lawson and USDA Secretary Yeutter

Lawson at St. Joseph's Elementary School

Lawson as a high-school student at St. Paul's School

Recent photograph of Lawson

Lawson and me

In his school years, he received a very good education. While I served as a faculty member at Tuskegee Institute, he attended the Tuskegee campus kindergarten, and when he was ready for elementary school, he attended St. Joseph's Catholic School in Tuskegee. During the times that Mama and Daddy Cook kept him, he was enrolled in a school in Suffolk, Virginia. When I moved to Tallahassee, he was enrolled in the school near the Florida A&M University campus. Also, while I was in Tallahassee, he studied piano lessons after school.

In later years, when I returned to Tuskegee Institute to serve as CRF director, Lawson was enrolled again in St. Joseph's Catholic School in Tuskegee, Alabama, after a short period at the Tuskegee Laboratory Learning Center. When he completed the eighth grade—the highest grade offered at St. Joseph's—he spent his ninth grade in public school in Tuskegee; this was followed by his enrollment and completion of his last high-school years at St. Paul's High School, a boarding school in Covington, Louisiana.

Our selection of a boarding school was well planned. Since my position at Tuskegee Institute required a great deal of travel, often I would take Lawson with me on my business trips whenever my itinerary enabled me to be near a boarding school. This enabled him to have interviews at several of those schools. We narrowed our list of desired schools to three that met our criteria of being near Tuskegee Institute. This was important for several reasons, including 1) ease of visits and attendance at parent-teacher meetings, 2) easy travel to Tuskegee, and 3) affordability. The expense of the boarding school was partially offset by the child support that his stepfather provided for him.

Our final choice of a boarding school for Lawson was St. Paul's Catholic School in Covington, Louisiana. He attended grades ten through twelve there. While he was enrolled there, Mama and Daddy Cook and I visited him often and talked to his teachers and counselor. On occasion, I would take him and some of his school mates to New Orleans for tours and meals. In the late 1980s, he graduated from that school. While living in Ohio with me for a summer, he completed a course in finance at Dyke College in

Cleveland. The following fall, he enrolled at Howard University. Although he did not complete the curriculum for earning a college degree, he completed several courses in computer-based information systems, finance, and accounting.

Now, he is making a way for himself and his children.

Appendix 3
Biography of Dr. Margaret Ellen Mayo Tolbert

D r. Margaret Ellen Mayo Tolbert earned her doctorate degree in biochemistry from Brown University. She earned her master of science degree in analytical chemistry from Wayne State University, and bachelor of science degree in chemistry with a minor in mathematics from Tuskegee Institute (now Tuskegee University) with high honors. Additionally, she completed a course in the principles of accounting at Dyke College in Cleveland, Ohio. For most of the positions she has held, she completed on-the-job training courses in leadership and management for career enhancement.

In 2002, she began her tenure as senior advisor in the Office of Integrative Activities at the National Science Foundation (NSF), from which she retired in 2011. She served as a senior-level agency spokesperson for NSF efforts to increase the participation of underrepresented minority groups, women, and persons with disabilities in science and engineering research and education, particularly in NSF programs. She oversaw activities of the congressionally mandated Committee on Equal Opportunities in Science and Engineering while acting as its executive liaison. As senior advisor, Dr. Tolbert provided leadership and oversight for mission-critical NSF-wide programs. She managed six research centers funded through the multi-million-dollar Science and Technology Centers Program. She was also responsible for policies and procedures focused on enhancing customer services and program performance.

Prior to joining the NSF staff, Dr. Tolbert was the first African American and the first female to serve as director of the U.S. Department of Energy's New Brunswick Laboratory, a nuclear analytical chemistry laboratory. Her work involved management and policy functions pertinent to the U.S. nuclear energy programs. She oversaw the laboratory's functions: to prevent the spread of nuclear materials, prepare and certify nuclear reference materials for use in the standardization of instruments, evaluate the measurement capabilities of different nuclear laboratories worldwide, and measure the amount of nuclear material in samples from various sources throughout the world. For a few months in 2001, she served a temporary assignment as acting associate director of the U.S. Department of Energy's Office of Laboratory Operations and Environment, Safety and Health.

Dr. Tolbert's other significant accomplishments include: the first African-American female to serve as director of the Division of Educational Programs at Argonne National Laboratory; the first African American to serve as special assistant to the vice chairs of the Presidential Committee on Education and Technology, of the Federal Coordinating Council for Science, Engineering, and Technology; the first female to serve as director of the Research Improvement in Minority Institutions Program at NSF; and the first female to serve as director of the Carver Research Foundation of Tuskegee Institute, which is the research foundation established in 1940 by Dr. George Washington Carver. This position was concurrent with that of Associate Provost for Research and Development and Professor at Tuskegee University.

From 1988 to 1990, she was the highest ranking African-American female employed at the BP America Research Center. There she served as senior planner and senior budgets and control analyst. In academia, she has served as visiting associate professor of medical sciences (Brown University), professor of chemistry and associate provost for R&D (Tuskegee University), instructor in mathematics and science (Opportunities Industrialization Center), and associate dean of the School of Pharmacy and professor of pharmaceutical science (Florida A&M University).

Dr. Tolbert has served as guest scientist at the International Institute for Cellular and Molecular Pathology in Brussels, Belgium, and completed work assignments in several countries, including Ghana, Liberia, Libya, Sudan, South Africa, Senegal, Austria, and Belgium. She has established national and international linkages among scientists, science administrators, and educators. Additionally, she has served as research advisor to graduate students.

Prior to her retirement, Dr. Tolbert was a member of the American Chemical Society, the American Association for the Advancement of Science, New York Academy of Sciences, Sigma Xi, the Institute of Nuclear Materials Management, and the Chicago Chemists' Club.

She has received numerous honors and awards for her contributions to society, and her biography appears in several publications. Dr. Tolbert has served as invited speaker at numerous conferences and at universities, and she has published papers on scientific as well as non-technical topics in peer-reviewed journals (e.g., *Journal of Biological Chemistry, Metabolism, Journal of Nuclear Materials Management, Journal of the National Technical Association*, and *Journal of College Science Teaching*). She has written numerous annual reports, books, and an article in a book. She continues to serve as a mentor for students interested in science and mathematics, and she continues to assist her family members with their formal education efforts.

Dr. Tolbert (Margaret Ellen Mayo) was born in the Saratoga section of Suffolk, Virginia.

Biography Details in List Format

Distinctions:

- One of six African Americans out of 400 Senior Executives at the National Science Foundation.
- First African-American female to serve as director of the New Brunswick Laboratory, U.S. Department of Energy.
- Highest ranking African-American female on the staff of the Chicago Operations Office, U.S. Department of Energy.
- First African-American female to serve as director of the Division of Educational Programs at Argonne National Laboratory.

- First African American to serve as special assistant to the vice chairs of the Committee on Education and Technology, Federal Coordinating Council for Science, Engineering, and Technology – a council of the U.S. President.
- First female to serve as director of the Research Improvement in Minority Institutions Program at the National Science Foundation.
- The first African American and the highest ranking female to serve as senior planner and senior budgets and control analyst at the British Petroleum Company of America Research Center in Ohio.
- First female to serve as director of the Carver Research Foundation of Tuskegee Institute (currently Tuskegee University).
- First female graduate student at Brown University to publish three full manuscripts—based on original laboratory research results—in the *Journal of Biological Chemistry* during a three-year doctoral study period.
- First member of the Mayo family—descendants of Fannie Mae Johnson Mayo and Benjamin Mayo of Suffolk, Virginia—to have had multiple careers in the academic, private, philanthropic, and Federal sectors.
- First member of the Mayo family to earn a doctorate degree.

Positions Held:

1969 – Research technician in the School of Agriculture at Tuskegee Institute in Tuskegee, Alabama

1969-1970 – Faculty member in the Mathematics Department at Tuskegee Institute

1970-1973 – Graduate student in the Division of Medical Sciences at Brown University in Providence, Rhode Island

1971-1972 - Instructor of science and mathematics (night classes) at the Opportunities Industrialization Center in Providence, Rhode Island (concurrent with graduate studies)

Summer of 1973 - Instructor of chemistry in the Transitional Program at Brown University

1973-1977 – Faculty member in the Department of Chemistry at Tuskegee Institute

Summer 1974 – Guest faculty researcher in the Biomedical Institute at Lawrence Livermore National Laboratory in Livermore, California

Summer of 1977 – Guest research scientist in the Neurobiology and Anatomy and the Pharmacology departments at the University of Texas Medical School at Houston, Texas

1977-1979 – Professor of pharmaceutical chemistry and associate dean in the School of Pharmacy at Florida A&M University in Tallahassee, Florida

1977-1978 – Instructor of chemistry in the Special Health Careers Opportunity Grant Program at Florida A&M University (concurrent position with the preceding one)

Five months in 1978-1979 – Guest scientist at the International Institute of Cellular and Molecular Pathology in Brussels, Belgium

Seven months in 1979 – Research scientist in the laboratories of Dr. Elizabeth LeDuc and Dr. John Fain at Brown University

1979 – Visiting associate professor of medical sciences at Brown University (concurrent position with the preceding one)

1979-1988 – Director of the Carver Research Foundation of Tuskegee Institute, professor of chemistry (full professorship as of 1980) in the Department of Chemistry at Tuskegee Institute, and associate provost for research and development at Tuskegee Institute; member of the Carver Research Foundation Board of Trustees; member of the University of Alabama System Board of Trustees (several months in 1985); a director of the Birmingham Branch of the Federal Reserve Bank of Atlanta (1985-1987)

Several summers between 1980 and 1985 – Research scientist at the Army Research Institute of Environmental Medicine in Natick, Massachusetts (projects conducted at Tuskegee Institute and at the Army Research Institute); adjunct professor of pharmacy at the University of Oklahoma in Oklahoma City (served on a PhD dissertation committee)

1987-1988 – Sabbatical leave (from Tuskegee University) at the Standard Oil Company of Ohio, which became BP America, Inc., in Warrensville Heights, Ohio

1988-1990 – Senior budgets and control analyst and senior planner at BP America Research Laboratory in Warrensville Heights, Ohio

September 1990 to December 1993 – Director of the Research Improvement in Minority Institutions Program; staff associate for Science, Mathematics, Engineering, Technology, and Education; and member of committees and subcommittees of the Federal Coordinating Council for Science, Engineering, and Technology at the National Science Foundation in Washington, DC

January to March 1994 – Consulting scientist (through TeleSec Services, Inc.) at the Howard Hughes Medical Institute in Chevy Chase, Maryland

1994-1996 – Director of the Division of Educational Programs at Argonne National Laboratory in Argonne, Illinois

1996-2002 – Director, New Brunswick Laboratory of the U.S. Department of Energy in Argonne, Illinois; member of the executive board of the Chicago Operations Office/U.S. Department of Energy; member of several standing committees of the Chicago Operations Office

2002-2011 – Senior advisor in the Office of Integrative Activities at the National Science Foundation in Arlington, Virginia

December 31, 2011 – Retired from the National Science Foundation

International Tours of Duty:

<u>Five months in 1978-1979</u>: As a National Institutes of Health/ National Institute of General Medical Sciences--Maximizing Access to Research Faculty Fellow, guest research scientist at the International Institute of Cellular and Molecular Pathology in Brussels, Belgium. Toured London and Cambridge, England; Paris, France; and Lausanne, Switzerland.

<u>August 2-21, 1981</u>: Team leader of a group of Tuskegee Institute specialists in the health professions and related fields. The team assessed the possibilities of linkages between academic and government agencies. My tours of duty, which were sponsored by the U.S. Agency for International Development (122-d Program), took place in Liberia, Senegal, Sudan, and Kenya.

<u>1981</u>: Organized and implemented the formal linkage agreement among Cuttington University College in Liberia, Tuskegee University, and other institutions. This linkage has enabled faculty exchanges, strengthened international capabilities, and enhanced research.

<u>April 24-May 5, 1981</u>: Member of a national team of female experts that visited Libya and gave workshop speeches on various topics for Libyan women to stimulate their interest in professional careers. At the workshop, Dr. Tolbert made presentations on diabetes, stress control, nutrition, and rural development issues.

<u>May 29-June 11, 1983</u>: Co-leader of a team, which traveled to Liberia to participate in planning sessions pertinent to the linkage of educational institutions and to participate in the signing ceremony linking Cuttington University College and Tuskegee University.

<u>1994-1996</u>: Served as principal investigator for the program "Support for U.S. Participation" in the International Atomic Energy Agency, a U.S. Department of State contract to Argonne National Laboratory.

<u>November 27-December 8, 1995</u>: Led the organization and implementation of a two-week workshop on radiotherapy and cancer incidence in Accra and Kumasi, Ghana; accompanied

by five U.S. experts. The workshop heightened the awareness of cancer prevention and control, thereby strengthening the National Cancer Program of Ghana.

November 30–December 3, 1995: Served as a member of the U.S. Department of Energy delegation that reviewed science and technology programs at selected historically disadvantaged universities in South Africa.

May 16-18, 1995: Served as a member of the 17th Advisory Committee on Radiation Protection and Nuclear Safety, International Atomic Energy Agency, Vienna, Austria.

October 1997: Participated in the International Atomic Energy Agency Symposium on International Nuclear Safeguards in Vienna, Austria, then traveled to Geel, Belgium, to participate in discussions on the management of nuclear materials with scientists and administrators at the Institute for Reference Materials Measurements.

1999-2002: Participated in discussions on nuclear safeguards measurement issues with scientists at the International Atomic Energy Agency headquarters in Vienna, Austria; at its Safeguards Analytical Laboratory in Seibersdorf, Austria; and at the Institute for Reference Materials Measurements in Geel, Belgium.

2002-2011: By invitation from the Office of International Science and Engineering and the Office of Integrative Activities at the National Science Foundation, gave briefings on Foundation policies and programs to foreign dignitaries from such countries as Finland, Norway, Uganda, Nigeria, Kenya, and Cameron. Also, gave briefings to congressional staffers on topics pertinent to the STC Program and CEOSE.

Publications (Partial List, Excluding Published Abstracts):

o Books:

S. Krishnamurthy and M. E. M. Tolbert, <u>Stereochemical Insights into Biochemistry</u>, a Hearthstone Book, Carlton Press, New York, NY (1983).

M. E. M. Tolbert, Editor, <u>Focus: Energy Issues for the Eighties</u>, Alabama Printers, Montgomery, AL (1984).

o Manual, Conference Proceedings, and a Review:

M. E. M. Tolbert and P. A. Loretan, "User's Manual for Applicants Proposing On-Site Burial of Self-Generated Radioactive Waste," Tuskegee Institute, AL (1986).

M. E. M. Tolbert, "Mobilizing Small Farmers to Meet the World Food Crisis," *Proceedings of the Tuskegee Institute Small Farms Conference*, Tuskegee Institute, AL (February 13-15, 1983).

"Practical Applications of Prostaglandins," reviewed by M. E. M. Tolbert for the *American Journal of Pharmaceutical Education*, **44**:223 (1980).

o Journal Publications on Biomedical Research:

M. E. M. Johnson (Currently M. E. M. Tolbert), N. M. Das, F. R. Butcher, and J. N. Fain, "The Regulation of Gluconeogenesis in Isolated Rat Liver Cells by Glucagon, Insulin, Dibutyryl Cyclic Adenosine Monophosphate, and Fatty Acids," *Journal of Biological Chemistry*, **247**:32293235 (1972).

M. E. M. Tolbert, F. R. Butcher, and J. N. Fain "Lack of Correlation between Catecholamine Effects on Cyclic Adenosine 3',5'Monophosphate and Gluconeogenesis in Isolated Rat Liver Cells," *Journal of Biological Chemistry*, **248**:56865692 (1973).

M. E. M. Tolbert and J. N. Fain, "Studies on the Regulation of Gluconeogenesis in Isolated Rat Liver Cells by Epinephrine and Glucagon," *Journal of Biological Chemistry*, **249**:11621166 (1974).

J. N. Fain, M. E. M. Tolbert, R. H. Pointer, F. R. Butcher, and A. Arnold, "Cyclic Nucleotides and Gluconeogenesis by Rat Liver Cells," *Metabolism*, **XXIV**:395407 (1975).

M. E. M. Tolbert, A. C. White, K. Aspry, J. Cutts, and J. N. Fain, "Stimulation by Vasopressin and Alpha Catecholamines of Phosphatidylinositol Formation in Isolated Rat Liver Parenchymal Cells," Journal of Biological Chemistry, **255**:19381944 (1980).

M. E. M. Tolbert, "The Subclassification of the AlphaAdrenergic Receptors of Isolated Rat Hepatic Parenchymal Cells," *Proceedings of the Fourth Annual ACHE Faculty/Student Symposium in Science 19791980* (1980).

B. B. Hoffman, T. Michel, D. M. Kilpatrick, R. J. Lefkowitz, M. E. M. Tolbert, H. Gilman, and J. N. Fain, "Agonist Versus Antagonist Binding to AlphaAdrenergic Receptors," *Proc. Natl. Acad. Sci.*, **77**:45694573 (1980).

E. L. Cook and M. E. M. Tolbert, "Prostaglandins: Potential CureAll Compounds," *FAMU Research Bulletin*, **XXIV(1)**:3544 (1980).

M. E. M. Tolbert, G. D. Draper, and J. A. Kamalu, "Effects of Cadmium, Zinc, Copper, and Manganese on Hepatic Parenchymal Cell Gluconeogenesis," *Journal of Environmental Science and Health*, **B16(5)**:575585 (1981).

M. C. Datta, J. Josephs, M. E. M. Tolbert, J. Andrews, and H. Dowla, "Acetylsalicylic Acid Antagonizes the BleedingInduced Changes in Hemoglobin Proportions in Normal Adult Rats," *Biochem. & Biophys. Res. Comm*, **137(1)**:6975 (1986).

o NonBiomedical Research Publications Based on Laboratory Research:

M. E. M. Tolbert, S. Bhattacharya, and P. K. Biswas, "Enzymic Saccharification of Cellulose and Cellulosic Biomass of Sweet Potato (Ipomoea batatas L.)Two Step Hydrolysis," *Biomass*, **11**:205213 (1986).

S. Bhattacharya, P.K. Biswas, and M. E. M. Tolbert, "Comparison of the Effectiveness of Various Pretreatment Methods on the

Enzymatic Hydrolysis of Sweet Potato (<u>Ipomoea batatas</u> L.) Biomass," *Biological Wastes*, **19**:215226 (1987).

S. Bhattacharya, J. F. Eatman, P. K. Biswas, and M. E. M. Tolbert, "CO_2 Enrichment and Its Relationship to Bioconversion of Cellulosic Biomass of Sweet Potato (<u>Ipomoea batatas</u> L.) into Fermentable Sugars," *Biomass*, **15**:259268 (1988).

o Non-Technical Publications (Full Manuscripts):

M. E. M. Tolbert, "Minority Women in Science and Engineering: A Review of Progress," *Journal of the National Technical Association*, **66(2):**4-15 (Spring 1993).

M. E. M. Tolbert, "Strengthening the Nation's Educational System through Programs at Argonne National Laboratory," *Journal of College Science Teaching*, **XXVI(1)**:18-25 (Sept./.Oct 1996).

M. E. M. Tolbert, "Human Resource Challenges for the 21st Century" (Workshop Summary)," *Proceedings of the National Science Foundation and Department of Energy Sponsored Conference Titled Organizing for Research and Development in the 21st Century*, M.L. Knotek and P. Eisenberger, Conference Co-Chairs and Editors, Washington, D.C. (April 24-25, 1997).

M. I. Spaletto, M. Clapper, and M. E. M. Tolbert, "Second NBL Measurement Evaluation Program Meeting: A Summary," *Journal of Nuclear Materials Management*, **XXVI(1)**:16-20 (Fall 1997).

M. I. Spaletto and M. E. M. Tolbert, "A Safeguards Measurement Evaluation Program with International Significance," *Proceedings of the Symposium on International Safeguards,* International Atomic Energy Agency, Vienna, Austria (October 14, 1997).

K. Mayer, M. E. M. Tolbert, R. Wellum, S. Deron, R. E. Perrin, and B. Mitterrand, "Preparing for the Future Today," *Journal of Nuclear Materials Management*, Pages 4 and 18 (Spring 1999).

R. Wellum, J. Tushingham, and M. E. M. Tolbert, "International Certified and SI Traceable: The Ultimate Aim for Reference Materials," International Safeguards V – II – Panel Discussion," *Journal of Nuclear Materials Management*, **XXVIII(1)**:23-24 (Fall 1999).

M. E. M. Tolbert, "Organization and Implementation of the Full-Day Session on Reference Materials," in Session H: International Safeguards IV – International Certified and SI Traceable: The Ultimate Aim for Reference Materials I, *Proceedings of the INMM 40th Annual Meeting,* **on CD ROM** (July 1999).

D. Donohue, M. E. M. Tolbert, and P. De Bievrè, "Deliberations on Safeguards Measurement Uncertainty," *Journal of Nuclear Materials Management,* **XXIX(2)**:27-30 (Winter 2001).

M. E. M. Tolbert, "Brown, Jeannette Elizabeth," in <u>African American National Biography</u>, Henry Louis Gates, Jr and Evelyn Brooks Higginbotham, Editors, Vol. 1, Oxford University Press, Pages 617-619 (2008).

Honors and Awards (Partial List)

Presented an appreciation plaque by former chairs of the national Committee on Equal Opportunities in Science and Engineering, 2012

Presented a plaque containing a copy of the Talladega College Slavery Library Mural painted in 1939 (This followed Dr. Tolbert's honors convocation speech at the Alpha Chi National Honor Society Initiation Ceremony held at Talladega College), March 9, 2011

Presented the Dr. George Washington Carver Distinguished Service Award after giving the Carver Convocation speech at Tuskegee University, January 2007

Presented a plaque by the East Suffolk High School Alumni Association, Inc., in recognition of outstanding achievement, July 20, 2002

Presented the Women of Color, Government and Defense Award in Managerial Leadership in Government, 2001

Presented Chicago Operations Office/U.S. Department of Energy Performance Awards, each year from 1997 to 2001

Presented an Appreciation Plaque by the Albuquerque Operations Office/U.S. Department of Energy following a speech Dr. Tolbert gave at the Albuquerque Operations office facility in Albuquerque, New Mexico, February 2001

Served as an honoree in the Museum of Science and Industry's "Black Creativity Exhibit: African American Women in Science and Technology," March 2000

Honored by the U.S. Department of Energy as it focused on advancing the status of women in the program titled "Women in Science," 2000

Recipient of the Chicago-Tuskegee Club President's Merit Award, 1999

Recipient of the Secretary of Energy Pride Award for community service, 1998

Honored by being among the few women invited to attend a luncheon and celebration program—"Women Making History"— given for women, the White House, Washington, DC, 1996

Recipient of a certificate for Women in Science Technology in commemoration of Women's History Month, Argonne National Laboratory, 1996

Recipient of a certificate of Distinguished Service to the Federal Reserve System and excellent contributions to the Federal Reserve Bank and to economic progress of the Sixth Federal Reserve District, 1987

Earlier awards and recognition include the following: Brown University Fellowship, 1970; Southern Fund Fellowship, 1971-1973; Outstanding Teacher, College of Arts and Sciences, Tuskegee University, 1975; NIH-MARC Faculty Fellow/Guest Scientist, International Institute for Cellular and Molecular Pathology in Brussels, Belgium, Five Months in 1978-1979, and Brown University in Providence, Rhode Island, Seven Months in 1979; Carver Research Associate 1981-1987; Plaque for service to Tuskegee Public Schools, 1982; Faculty Achievement Award, Tuskegee University, 1983; Delta Sigma Theta Sorority Award for Outstanding Service and Contributions to Education, 1983; Tuskegee Lions Club President's Award, September 1, 1983; Certificates of Service, 1983 and 1984-1985, awarded for outstanding service in lionism and the Tuskegee Eye

Bank; The Woman of the Year Award from the Alpha Xi Chapter of the Zeta Phi Beta Sorority, 1984; Tenure Granted by Tuskegee University, 1985; Certificate of Appreciation and Recognition awarded for eminent volunteer services and sincere dedication in the District Court of Macon County-Juvenile & Outreach Service, June 19, 1985; plaque awarded by the East Tennessee Chapter of the National Contract Management Association, April 16, 1985; elected a Fellow of the American Association for the Advancement of Science for distinguished efforts on behalf of the advancement of science, February 15, 1988

Appendix 4
Book Chapters, Articles, and Other Information Published about Dr. Margaret Ellen Mayo Tolbert

T he following two lists are included in this book as resources. Enjoy the reading!

In Books (Partial List)

Jeannette E. Brown, "Margaret Ellen Mayo Tolbert," African American Women Chemists, Oxford University Press Inc., New York, NY, 2012, pages 123-135.

Margaret E. M. Tolbert, interview by Jeannette E. Brown at the National Science Foundation, Arlington, Virginia, August 13, 2009 (Philadelphia: Chemical Heritage Foundation, Oral History Transcript #0648); Date of First Printing of Margaret E. M. Tolbert: Oral History by the Chemical Heritage Foundation, January 24, 2011.

Jeannette Elizabeth Brown, African American National Biography, Vol. 7, Henry Louis Gates Jr., and Evelyn Brooks Higginbotham, Editors, Oxford University Press, New York, NY, 2008, pages 613-614.

Diann Jordan, Sisters in Science, Purdue University Press, West Lafayette, IN, 2006, page 36.

Ray Spangenburg and Kit Moser, "Tolbert, Margaret Ellen Mayo," African Americans in Science, Math, and Invention, Facts on File, Inc., New York, NY, 2003, pages 211-212.

55th, 56th, 57th, and 58th editions of Who's Who in America.

Wini Warren, "Margaret Ellen Mayo Tolbert: Biochemist and Administrator," Black Women Scientists in the United States, Indiana University Press, Bloomington, IN, 1999, pages 263-264.

Sally Cole-Misch, (Kristine Krapp, Editor), Notable Black American Scientists, Gale Research, Farmington Hills, MI, 1999, pages 299-301.

R. R. Bowker, American Men & Women of Science, 1998-99, 20th Edition, Vol. 7, New Providence, NJ, 1998, page 182.

James H. Kessler, J. S. Kidd, Renée A. Kidd, and Katherine A. Morin, "Margaret E. M. Tolbert," Distinguished African American Scientists of the 20th Century, Oryx Press, 1996, pages 317-320.

Vivian Ovelton Sammons, Blacks in Science and Medicine, Hemisphere Publishing, New York, NY, 1990, page 233.

The Outstanding Young Women of America Program, Outstanding Young Women of America, Washington, DC, 1976, page 753.

In Periodicals, Online, and in Special Events (Partial List)

The League, Margaret Ellen Mayo Tolbert, www.theleagueonline. org/ASmtolbert.php (as of October 15, 2014).

Wikipedia, Margaret E. M. Tolbert, www.wikipedia.org/wiki/ Margaret_E._M._Tolbert (as of October 15, 2014).

Managerial Leadership in Government, Margaret E. M. Tolbert, PhD, www.blackengineer.com/events/winners bios/margaret tolbert.shtml (as of October 15, 2014).

Institute for Broadening Participation, Margaret Tolbert, www. pathwaystoscience.org/profiles.aspx?ind=TolbeMarga (as of October 15, 2014).

Chemistry Connections: Our Roots—Our Future, MyRSC, Margaret E. M. Tolbert, http://my.rsc.org/reviews/item/1/7272 (as of October 15, 2014).

Zoominfo, Dr. Margaret E. M. Tolbert, www.zoominfo. com/p/Margaret-Tolbert/97939379 (as of October 15, 2014; contact information obsolete).

Chemical Heritage Foundation, Margaret E. M. Tolbert, www. chemheritage.org/discover/online-resources/chemistry-in-history/ themes/chemical-education-and-public-policy/public-policy/ tolbert.aspx (as of October 15, 2014).

TRUST, Team for Research in Ubiquitous Secure Technology, a Biographical Sketch of Margaret E. M. Tolbert, www.truststc.org/people/directory/mtolbert (as of October 15, 2014).

Photograph and biographical sketch included as a part of the NEW CENTURY LEADERS Exhibit, unveiled at Ortho Biotechnology/Johnson & Johnson Company, March 17, 2003.

Biographical information included in the careers section of the traveling exhibit titled "Women in Chemistry," the Chemical Heritage Foundation of Philadelphia, PA, June 2003.

Biographical sketch included in *U.S. Black Engineer Information Technology,* June/July 2001, pages 23 and 25.

Featured in "Lab Coats and Space Suits," *Chicago Tribune,* Section 8, February 2, 2000, Pages 1-2.

Journal of College Science Teaching, May 1998, page 371.

Pietri, Charles E., "JNMM Interview with Margaret E. M. Tolbert," *Journal of Nuclear Materials Management,* Vol. XXVI, No. 1, Fall 1997.

DOE This Month, January 1997, page 18.

DOE This Month, July 1997, page 15.

DOE This Month, April 1996, page 17.

"Best Bets for a Successful Career in the 21st Century," *Ebony,* August 1985, two photos with legends on page 93.

Chris Benson, "Tuskegee: City of History and Hope," *Ebony,* July 1982, one photo with legend on page 59.

Flanagan, Brenda, "Essence Women," *Essence,* August 1980, pages 37-38.

Maguire, Carole, "Former Suffolkian Studies Common in Uncommon Way," *The Suffolk News-Herald,* August 24, 1980, page 11.

Reference to Dr. Tolbert's scientific work appears in several journal articles and in the book, <u>The Pharmacological Basis of Therapeutics</u>, fifth edition, page 489 (1975).

Dr. Tolbert's film and television appearances to discuss her background, Tuskegee University work, and the research of the Carver Research Foundation include the following:

- Appeared in the Human Interest Series of the Columbia Broadcasting System's "On the Road to 1976 with Charles Kuralt,"
- Narrated and appeared in part of the research section of "Lifting the Veil: The Tuskegee Tradition," a color documentary film of the Screen News Digest-Hearst Metrotone News, produced by Cloyd Aarseth,
- Appeared (June 1984) on a WSFA-TV (Montgomery, Alabama) live talk show with Lisa Walsh, program hostess,
- Appeared (January 1985) on the WSFA-TV program, "Focus," with Kim Davis and on an earlier production of "Focus" with Janet Maye, program hostess,
- Appeared (1986) on Alabama public television with Mary Gaines, program hostess.

Appendix 5
Abbreviations and Explanations

The following abbreviations and explanations are provided for the convenience of the readers of this book. Hopefully, this will enable clarity and facilitate ease of reading and understanding of the contents of this book.

AAAS: American Association for the Advancement of Science

ACS: American Chemical Society

AMP: Adenosine Monophosphate

ANL: Argonne National Laboratory

BP: British Petroleum Company

CEOSE: Committee on Equal Opportunities in Science and Engineering

CLiPS: Center for Layered Polymeric Systems (This is the STC for which Case Western Reserve University has the lead role.)

CMMAP: Center for Multi-Scale Modeling of Atmospheric Processes (This is the STC for which Colorado State University has the lead role.)

CMOP: Center for Coastal Margin Observation & Prediction (This is the STC for which Organ Health and Science University has the lead role.)

C-MORE: Center for Microbial Oceanography (This is the STC for which the University of Hawaii at Manoa has the lead role.)

CReSIS: Center for Remote Sensing of Ice Sheets (This is the STC for which the University of Kansas has the lead role.)

CRM: Certified Reference Material

While Dr. Tolbert was NBL director, the following CRMs were developed and issued, or recertified and reissued by NBL staff members:

- CRM 145 Uranium (Normal) Assay Solution Standard, September 1996
- CRM U930-D, Uranium Isotopic Standard, September 1997

- CRM 125-A Uranium (Enriched) Oxide – (UO2) Assay and Isotopic Standard, December 1997
- CRM U010, Uranium Isotopic Standard, September 30, 1998 (CRM U010 is a reissue of CRM U010 issued originally in 1970)
- CRM 146, Uranium Isotopic Standard for Gamma Spectrometry Measurements, July 30, 1999
- CRM 149, Uranium (93-percent Enriched) Oxide – U3O8 Standard for Neutron Counting Measurements, November 30, 1999
- CRM 42A (1-4) Uranium (Normal) Counting Standard, March 30, 2001, and
- CRM 115 Uranium (Depleted) Metal, July 2002. (CRM 115 is a reissue of CRM 115 issued originally in June 1978)

Dan Doodle: a savory product made by stuffing the cleaned large intestine or stomach of a slaughtered pig with meat from various parts of that animal. The meat is first cut or ground into small pieces and seasoned well. The resulting product is placed into a smoke house for curing or cooked for hours on a stove, after which it is used to season vegetables by cooking them together. Sometime the Dan Doodle is sliced and the pieces fried for eating, primarily as a breakfast food.

DEP: Division of Educational Programs, a division of Argonne National Laboratory that is owned by the U.S. Department of Energy and operated under contract by the University of Chicago

DOE: U.S. Department of Energy

HBCUs: Historically Black Colleges and Universities

Hoochie Coochie: a sensual and provocative belly dance performed by women

IAEA: International Atomic Energy Agency, located in Vienna, Austria

INMM: Institute of Nuclear Materials Management, an international organization that has the primary role of ensuring the safe, secure and peaceful stewardship of nuclear materials

IRMM: the Joint Research Centre's Institute for Reference Materials and Measurements

Knee Baby: the child that precedes the last one born in a family

Mary Jane: a candy with a taffy consistency, flavored with peanut butter and molasses with a center of peanut butter. Delicious!

MOU: Memorandum of Understanding

NAS/COSPUP: National Academy of Sciences/Committee on Science and Public Policy

NBL: New Brunswick Laboratory, a government-owned and -operated laboratory located in Argonne, Illinois

NIST: National Institute of Standards and Technology, an agency of the U.S. Department of Commerce

NRCEN: National Science Foundation Research Center Educators Network

NSF: National Science Foundation, an independent agency of the United States located in Arlington, Virginia, with offices in selected foreign countries

OIA: Office of Integrative Activities, a former office of the National Science Foundation (the name of this office has changed in recent times to Office of International and Integrative Activities, and its role has been expanded)

PNNL: Pacific Northwest National Laboratory, a U.S. Department of Energy research laboratory located in Richland, Washington

Put her foot in it: a phrase used to indicate that the food prepared by a given person is delicious

Saratoga: a section of Suffolk, Virginia, with a majority population of African Americans

SES: Senior Executive Service, a corps of executives selected for their leadership qualifications

STCs: Science and Technology Centers, a program sponsored by the National Science Foundation

STEM: Science, technology, engineering, and mathematics

Stilts: Two long sticks, each of which had a tin can mailed to the lower half of the sticks. To use stilts, one would put one foot on each of the cans and balance while walking by holding onto the upper part of each stick. Some kids would dance using stilts. It was a fun thing to do.

Sweet Potato Jacks: a combination of mashed sweet potatoes, eggs, small amount of lemon juice, sugar, cinnamon, nutmeg, and vanilla extract, which is put inside a pocket of dough and fried

TB: Tuberculosis

Tootsie Roll: a chocolate candy whose texture is a cross between caramel and taffy. In the early days, these sold two for a penny.

TRUST: Team for Research in Ubiquitous Secure Technology (This is the STC for which the University of California at Berkeley has the lead role.)

TV: Television; in the early days, there was only black-and-white television, in contrast to full color that is currently available

USAID: U.S. Agency for International Development

About the Author

D r. Margaret E. M. Tolbert is a biochemist and expert manager of complex science and engineering programs. She has experience in academia and the private and federal sectors. Working in these sectors has enabled her to address diversity issues at local and national levels. She has published scientific and non-scientific articles and books and has served as a speaker at conferences and universities. Additionally, she has completed several tours of duty in foreign countries. For her significant contributions to society, she has received numerous awards.